Framing African Development

Africa-Europe Group for Interdisciplinary Studies

VOLUME 16

The titles published in this series are listed at *brill.com/agis*

Framing African Development

Challenging Concepts

Edited by

Kjell Havnevik
Terje Oestigaard
Eva Tobisson
Tea Virtanen

BRILL

LEIDEN | BOSTON

Library of Congress Cataloging-in-Publication Data

Framing African development : challenging concepts / edited by Kjell Havnevik, Terje Oestigaard, Eva Tobisson, Tea Virtanen.
pages cm -- (African-Europe Group for Interdisciplinary Studies)
"This book is based on contributions to a series of seminars organized by the Rural and Agrarian research cluster at the Nordic Africa Institute (.nai), Uppsala, between 2011 and 2013."
Includes bibliographical references and index.
ISBN 978-90-04-30541-0 (pbk. : alk. paper) 1. Economic development--Africa. 2. Economic development--Africa--International cooperation. I. Havnevik, Kjell J., editor. II. Oestigaard, Terje, editor. III. Tobisson, Eva, editor. IV. Virtanen, Tea, editor. V. Series: African-Europe Group for Interdisciplinary Studies (Series)
HC800.Z9E4442 2015
338.96--dc23

2015031743

This publication has been typeset in the multilingual "Brill" typeface. With over 5,100 characters covering Latin, IPA, Greek, and Cyrillic, this typeface is especially suitable for use in the humanities. For more information, please see www.brill.com/brill-typeface.

ISSN 1574–6925
ISBN 978-90-04-30541-0 (paperback)
ISBN 978-90-04-30546-5 (e-book)

This book is printed on acid-free paper.

Contents

Acknowledgements

This book is based on contributions to a series of seminars organized by the Rural and Agrarian research cluster at the Nordic Africa Institute (NAI), Uppsala, between 2011 and 2013. We are grateful to the presenters who, following discussion and comments from seminar participants, further developed their contributions into chapters that have resulted in this book. We are grateful to the NAI as a whole for its support in preparing this book, and also for the practical help we received in organizing the series of seminars from two of its members – Kent Eriksson and Inga Britt Isaksson Faris.

We would like to thank the book's two anonymous reviewers, who provided helpful ideas about its structure and framing, and who also suggested ways of improving a number of chapters. Thanks also must go to the contributors for following up on these suggestions. We are grateful to Clive Liddiard for his competent language editing, and also for his constructive ideas on how to improve certain aspects of the book. Susanna Dukaric of the NAI assisted importantly in designing the front cover of the book.

We thank Brill for the opportunity to publish this book – in particular Franca de Kort, who has provided us with professional assistance throughout the process of preparing for publication.

Uppsala, 23 June 2015
The editors

List of Contributors

Deborah Fahy Bryceson
did her Bachelors and Masters degrees in geography at the University of Dar es Salaam followed by a D.Phil from the University of Oxford. She is currently an Honorary Research Fellow at the Centre of African Studies at the University of Oxford as well as Deputy Director of the International Gender Studies Centre at the University of Oxford. She has published extensively on labour trends in the fields of rural as well as urban studies. She is currently researching African artisanal mining and has recently co-published an edited collection entitled *Mining and Social Transformation in Africa* (Routledge 2014).

Rosalind Eyben
is a feminist anthropologist with long experience of development practice, teaching and research. Her most recent books are *International Aid and the Making of a Better World, Feminists in Development Organizatons* (with Laura Turquet), and *The Politics of Evidence and Results* (with I. Guit, C. Roche and C. Shutt).

Kjell Havnevik
is a professor and senior researcher currently with the Nordic Africa Institute (NAI), Sweden and the University of Agder, Norway. He holds a PhD from the University of Bradford (UK) 1988 and has for four decades been conducting research and education work with a focus on rural and agrarian change in Africa at the Universities of Bergen and Agder in Norway, the University of Dar es Salaam, Tanzania, the Swedish University of Agricultural Sciences, Uppsala and the institutes CMI, Bergen and NAI. Some of his recent publications include the co-edited books *Biofuels, Land Grabbing and Food Security in Africa*, Zed Books 2011, *African Engagements*, Brill 2011, and the study *Responsible Agricultural Investments in developing countries – how to make principles and guidelines effective*, for the Swedish FAO Committee 2014 and the article "The Current Afro-Optimism – A Realistic Image of Africa?" *FLEKS – Scandinavian Journal of Intercultural Theory and Practice*, 2015.

Amanda Hammar
is currently MSO Professor and Director of the Centre of African Studies, Copenhagen University. She has a Masters in Social Policy and Planning from LSE and a PhD in Development Studies from Roskilde University. Among other things, she has researched and published on agrarian change, state making,

belonging and exclusion, the Zimbabwe crisis, and political economies of displacement. Recent publications include *Displacement Economies in Africa: Paradoxes of Crisis and Creativity* (Zed Press, 2014), 'Ambivalent Mobilities: Zimbabwean Commercial Farmers in Mozambique' (*Journal of Southern African Studies,* 2010), and several edited special issues of and articles in journals (Journal of Southern African Studies, 2010, and Journal of Contemporary African Studies 2008) on themes of crisis and displacement in southern Africa. Her current research concerns urban displacement and resettlement and changing modes of governance and citizenship in Zimbabwe.

Mats Hårsmar, PhD
is affiliated with the Swedish Expert Group for Aid Studies (EBA), as well as with the Stockholm International Water Institute (SIWI). His research interests include issues related to technical change in agriculture, poverty issues and development processes more broadly, with a particular geographic focus on West Africa. Previously, Hårsmar has held positions as chief analyst for development policies with the Swedish Ministry for Foreign Affairs and as researcher with the Nordic Africa Institute. A major focus in Hårsmar's work has been to bridge research and policy making, hence moving in between academia and policy organisations.

Terje Oestigaard, Dr. art
is a senior researcher and the cluster leader of the 'Rural and Agrarian Change, Property and Resources' cluster at the Nordic Africa Institute (Uppsala), and docent in archaeology at Uppsala University, Sweden. He has conducted fieldworks in Bangladesh, Egypt, Ethiopia, Greece, India, Jordan, Nepal, Palestine, Tanzania and Uganda. His recent books include *Religion at Work in Globalised Traditions – Rainmamking, Witchcraft and Christianity in Tanzania* (2014), *A History of Water: Water and Urbanization: Series III, Volume 1* (2014) edited with Terje Tvedt, *Water, Christianity and the Rise of Capitalism* (2013), and *The Source of the Blue Nile – Water Rituals and Traditions in the Lake Tana Region* (2013) together with Gedef Abawa Firew.

Rune Skarstein
is Associate Professor Emeritus at the Department of Economics, The Norwegian University of Science and Technology (NTNU), Dragvoll Campus, Trondheim, and Associate of the Nordic Africa Institute, Uppsala. His primary research focus is development economics and macroeconomics. He has spent long periods doing research in Tanzania and has been visiting researcher at universities or research institutes in Argentina, India, Mexico, Germany and Austria.

Eva Tobisson
has a PhD in social anthropology from Göteborg University. Since 2002, she holds a position as senior advisor in the Department for Aid Management at the Ministry for Foreign Affairs, Sweden, where she works on development policy with particular focus on research of relevance for development, as part of Sweden's international development cooperation. In 2010–2012, she was seconded to the Nordic Africa Institute (NAI) to pursue her research interest in livelihood strategies among coastal populations in Zanzibar, in perspective of national and global drivers of change,[1] and to help bridge the gap between research and policy. Her participation in the work on the current book was part of her affiliation to NAI.

Tea Virtanen
is currently a Finnish Academy research fellow based at the University of Helsinki. She received her PhD in cultural anthropology from the University of Helsinki in 2003. She has worked earlier e.g. as an Assistant Professor of Cultural Anthropology at the University of Joensuu (2002–2005) and a Nordic researcher (Finland) at the Nordic Africa Institute in Uppsala (2010–2013). Virtanen has done extensive fieldwork among the Mbororo people in Cameroon since 1994. Her research interests include pastoralism, ritual and performance, Islamic religiosity, rural–urban dynamics, and popular conceptualization of indigeneity.

1 Tobisson, E (2014) Consequences and Challenges of Tourism and Seaweed Farming: A Narrative on a Coastal Community in Zanzibar. *Western Indian Ocean Journal of Marine Sciences*. Vol. 12. No. 2, pp. 169–184.

CHAPTER 1

Framing African Development – Challenging Concepts

Kjell Havnevik[1]

Over time, the African continent has been framed by concepts that relate to its development, with some more comprehensive than others. The concepts were initially created outside the continent, primarily in Western institutions and agencies, and sought to describe and understand Africa, but also to legitimize external interventions driven by religious, military, political, economic, exploitative and altruistic motives.

The concepts addressed in this book capture four themes that represent central aspects of the West's framing of African development: (i) the concept of the "**other**", addressing the question of culture and representation in the context of development, (ii) the concept of **poverty** and how to address it, i.e. the **empowerment** and **livelihood** concepts, (iii) concepts addressing **displacement** and comprising the concept of **primitive accumulation**, and (iv) concepts relating to **food security and food sovereignty** that connect to agricultural production-, sustainability-, rights- and power issues.

In order to challenge the concepts selected and relating to the framing of African development, we find it necessary to understand their logic and the underlying process of their construction. In brief, to challenge the concepts mentioned above necessarily implies reflecting on the ways in which we in the West have historically developed our narratives in the social, economic, technological and cultural fields. This leads us to a critical analysis of the Western vision of Africa, its development and people.

Addressing the Logic and the Underlying Process of Construction of the Concepts

Reflecting on the mythification of optical technology, we find that its development could serve as a metaphor or a departure point to understand how

1 I am grateful for comments to this introductory chapter, in particular regarding the example of the construction of the Western visual technology to Edyala Lima de Iglesias. I am also thankful to Deborah Bryceson for comments to this version of the chapter and to Mats Hårsmar, Terje Oestigaard and Clive Liddiard for comments to earlier versions.

 | DOI 10.1163/9789004305465_002

Western civilization has built up some concepts to make them to be perceived as the significant of "real", of "true" and of "universal". As we know, within Western civilization the duality "reality" and "truth" operates as if it was "natural": what our eyes see is perceived to be "real" and therefore represents "truth" (Barthes 1972).

To point out some aspects of the Western narrative logic that interests us, we chose the historical period of the Renaissance, characterized by the advent of the *camera obscura*[2] and of *perspectiva artificialis*[3] as well as the emergence of the Cartesian subject (Grosholz 1991). The construction of this Western "look" interests us less as a technical device *per se*, and more on account of its consequences in the structuring of a logic and a perspective that reflect Western cultural values and visions. The images produced by this strictly codified perspective, or frame, were considered a physiological reproduction of what the human eye could "naturally" see, therefore approaching "representation" of "reality", naturalizing an ideological perspective – making believe that the image really reproduces what the human eye "naturally" captures.

This ideological aspect of the technology used in the manufacture of photographic and cinematographic cameras reveals the maintenance of the parameters and codes of the specular vision defined by the Renaissance. In a way, from the *camera obscura* through the optical engineering applied to photographic, cinematographic and TV lenses, right up to digital technology, the axis of visual technological development reveals the Western ambition to attain the most "exact" representation of reality. In fact, the technology present in the camera lenses of today obeys the principles already existing in the technique used by many painters of the Renaissance, giving continuity to a certain way of constructing "reality" – of "seeing" the world and identifying it with a "neutral" and "scientific" vision of the world – although in fact it is generated by culture.

The central point (the eye-subject) constructed by the *perspectiva artificialis* corresponds to the place that Western, white, Christian Man has assigned to himself. He is not only "the centre", but also the origin of all sense – a sort of

2 Latin expression that signifies "dark chamber" – the basis for the modern photographic camera. The *camera obscura* meant the existence of a device that mechanically reproduces the perspective from a central point, as the way "man sees the world". It appears that a number of artists during the 17th and 18th centuries secretly employed the technique in order to draft with "photographic" precision landscapes, nature and portraits. See Lacorre (2010).

3 A technique in which the current Western system of representation has its origin. The *perspectiva artificialis* is meant to create the impression of a third dimension in the two-dimensional frame of a painting or a photograph.

transcendent consciousness of the world. From his narcissistic perspective, the world is envisaged as "an object", and is reduced to the status of a mirror, reflecting his own myths and traditions (see also Oestigaard, Chapter 2). In the history of the development of this technology, it is undeniable that one of the ambitions of Western civilization has been to guarantee the status of "reality" for its images, representations and narratives, and to relate this perspective to a "universal truth" (Comolli 1971–72). It is thus no mere chance that camera lenses are also known as "objectives" – identifying the technique with a "neutral" and a "scientific" vision of the world.

To round off this example, those with experience of photography will know that lenses are not designed to reproduce black and white subjects with the same sharpness: a black subject requires a different set of lighting for its features to be reproduced clearly. In other words, we should avoid universalizing our technical, scientific and cultural developments as if they could be applied to other cultures without critical reflection. In our opinion, this "naturalization" of Western values and perspectives needs to be discussed and understood more deeply in order to avoid the error of reducing other cultures to a mirror image of our own ideas, needs and concerns.

We hope that the logic revealed by this example[4] – construction of the visual technology – will help us to perceive and to explain the process underlying the mythification of Western notions present in other fields of knowledge. In challenging these Western perspectives and narratives, the chapters of this book aim to open a discussion surrounding the origin of some concepts used to frame African development, their evolution over time, and their usefulness and relevance for understanding and describing the continental realities. We hope that such a discussion may also lead to improvements in policy prescriptions and assistance interventions that aim to support African development.

The Background and Process Leading to Challenging of the Concepts

The challenge taken up by the authors of this book is undoubtedly considerable, since – with one exception – all the authors grew up in Western cultural contexts, and all of them subsequently studied at Western, primarily Nordic,

4 Although the example is presented only briefly, it allows us to perceive the logic underlying the construction of some Westerne concepts of "the other". For a further discussion of this issue, see Lima de Iglesias 2014.

universities. In the course of their research careers, the authors have conducted field work in one or more African countries, often in cooperation with African universities and researchers. Some of the authors have also worked for African public institutions and universities. Many of them also gained insights into the workings of international institutions and aid donor activities through their studies of the policies and strategies of such institutions, which have primarily sought to develop Africa.

These experiences have given the contributing authors knowledge of the use of central Western concepts in the framing of African development to explain and understand African societal realities. By engaging with these Western concepts, the primary aim is not to reveal their weaknesses, but rather to assess their relevance: they are regarded as a point of departure for the authors' own research activities. The challenges to the central Western concepts is thus most often based on an analysis of the mainstream Western definition of the concept, which then is confronted with the authors' experiences in the field.

From this confrontation (or juxtaposition), many of the authors try to integrate or merge the Western concept with the new knowledge and insights, so as to create new ways of seeing and understanding African development. This process has also led some of the authors to contribute to the adoption or creation of new concepts that can better capture the conditions and dynamic processes that relate to African development. Improvements in the Western concepts used to frame African development have, of course, also been presented by researchers from Africa and other continents. Their contributions are documented in various chapters of this book.

The Urgency of the Critical Inquiry – Africa Opening up: Can the Continent Embark on a Sustainable Development Path?

We believe that our critical inquiry into the central concepts used to frame African development is urgent, both because of the intensification over the last decades of the relationships between Africa and the world, and because of Africa's problem to embark on a sustainable development path based on substantial democracy (Bangura 1992, 2011, Mkandawire 2001 and Rudebeck 2015). In the case of the latter point, this has occurred in spite that Africa since the early 1960s has received considerable development assistance and advice from the West – i.e. the institutions that it dominates, for example the International Monetary Fund (IMF) and the World Bank, donor agencies and non-governmental organizations.

Poverty reduction has been the primary focus of Western development assistance to Africa from the 1970s (first the targeting of absolute poverty) and again from the early 1990s (poverty assessments, the linking of debt reduction to growth strategies, pro-poor growth strategies, and more recently inclusive growth strategies). In spite of this effort to reduce African poverty over time, the situation in 2015 is still that 41 per cent of the continent's population live below the poverty threshold of USD 1.25/day (World Bank 2015). Mats Hårsmar in Chapter 3, however, shows the limitation of this quantitative concept for understanding African poverty although it has gained a central position in global development strategies, including the first set of Millennium Development Goals to be attained in 2015.

The urgency also stems from our doubts as to the sustainability of African growth over the past decade of around 5 per cent annually. One reason is that it has largely been based on the exploitation of natural resources: this currently constitutes about 40 per cent of African Gross National Product (GNP), though it employs less than 1 per cent of those formally employed (McKinsey 2012; Havnevik 2015).

The number of people who go hungry every day in Africa has not diminished in absolute terms for decades (Havnevik, Chapter 8). And in terms of future population growth, the estimate is that Africa's population will increase from 1 billion today to 2 billion in 2050. This growth will account for half of the global population growth in the period.

The capital-intensive large-scale investment that has been undertaken in Africa in mineral exploitation, land-based energy and food production over the past decade is unlikely to contribute to inclusive economic development, or to meeting the need for increased employment opportunities. Research shows that such large-scale investments often displace or alienate smallholders from their land without providing proper compensation or compensating employment opportunities (Matondi et al. 2011; FAO 2013; Havnevik 2014; Hammar, Chapter 6; Skarstein, Chapter 7). The decline documented in African manufacturing over recent decades also implies that formal work opportunities in urban areas are limited. Overall, such a development trajectory is likely to increase rural migration to African cities and as well beyond the continent.

We hope that our critical examination of the central concepts for the framing of African development can result in a deeper discussion of what current development models for Africa could lead to. For instance, the West's framing of the modernization of African agriculture, based on large-scale investments, is posited as a win–win narrative. This is in spite of research from other countries and continents – e.g. the experience of Brazil shows that large-scale agriculture requires two workers to cultivate 100 hectares, whereas smallholder farming regimes require 15 – seven times as many (Fernandes et al. 2012). How can the development of Africa – with its high levels of poverty and food insecurity and its rapid population growth – be conceived of without structural change to broaden the continent's economic basis, at the same time as sustainable food and agricultural production and increased employment generation are secured? It seems that the discussion of African development alternatives should be linked more to African realities and aspirations that go beyond notions of win–win narratives that find little support in empirical investigation (FAO 2013; Havnevik 2014, 2015).

The Concept of the "Other" and African Development

Terje Oestigaard in Chapter 2 shows that an important feature of the framing relationships with Africa is the asymmetrical power representations between the West and the "other". The West's dominance made it possible for it to frame the "other" without a deeper understanding of the framed. Instead "the other" appeared as a mirror-self of the West, reflecting its own expectations and aspirations.

At an early stage in the West's framing of the "other", the notion emerged of the backwardness of the "other" – culturally, economically and socially. As a corollary, the West claimed that "development" in these other continents, territories and cultures had not yet begun. This perspective of the backwardness of the "other", subsequently legitimized Western colonization of Africa and other territories, as well as post-colonial interventions (Oestigaard, Chapter 2).

The process of creating the "other", has, over time, been particularly discussed within the discipline of social anthropology. Oestigaard shows that outstanding representatives of the discipline – one from the West (Sahlins 1995) and one from Asia (Obeyesekere 1992) – present completely different views of the relationship between the European (Captain Cook, who visited Hawaii in 1778–79) and the native. Sahlins claimed that natives saw Captain Cook as a god, while Obeyesekere argued that he was merely considered a chief. However, according to Obeyesekere, if Captain Cook was seen as a god, it was the Europeans themselves who created the idea. This fitted well with the European self-image. This "European god" is, in the words of Obeyesekere, a myth of "conquest, imperialism and civilization" (Obeyesekere 1992).

Are all cultures similar because we are all human beings, or do some cultures contain different logics? How can different cultures be understood, and what does cultural difference mean? Sahlins argues in favour of cultural relativism (cultures have their own logic) while Obeyesekere favours a more essentialist or universal understanding of culture. On what empirical basis can one argue for the one or the other position with regard to cultural understanding? And how do the Western concepts employed relate to the cultural question?

These questions remain unresolved in Western sciences. Whereas anthropology as an academic discipline aims to understand the "other" by focusing on understanding change, the West's framing of African development aims directly at changing the "other". But on whose terms, and with reference to what, are the West and its institutions aiming to change the "other" – in our case Africa? Is the understanding of change a prerequisite for initiatives and interventions that aim to change the "other"? The content of Chapter 2, as well as of many others in the book, is located in the ambiguous interface between understanding change and changing the "other".

Poverty, Empowerment and Livelihood Concepts and Their Interlinkages

In Chapters 3, 4 and 5 the nexus between poverty, empowerment and livelihood concepts becomes evident. Support for local empowerment and rural livelihoods can be seen as a way of helping to reduce poverty. International development agencies' raison d'etre over the past four decades has been to reduce poverty. But in spite of continuous improvements in the concept and associated intervention strategies, poverty has only been reduced marginally in Africa. Part of the explanation may be revealed by an analysis of the empowerment concept, which shows that the original meaning of the concept has been turned upside down: rather than implying power and space for development from below, in the streamlined version of the Organisation for Economic Co-operation and Development's Development Assistance Committee (the OECD's DAC) it came to mean delegation of power from the top to the bottom. The livelihood chapter shows that the livelihood concept was basically descriptive and schematic: it was useful for data collection and for designing broad-based development interventions; however, it has seemingly had a limited impact on poverty reduction.

The concept of poverty came to the fore in the early 1970s, when the World Bank launched a strategy to reduce absolute poverty. In its early phase, the definition of poverty was purely quantitative: a person was poor if he or she was earning less than a dollar a day (later increased to USD 1.25/day). In Chapter 3, Mats Hårsmar shows that the efforts of international institutions and donors to reduce poverty in Africa over the past four decades have fallen short of expectations.

Hårsmar traces how donors' poverty approach has shifted over time, from emphasizing income/consumption (I/C), to participation and, more recently, capability aspects. He argues that the capability approach reaches out for a third way of understanding poverty, in that it provides an arena where the gaps/tensions between different epistemological approaches can be discussed, instead of being perceived as fundamental divisions.

Although the **poverty concept** has been central to the West's framing of African development, it was not until the mid-1990s that the World Bank initiated large-scale field research that acknowledged the importance of the voice to the poor in defining poverty (Narayan 1997; Narayan et al. 2000). These studies led to a much more nuanced picture of what poverty implies, and the capability approach made it possible to use a multitude of methods and data. These factors can, according to Hårsmar, constitute an important platform for taking multi-disciplinary, multi-dimensional and dynamic approaches to the study of poverty.

The challenge to the poverty concept, as put forward by Hårsmar, comes from within the discipline of development economics itself led by Amartya Sen, who, though based at Western universities/institutions, is of Indian origin (Chapter 3). His profound understanding of Indian culture where poverty is of layered complexity gave impetus to his conceptual contribution to the study of poverty in cooperation with Martha Nussbaum (e.g. Nussbaum 2003). This helped the discipline of development economics adopt a more empirical and open approach to the multidisciplinary dynamics of poverty.

The **empowerment concept** emerged in the writings of Paulo Freire (1970). Freire saw empowerment as a process of liberation from structural oppression, through collective critical awareness or "conscientization". The streamlining of the concept in Western institutions, including the OECD's DAC, however, changed its meaning to signify those in authority giving power to marginalized or discriminated groups.

As Rosalind Eyben demonstrates (Chapter 4), her facilitation of the task force on empowerment under the OECD's DAC succeeded in constructing an official policy text which ran counter to the Western mainstream neo-liberal environment. But alas a few months after the submission of the task force report on empowerment, the DAC abolished the task force and shifted its development concern away from empowerment. Was the task force's insistence in center-staging power in the development agenda too much of a threat to the OECD, one of the most powerful institutions in influencing the global development agenda?

Deborah Bryceson (Chapter 5) traces how the **livelihood concept** used in the framing of African development emerged in the early 1990s. The conceptualization of a sustainable livelihood framework provided a household decision-making model and community-based analysis that focused on five types of household assets/capital (human, natural, financial, social and physical).

Its schematic character, however, made it difficult for the framework to address the complex processes of de-agrarianization and de-peasantization, which had already started to unfold in Africa during the "lost development decade" of the 1980s (Bryceson 1999; Bryceson et al. 2000).

The descriptive and schematic character of the framework rendered the concept useful in facilitating the rapid collection of data on changing work patterns, and in designing broad-based development agency interventions. However, the author regrets that few studies have so far sought to question or document the approach's utility in terms of what cumulative findings have revealed about development and its converse, impoverishment.

Drawing on her own research, Bryceson shows that the complex realities and intricate dynamics of change in rural Africa have not been adequately apprehended by the sustainable livelihood framework. Her research focuses on the social tensions along the path of non-agricultural income diversification, as people's sense of family and community are increasingly challenged by individual family members' efforts to seek sources of individual income to compensate falling earnings from farming. The relatively low returns of most rural income-generating activities have been frustrating. There is little evidence to support earlier agricultural economics research, which predicted increasing forward and backward linkages between non-agricultural and agricultural activities that were hypothesized to raise the productivity of smallholder farming. The trend towards rural labour diversification is primarily a project of survival, rather than productivity-raising development.

The author stresses the need to shift livelihood research in the direction of concepts linked to occupationality, which allows examination of the nature of the change in people's identity as they experiment with new forms of livelihood. This approach further entails consideration of the dynamism of collective groups of people engaged in livelihood searches, which is not possible by employing the livelihood concept. The author shows, through a case study of Tanzanian artisanal gold miners, how it is possible to find crossover from a livelihood context to a specialized work career in the embryonic formation of an informal, but increasingly professional cadre of miners.

The Displacement and Primitive Accumulation Concepts – Analyses of "Undesired" Outcomes

The chapters on the concepts of displacement and primitive accumulation relate to processes of change that undermine people's livelihood or their access to land and resources. Amanda Hammar (Chapter 6) focuses primarily on displacement in the African context, while Rune Skarstein (Chapter 7) presents a more global overview and analysis, which has the capitalist system as a point of departure (primitive accumulation). We learn from the chapters that displacement – large in scale, both historically and currently – is an outcome that runs counter to the ideas and objectives of Western concepts used in the framing of African development.

The focus on the "flip side" of development may explain why the streamlined concept of displacement stands out as technocratic and partial (Chapter 6) and why the concept of primitive accumulation is simply overlooked or sidelined (Chapter 7) in the West's framing of African development. The analysis of the concept of primitive accumulation indicates that there exists a limited space for alternative theories and perspectives (alternative to those of the dominant Western institutions and agencies) in the framing of African development. This observation is also reflected in the content of the curricula of Western educational institutions and the prioritization of Western research funding. There may, in our assessment, be two reasons for this: (i) the alternative theories and perspectives emphasize or acknowledge the critical role of conflict in societal processes of change, and (ii) many of the assumptions of theories that guide the content of the streamlined concepts of the West underline values or human behaviour of universal character. This makes it difficult for the concepts to capture the understanding of historical processes that comprise interlinked changes of economic, social, spatial and cultural character. Reflecting on this problem, it could be that invoking universal assumptions for the modelling of complex societal contexts and processes implies the substitution of history for nature (see Barthes 1972).

In her chapter on the **concept of displacement**, Hammar (Chapter 6) challenges the more standard technocratic and humanitarian perspectives on displacement. These perspectives tend to promote mono-dimensional and stale paradigms which result in distortions and stereotyping of the causes, processes and outcomes of displacement. According to Hammar, these perspectives echo aspects of the UN Convention Relating to the Status of Refugees of 1951 and subsequent amendments, rather than the complexities and the multiple dimensions of displacement that have emerged over recent decades.

The scale and diversity of the problem of displacement in Africa cannot be denied, since even official counts show that in 2009/2010 there were 2.3 million refugees and about 11.5 million internally displaced persons across the continent (IDMC and Norwegian Refugee Council 2010: 2–3).

Hammar's own experience drawn from field research (Zimbabwe and Mozambique) led her to challenge the streamlined concepts relating to displacement. She argues for a more nuanced perspective on displacement, comprising several elements and their relationships. In particular, she underlines the need to shift the focus of the concept from primarily forced displacement (or migration) to enforced changes that can open up the concept to the complexities, multiple aspects and relationships of displacement. She proposes, based on her field experience, three important entry points to the understanding of displacement that reflect paradoxical dimensions linked to place, positionality and productivity. As to place, it is critical to engage closely with the actual sites of displacement. Positionality underlines the need to analyse both the former and changing social positions of people, since they impact on people's experience and management of their displacement. And on the issue of productivity, Hammar also includes the idea that displacement may generate new capacity and opportunity. She provides empirical examples from Zimbabwe (see also Hammar 2014). Her field research experiences thus led Hammar to a rethinking of the conceptualization of the concept as "enforced changes in interweaving spatial, social and symbolic conditions and relations".

Skarstein's presentation of the **concept of primitive accumulation** (Chapter 7) also relates to issues of displacement, but from a different perspective. He challenges the contribution of mainstream development economics, arguing for a Marxist historical understanding that distinguishes pre-capitalist and capitalist markets and different forms of capitalism rather than a simplistic view of market expansion based on mainstream development economics that treats land and labour as any other commodity. This assumption, according to Skarstein, will render the discipline unable to capture and explain critical features of historical processes.

He also refers to Karl Polanyi, who, like Marx, emphasizes that a basic feature of capitalism is the commodification of land and labour. It is this process of commodification that Marx denotes as "primitive accumulation". Marx sees capitalism as the accumulation of capital proceeding in a never-ending circle. However, its point of departure, and a primary condition for its expansion, is the process of primitive accumulation. This process consists of: (i) expropriation of the means of production, livelihood and labour of pre-capitalist producers and their transformation into commodities, with (ii) the outcome that formerly autonomous producers will have nothing to sell but their labour power. This process opens them up to exploitation by capital as wage labour. The continuous conquering of pre-capitalist modes of production by capitalism will in this way feed the expansion of the system.

Polanyi analyses the transition from the pre-capitalist to the capitalist system of production somewhat differently. Polanyi (1957) argues that economic life was governed by three principles: (i) householding, (ii) reciprocity, and (iii) redistribution. Skarstein shows that Polanyi asserts that gain and profit on exchange "never before played an important part in human economy" before capitalism. This is in spite of the fact that the institution of the market had been fairly common since the Stone Age. What has happened in modern times, according to Polanyi, is that the market has gone from being the servant of society to its master: "The control of the economic system by the market is of overwhelming consequence to the whole organization of society" (ibid.: 57, 71).

Whereas Marx emphasizes that the continuous expansion of the capitalist system will lead to its destruction, Polanyi, according to Skarstein, ends on a hopeful note: "But no society could stand the effects of such a system of crude fictions [i.e. the commodification of land and labour] even for the shortest stretch of time unless its human and natural substance as well as it business organization was protected against the ravages of 'this satanic mill'" (ibid.: 72–73).

Skarstein (Chapter 7) analyses how the process of primitive accumulation has played out historically in Great Britain (the enclosure movement), the USA (external and internal colonization of the native population), India (displacement of lower castes and peasants) and Africa (the impact of large-scale foreign investments in land and energy for exports and the impact on smallholder farmers and the environment).

From Food Security to Food Sovereignty?

The **concept of food security** has, over the past two decades, come into increasing focus on the global development agenda. This rise in interest in the concept has followed from the inability to reduce global hunger, the rapid increase and variation in food prices globally, and the competition for agricultural land from increasing energy production, as a consequence of climate change and the attainment of 'peak oil'. The rising global interest in investment in land, with a particular focus on Africa, has followed from these emergent concerns. The West has, however, framed this development in a "win–win" narrative, implying that all stakeholders in the process – including international investors, host country governments and smallholder farmers – will benefit.

This development is of particular concern for Africa, since the continent accounts for a major share of the hungry population of the world, as well as large proportion of what is conceived as globally "available" agricultural land. In Chapter 8, Havnevik addresses the changing content of the concept of food security over time: the emphasis on storage, the nutritional value, access to food, food safety and cultural acceptance of food. On the basis of this historical exposé, Havnevik outlines a conceptualization of food security that reflects the more general definition that the FAO Food Summit arrived at in 1996, which states that food security is attained "when all people at all times have access to sufficient, safe, nutritious food to maintain a healthy and active life".

Havnevik argues, however, that this way of defining food security is descriptive and incapable of capturing the causes and power relations that generate and sustain hunger over time. Also increasing external investment in African land for export has caused growing conflict between large-scale investors and smallholder producers – not just over land, but over water as well.

Against this background, Havnevik argues for a paradigmatic shift in the understanding of food security that places less emphasis on descriptive definitions and win–win type narratives, and instead moves in the direction of environmental sustainability, global social justice, human rights and fair trading agreements relating to food – its provision and distribution. Incorporating power, rights and sovereignty issues in the discussion of food security necessitates a shift to the concept of **food sovereignty**. This concept, which is increasingly supported and promoted by smallholder farmers' associations worldwide, helps explain the causes of hunger and recognizes the importance of smallholder farmers in generating a global sustainable food supply. This will require support for securing smallholders' land rights and improving their production conditions relating to technology, infrastructure, credit lines and market access. Labour-intensive smallholder production regimes in Africa are relevant not only to the provision of food in Africa and beyond, but also to addressing climate change and the need to increase employment opportunities in Africa in the future. As well this will be a most important way in the longer run to halt migration out of Africa.

References

Bangura, Y. (1992). "Authoritarian Rule and Democracy in Africa: a Theoretical Discourse". In Rudebeck, L. (ed), *When Democracy Makes Sense. Studies in the Democratic Potential of Third World Popular Movements*, AKUT, Uppsala University, Uppsala, pp. 69–104.

Bangura, Y. (2011). "Inequality and the Politics of Redistribution". In *European Journal of Development Research*, no. 4, vol. 23, pp. 531–536. www.palgrave-journals.com/ejdr/.

Barthes, R. (1972). *Mythologies*. Hill and Wang. New York (first published in 1957, translated from French by Annette Lavers).

Bryceson, D.F. (1999). "African Rural Labour, Income Diversification and Livelihood Approaches: A Long-Term Development Perspective." In *Review of African Political Economy*, No. 80, pp. 171–89.

Bryceson, D.F., C. Kay and J. Mooij (2000) (eds). *Dissappearing Peasantries? Rural Labour in Africa, Asia and Latin America.* Intermediate Technology Publications, London.

Comolli, J.-L. (1971–1972). "Technique et Idéologie." In *Cahiers du Cinéma*, pp. 229 á 240. Paris.

FAO (Food and Agricultural Organization) (2013). *Trends and Impacts of Foreign Investments in Developing Country Agriculture. Evidence from case studies.* FAO, Rome.

Fernandes, B.M., C.A. Welch and E.C Goncalves (2012). *Land Governance in Brazil. A geo-historical review of land governance in Brazil.* International Land Coalition Framing the Debate Series no. 2, Rome.

Freire, P. (1970). *The Pedagogy of the Oppressed.* Continuum, New York (first published in Portuguese in 1968).

Grosholz, E. (1991). *Cartesian method and the problem of reduction.* Oxford University Press, Oxford.

Hammar, A. (ed) (2014). *Displacement Economies in Africa – Paradoxes of Crisis and Creativity.* Zed Books, London and New York.

Havnevik, K. (2014). "Responsible agricultural investments in developing countries – how to make principles and guidelines effective." Swedish FAO Committee Publication Series 9. Ministry of Rural Affairs, Stockholm.

Havnevik, K. (2015). "The Current Afro-Optimism – A Realistic Image of Africa?" In *FLEKS – Scandinavian Journal of Intercultural Theory and Practice,* Oslo and Akershus University College of Applied Sciences, autumn 2015 Festskrift in honour of professor Tore Linné Eriksen. https://journals.hioa.no/index.php/fleks.

IDMC and Norwegian Refugee Council (2010). Internal Displacement in Africa, at: http://www.internal-displacement.org/publications/global-overview-210-africa.pdf.

Lacorre, B. (2010). *L'image et le fantasme.* Cahiers Philosophiques Hors-série; Paris.

Lima de Iglesias, E. (2014). *Le labyrinth en miroirs d'Eva. Le Mythe de L'eternel Feminin et L'anti-Heroine.* École Doctorale 267 – Arts du Spectacle, Sciences de L'Information et de la Communication (ASSIC). Université Sorbonne Nouvelle – Paris 3. Thesis available at http://www.univ-paris3.fr.

Matondi, P., K. Havnevik and Atakilte Beyene (eds) (2011). *Biofuels, Land Grabbing and Food Security in Africa.* Zed Books, London and New York.

Mkandawire, T. (2001). "Thinking about developmental states in Africa". In *Cambridge Journal of Economics* 25 (3): 289–314.

McKinsey Global Institute (2012). "Africa at work: Job creation and inclusive growth in Africa". August. McKinsey & Company.

Narayan, D. (1997). *Voices of the Poor. Poverty and Social Capital in Tanzania.* World Bank. Washington D.C.

Narayan, D., R. Patel, K. Schafft, A. Rademacher and S. Koch-Schulte (2000). *Voices of the Poor. Can anyone hear us?* Published by the Oxford University Press for the World Bank.

Nussbaum, M. C. (2003). "Capabilities as Fundamental Entitlements: Sen and Social Justice". In *Feminist Economics*, Vol 9.2–3: 35–59.

Obeyesekere, G. (1992). *The Apotheosis of Captain Cook: European mythmaking in the Pacific*. Princeton University Press.

Polanyi, K. (1957). *The Great Transformation. The Political and Economic Origins of Our Time*. Beacon, Boston, MA.

Rudebeck, L. (2015). "Democracy and Development – two concepts and their linkages". mimeo. Center for Environment and Development, CEMUS, Uppsala University.

Sahlins, M. (1995). *How 'Natives' think: About Captain Cook, for example*. University of Chicago Press.

World Bank (2015). *Global Monitoring Report 2014/2015 – Ending Poverty and Sharing Prosperity*. Washington D.C.

CHAPTER 2

Developing the 'Other': Perceptions of Africans and change

Terje Oestigaard

Introduction[1]

Developing the 'other' – in this case Africans – should here be understood in two distinct ways that partly overlap and depend upon each other. On the one hand, the rationale for development aid is that there is someone somewhere – countries or people – who can develop. On the other hand, for this kind of development to happen there needs to be another group of 'others' – the donors, in this case the broadly defined 'West' – who will take part in facilitating the development. Thus, at the outset, there are two categories of 'others' – the Africans and the Westerners. Both parties are dependent upon each other and have to be 'developed' as concepts prior to the actual 'development'.

But this relationship is largely an asymmetrical power dependency. Moreover, this dichotomy of the 'other' African seen in relation to the 'West' is a product of history that has developed over time. The perceptions of the African 'otherness' also constitute frames for understanding development practices. Although today the dark and murky colonial perceptions largely belong in the past, Africa and the African 'other' are still, to varying degrees, perceived as different. Various perceptions of the 'other' also have implications for understanding processes of change and the premises on which they occur, and this is also reflected in today's development discourse.

The overall aim of this chapter is to address the concept of the 'other' and 'otherness', as well as the development and the developing of the 'other' and how this relates to changes on the African continent – past and present. This will be analysed through four perspectives: first, a theoretical and anthropological discussion of how to approach the 'other'; second, a historical examination of the concept of the African 'other' from colonialism onwards; third, a look at whether Africans have contributed to these perceptions by developing a Pan-African ideology and philosophy; and finally, a presentation of images of 'others' in the

1 I would like to thank Professor Kjell Havnevik for his useful comments and suggestions; also Professor Axel Fleisch and the rest of the participants at the Concept Africa workshop in Johannesburg in November 2012 for fruitful discussions.

 | DOI 10.1163/9789004305465_003

development discourse, mainly as portrayed in the media, with examples drawn particularly from Norway. Taken together, this will form the basis for a comparative discussion of developing the 'other' as part of the development discourse.

Captain Cook and the Clash between Giants

Before entering the development discourse, it may be useful to approach the problem from a theoretical and anthropological standpoint. One of the last major clashes in anthropology between prominent and dominant anthropologists of our time took place in the early 1990s. One of the leading authorities on the history of the Pacific, Marshall Sahlins, had written extensively on the topic, including *Islands of History* (1985). In 1992, another distinguished anthropologist, Gananath Obeyesekere, published *The Apotheosis of Captain Cook: European mythmaking in the Pacific*, which featured a harsh critique of Sahlins.

Sahlins' first response was not to comment on Obeyesekere, preferring to leave that to other scholars and reviewers. But most of the thirty or so reviews of Obeyesekere's book were quite positive, and he was even awarded two prizes for it. So if anybody wanted to defend Sahlins, it had to be himself. His response was another book: *How 'Natives' Think: About Captain Cook, for example* (Sahlins 1995). This book has been labelled remorseless revenge (Borofsky 1997: 256).

As Obeyesekere notes (1997: 270), quoting Kerry Howe (1996: 116) in Sahlins' work:

> Obeyesekere's work is variously described (to give but a small alphabetical sample) as: absurd, anti-anthropological, blundering, blustering, careless, contradictory, defective, dubious, evasive, epistemic murk, falsely accusative, fictitious, highly righteous, helter-skelter, implausible, misrepresentational, pidgin-anthropology, quixotic, scattershot, slanderous, scholier-than-you, solipsistically fallacious, stratified palimpsest of confusion and contradiction, symbolically violent, ventriloquism, willy-nilly, wrong, unaware, unhistorical [and more].

On the other hand, Obeyesekere himself admitted that he had written, wittingly and unwittingly, in a 'satiric mode of shaming' (Obeyesekere 1997: 270). The language he used, and his wordplay, reflected this: in the second edition of his book, for instance, he added a 63-page reply to Sahlins entitled 'On de-Sahlinization'. He also admitted that the reason he wrote his book in such a polemical style was to 'stir things up' (Borofsky 1997: 261). How and why did it come about that two of the giants of anthropology should have written books targeting one another and using rather unpleasant language? What were the stakes involved?

The empirical point of departure of the debate was whether Captain Cook was seen as a god (Lono) when he went to Hawaii in 1778–79, or merely as a chief. Sahlins favoured the first position; Obeyesekere the second. Obviously, such an empirical or interpretative dispute would not have caused a disagreement of such magnitude. But Obeyesekere had another agenda, too. The idea of European colonizers being seen as gods was not the natives' view, he argued, but a view created by the Europeans themselves. It fitted the European self-image in their own conquests, legitimating the Europeans' worldview of superiority: 'To put it bluntly, I doubt that the natives created their European god; the Europeans created god for them. This "European god" is a myth of conquest, imperialism, and civilization' (Obeyesekere 1992: 3).

At the end of the day, as the battle of debate unfolded, most agreed that Sahlins was empirically right, and that Obeyesekere could not prove and document his hypothesis well enough. At the same time, many favoured Obeyesekere and his perspective, which fitted well with post-colonial theory. One of the other main controversies was about data and facts: what constitutes our empirics?[2] And how can one evaluate and judge another's (an anthropologist's) empirical facts, way of reasoning and presentation of an argument? The debate raised two questions: (i) the cultural question, and (ii) the question of representation – who can speak for the Hawaiians (or for the Others in general)?

Clifford Geertz summarized the debate in an article, 'Culture War', which emphasized fundamental aspects that have haunted anthropology since its dawn. One fundamental issue is what 'knowing' about 'others' implies and constitutes? Following Geertz, is it possible to know others – and if it is possible, is that good? Or should anthropologists work to advance the fortune and lives of the people being studied? Do anthropologists 'know better' the people and the processes they study than the people themselves? This was one of the important questions in the debate.

Perhaps the most fundamental question on which Sahlins and Obeyesekere disagreed was culture: how to understand cultural difference? What do cultural differences mean and what are the implications of different standpoints? According to Geertz, for Sahlins it represents substance; for Obeyesekere it represents surface. Or in other words: Sahlins argues that different cultures

2 Regarding the debate and the different empirical positions, see Borofsky (1997) for details.

have different rationalities; Obeyesekere contends that everybody is like ourselves and fundamentally thinks the same way, since we are all humans (Obeyesekere himself is Sri Lankan) (Geertz 1995). Later, Obeyesekere elaborated on this point. Based on an essentialist (or universalist) perspective, he argued that the idea that life-forms are incommensurable is wrong: 'quite the contrary, commensurability of forms of life is possible although those life-forms are enclosed in larger life-worlds that are different, even incommensurable' (Obeyesekere 2002: 354).

The other question also has direct relevance for the development discourse: who can speak for the Hawaiians or the Others – in this case the Africans? Despite the fierce debate between Sahlins and Obeyesekere on everything else, on this point they agreed (albeit from different perspectives): they do not want to speak for the Hawaiians.

Obeyesekere says: 'I find it utterly presumptuous that ethnographers should tell native peoples how they think or formulate their "classical rules" for them, without an iota of skepticism or tentativeness' (Obeyesekere 1997: 271). In *Medusa's Hair* (published earlier) he elaborated parts of his reasoning: 'Our informants are not passive objects out there, nor are we as anthropologists tools or objective others. They must think in some fundamental ways as we do, for *we* and *they* are constituted of the same essence, our human nature, our species being' (Obeyesekere 1981: 192). Thus,

> ethnography poses an enormous paradox: there is virtually no one, from Boas onwards, who really believes that natives are biologically different from Europeans. But this universalist assumption cannot be brought directly into our writing nowadays because it essentializes human beings, and 'essentialism' is a dirty word. Instead we have moved in the reverse direction and have celebrated *difference*; thus each culture is different, and we have proclaimed a doctrine of cultural relativism to rationalize that difference.
>
> OBEYESEKERE 1997: 271

Sahlins does not wish to speak for the Hawaiians either, but on different grounds:

> Yet, the issue is not, I think…who can speak for Hawaiians, whether back then or now… To assume the right to speak for Hawaiians would be morally repugnant as well as epistemologically madness. Nor is the problem whether they – the so-called…subalterns can speak. The problem is whether they can be heard and understood.
>
> SAHLINS 1997: 273

Whereas Obeyesekere argues in favour of a type of essentialism or universalism, Sahlins argues in favour of a type of relativism:

> Relativism is the simple prescription that, in order to be intelligible, other peoples' practices and ideals must be placed in their own context, thus understood as positional values in a field of their own cultural relationships, rather than appropriated in the intellectual and moral judgments of our own categories.
>
> SAHLINS 1997: 273

And he uses an example: 'Something like cannibalism or the eucharist can thus become anthropologically intelligible even if it is not to everyone's taste.' He adds: 'But then, cultural relativism has never meant for anthropology the vulgar moral relativity for which it is criticized by the defenders of Western-cum-universal virtues' (Sahlins 1997: 274).

Henceforth, both from an essentialist/universalist and a relativist perspective it is possible to argue strongly, on human and other grounds, that one should not speak for Others. Leaving behind the debate of Captain Cook as such, it nevertheless has relevance because of European (and/or Western) engagement and involvement in other parts of the world today. The advantage in the debate between Sahlins and Obeyesekere is that the positions are clear cut, representing opposites. One may assume that most people engaged in the development discourse will agree with Obeyesekere that people in, say, Africa are like us (meaning everybody else). But many will agree with Sahlins that 'they' are not like us – different cultures, different rationalities.

This difference between Obeyesekere and Sahlins also points to the core of discourses of culture, since the very concept carries with it ambiguity. Thus, on the one hand, every human is basically and essentially the same and equally 'cultural', in the sense that culture refers to the similarities between and within humans. On the other hand, there are also differences because of culture. 'Culture refers, in other words, both to basic similarities and to systematic differences between humans' (Eriksen 1995: 9). How is it possible to combine these two positions – essentialism/universalism and relativism – which in anthropology have caused such heated debate? Or is it, as many anthropologists claim, that anthropology is about discovering 'both the uniqueness of each social and cultural setting *and* the ways in which humanity is one' (Eriksen 1995: 13), thus uniting universalism and relativism?

Whereas anthropology aims to study cultures with the primary goal of *understanding* the Other, the development discourse aims to *change* the Other. This has implications for both the comprehension of and attitudes towards the 'other'. Changing is different from understanding; and connected with the latter, there is most often an inevitable asymmetry of power relations that enters into the picture. Whose voices are heard and whose are dominant?

The Historical African: An Archaeological Approach

Today, on whose terms do African engagements take place? Although the general consensus or perception within the development discourse is that African engagements are based on a mutual and equal basis in and between the different actors, this is not necessarily so (see Dietz et al. 2011). Notions linger on that Africa is the dark continent and is somehow backward – or at least has not fully progressed (except from an economic point of view). This was evident in a speech made by former French President Sarkozy in Dakar in 2007, when (among other things) he stated that '[t]he tragedy of Africa is that the African has not fully entered into history... They have never really launched themselves into the future.' This was, said Achille Mbembe, a professor at Witwatersrand University, an attitude 'worthy of the 19th century' (Ba 2007).

'The white man's burden' (as framed by Kipling in 1899) embodied the European colonial attitude at the time towards the perceived current state of development and the responsibility of Christians. Africa was primitive and backward. At the same time, the German philosopher Hegel stated that Africa 'is no historical part of the World; it has no movement or development to exhibit. Historical movements in it – that is in its northern part – belong to the Asiatic or European World' (Hegel 2007 [1899]: 99). Not only were Africans perceived as barbaric and lagging behind the rest of humanity in terms of evolution, but they were 'capable of no development or culture, and as we see them at this day, such have they always been' (ibid.: 98).

Ideologically, such perceptions of the 'other' Africans legitimized the colonial conquests, partly as a process of 'development'. Archaeology played a crucial part in creating this 'backward otherness', as the archaeologist Bruce Trigger states: 'Colonialist archaeology...served to denigrate native societies and peoples by trying to demonstrate that they had been static in prehistoric times and lacked the initiative to develop on their own' (Trigger 1984: 363). As a consequence:

> While the colonisers had every reason to glorify their own past, they had no reason to extol the past of the peoples they were subjugating and supplanting. Indeed, they sought by emphasising the primitiveness and lack of accomplishments of these peoples to justify their own poor treatment of them.
>
> TRIGGER 1984: 360

Archaeology has thus been central to the construction of the African 'otherness'. Without going further into the colonial perceptions of the Africans (elaborated at length elsewhere), it may be worthwhile dwelling on archaeology. Archaeology has been closely and intimately linked with nationalism and nation-building. By definition, in a world of nation states, a nation needs a past, for its own good and to create a sense of belonging for its members (Díaz-Andreu 1996: 68). Thus, regarding nationalism, 'it is…a concept of importance to modern people, including archaeologists, rather than to the people who created the archaeological record' (Trigger 1995: 276). Archaeologists (to some extent) and especially politicians make the past nationalistic. This is a political and ideological act, and Kaiser has pointed out some of the ways in which authorized versions of the past may legitimate the current order: first, by establishing a link between present governors and ultimate sources of power and legitimacy with their origins in the past; second, claiming that a nation's population is superior to others on the basis of past achievements and thereby inventing and creating (favourable) traditions; and third, glorifying the present by presenting the past in an unfavourable light. Thus archaeology may establish political and territorial legitimacy, support a political ideology, and create and maintain cultural identity and ethnicity (Kaiser 1995: 113).

Although the use of a country's past for political ends and for glorification cannot be defended scientifically if it distorts theoretical, methodological and empirical premises and data, archaeology has nevertheless been used for just such purposes. The aim here is not to criticize nation states' political use of archaeology,[3] but merely to indicate a noteworthy aspect in the history of ideas: whereas European (and some other) countries have used archaeology extensively to glorify their past, generally speaking the same is not true of African countries. This is not necessarily because African countries have been unwilling to use archaeology politically, but the role and significance of such political and nationalistic endeavours globally has been suppressed and their attempts have been largely unsuccessful. The glorious Africa has been denied global political importance.

The uniqueness and innovative cultures of Africa are commonly seen and understood on different premises than are developments elsewhere. If one defines archaeology broadly and includes cultural heritage in a wide sense, African art has had a prominent and peculiar position in the West and in modernity discourses. Mudimbe argues that *deviation* is what chiefly characterizes the idea of Africa in the West (Mudimbe 1994: xii). Implicit in this notion are the still lingering perceptions that Africans are on the lower rungs of the evolutionary ladder. As Baaz argues, historically 'Africans were defined

3 For a discussion of this, see, for instance, Oestigaard (2001; 2007).

in terms of their difference from the West, as the barbarian origin of man as opposed to civilisation, as body opposed to mind, as passive opposed to the active and innovative' (Baaz 2001: 8).

The African 'other' has, however, also been regarded with admiration and celebration, as something 'authentic' and untouched by modernity – in other words, representing 'nature' in a somehow vaguely defined form, reinforcing images of the 'noble savage' (ibid.: 8–9). Thus, the African 'otherness' created contradictory views and images of Africans as either noble or ignoble, although both perceptions were rooted in the derogatory view of the 'backward' continent. These images predominated until the era of the Enlightenment; but even today, anthropologists tend to describe African art and objects as something genuinely tribal, as opposed to something from the fragmented and individualistic West (Miller 1991: 186).

In short, for all the achievements and developments on the African continent that could have been interpreted as culturally innovative and unique contributions (not only to Africa, but to mankind and the world as a whole), these have tended to be regarded less favourably in the West and elsewhere. The mental perceptions in the West of the African 'otherness' have been difficult to change. However, using a musical paradox as an example, this otherness 'is "totally Other, but not quite"... [African] musicians have to adjust to the tourists' longing for an otherness that is not too disturbing, not too strange' (Baaz 2001: 17). The idea of the African 'otherness' is nurtured and continuously developed today, and even when such perceptions are changed and adapted to the global world, the distinctive 'otherness' is maintained.

Pan-Africanism – A Solution or Part of the Problem?

Are Africans partaking in the creation and development of this African 'otherness'? The answer is partly 'yes' (but in practice 'no'). In a broad sense, Pan-Africanism is a diverse movement, developed as a response and reaction to European colonialism and racism. The deprivation on the continent and the colonial legacy led Pan-Africanism as an intellectual movement to emphasize first racial and later cultural unity and solidarity among Africans. One of the main goals was to create political unity among the African states in relation to the wider world (Baaz 2001: 9).

Before proceeding with Pan-Africanism as a political and ideological movement, one might usefully examine one of the many degraded perceptions of African development: the ancient Egyptian civilization. This gives some idea of the urgent need and desire within and among intellectuals in Africa to change the premises and to turn the discourse upside down.

Ancient Egypt is one of the marvels of the world (perhaps even *the* marvel). Today the pyramids at Giza are the only one of the Seven Wonders of the Ancient World to survive. Given the afore-mentioned perceptions of Africa as backward, and bearing in mind Hegel's contention that no development can take place in Africa (and Sarkozy's more recent claim that Africa has not yet fully entered history), Egypt posed a serious problem for Western intellectuals at the turn of the last century. How was it possible for Africa to have developed such astonishing and wondrous monuments, and indeed one of the greatest civilizations in history? The solution was to exclude Egypt and its ancient civilization from African development. As Hegel wrote: 'Egypt will be considered in reference to the passage of the human mind from its Eastern to its Western phase, but it does not belong to the African Spirit' (Hegel 2007 [1899]: 99). Consequently, Africa was seen as incapable of independent, autonomous development and of cultural or technological innovation. Africa was the passive receiver of developments from elsewhere, in this case from the Near East. Not only was Africa denied engagements on equal human terms, but in practice Africans were stripped of their humanity.

This perception was rooted in the paradigm of that time, when technical, cultural and political achievements were seen as diffusion and migration from the north and were ascribed to the prehistoric Hamitic peoples (Trigger 1984: 362). According to the 'Ex Oriente Lux' ('Light from the East') school of thought, European civilization in the Bronze Age had its origins in the civilizations of the Near East. This perception also appealed to many Christians, with their biblical view of world history (Trigger 1994: 151, 160–61). The Egyptian civilization also fitted into this picture.

In the Old Testament there is the myth about the Hamites. Ham was one of Noah's three sons, alongside Japheth and Shem. (The descendants of the latter two brothers were supposed to be the Aryans and the Semites.) According to Genesis 10.6, the Hamites included Cush, Egypt, Put and Canaan. Understanding of the Hamites has changed several times throughout history, and in the early nineteenth century they were seen as Caucasians – whites in black skin. The Hamites were not like other black Africans, and hence they linked Egyptian civilization to the Bible and the Middle East. The Hamites were therefore seen as the great 'civilizers' of Africa (Mamdani 2001: 82–86). Consequently, the Egyptian 'problem' was solved: the Egyptian civilization was developed not by Africans, but by 'whites' (Dietz et al. 2011: 9).

Archaeologically, this interpretation was dismissed. Gordon Childe (1934) and Henri Frankfort (1956) conducted comparative studies of the early civilizations of ancient Egypt and southern Mesopotamia. They concluded that all civilizations had developed in distinct ways and were fundamentally different

(Trigger 2003). Apart from the archaeological discourse itself, the colonial perceptions of African developments have been challenged and turned upside down. Cheik Anta Diop (1974), for instance, contended that the Egyptians were black. This argument was pursued further by Martin Bernal in his *Black Athena* (Bernal 1987; 1991), where he advances the idea that ancient Greece and European civilization have their origins in Black Africa and Egypt; and moreover, that the Greek islands had been colonized by Africans. Where Diop focused mainly on contacts between Egypt and Sub-Saharan Africa, Bernal stressed contacts from Egypt towards the north, the west and the east.

The works of Diop and Bernal have been heavily criticized on empirical grounds, and Bernal admitted that part of his *Black Athena* project was an attempt to lessen European cultural arrogance (Bernal 1987: 73). Thus, academically they have turned out to be highly ideological and political models. Such theories often fail when the data is scrutinized, and they may even do the 'subalterns' few favours. They are often part of larger political and nationalistic processes and ideologies without scientific basis, and as such are highly problematic from an academic perspective. Still, such studies that aim to take African history and civilization back to an African context, where Africans are active and culturally innovative (e.g. Chami 2002), have, as Martin Hall pointed out, 'been highly effective in demolishing the tenets of colonial histories of Africa' (Hall 1986: 37).

Apart from mere academic perspectives, such studies also have to be seen in the context in which they originated. More often than not the intellectuals and scholars had to develop the space in which they could manoeuvre, which could imply demolishing colonial prejudices and perceptions. In retrospect, some of the approaches may have duplicated the colonial perspectives, but with opposite values. Thus, some of the inherited premises implied that Africans occupied the lowest rung of the evolutionary ladder and were culturally and intellectually incapable of promoting their own development. In trying to turn this tide, certain arguments may have gone too far in the other direction. This may be understandable and may have been necessary, since at the outset the discourse disfavoured Africa and Africans.

Pan-Africanism as a movement was initiated by Du Bois in Paris in 1891. The ideological unification 'emphasises the sameness and oneness of the African family, seeking from there to provide a framework for the unity and growth of African peoples' (Ugwuanyi 2011: 354). Politically, Pan-Africanism stresses the need for 'a continental government for Africans', as the first prime minster of independent Tanzania, Julius Nyerere, said; 'each of the African states is separately weak in relation to the outside world and so dependent on it' (Ugwuanyi 2011: 356).

There are several directions within this overall movement. First, there is Sub-Saharan Pan-Africanism, which seeks solidarity among black Africans in Sub-Saharan Africa. Second, there is Trans-Saharan Pan-Africanism, which seeks solidarity between south and north, in practice the whole of Africa. Third, there is Trans-Atlantic Pan-Blackism, which links Sub-Saharan Africa to the diasporas in the western hemisphere, mainly black Americans, West Indians and black Brazilians. And finally, there is Trans-Atlantic Pan-Africanism, which aims to bring together the black diaspora in the western hemisphere with the whole African continent, including both the blacks and the Arabs (Ugwuanyi 2011: 355).

However, Pan-African unity has been challenged from within Africa. As the first Nigerian prime minister said in 1960, when his country gained its independence: 'Nigeria has not the slightest intention of surrendering her sovereignty, no sooner has she gained independence [*sic*], to anyone else' (ibid.: 357). In other words, is there a need for a Pan-African platform, and can such a platform be the basis for meeting the needs of the respective countries?

Regarding African 'otherness', there are other challenges related to the Pan-African idea of unity, which ideally should lead to some kind of union, e.g. the United States of Africa. The main defect with this idea is, as Ugwuanyi has pointed out, that

> this unity is anchored in the principle of an assumed African family. What this means is that non-Africans are not eligible to be considered within the framework of Pan-Africanism... Thus the challenge that faces Pan-Africanism in this regard is how to achieve a sense of unity that will enable them to tap the wealth of non-Africans without losing the gains from African solidarity. For this reason, Pan-Africanism cannot serve this purpose.
>
> IBID.: 359

In other words, defining the uniqueness of black Africans in Africa is fraught with serious difficulties, partly because the line of reasoning bears strong similarities to earlier racial categorizations (although in the opposite direction). A central aspect of the presumed African unity is the sum of the cultural values in the black world; but, as has been pointed out by several researchers, these virtues are curiously similar to the sum of the non-virtues of the Africans in the colonial discourse. Thus, identifying such common African virtues (such as aesthetic feelings, rhythm, sensuality, mysticism, etc.) may rather support and confirm racist stereotypes than undermine them (for references see Baaz 2001: 11).

Has Pan-Africanism contributed to the creation of images of Africans as the 'other' and to the African 'otherness'? Superficially, it may appear that it has; but in practice the answer is most likely 'no' – for two reasons. First, those who are familiar with colonial history and with the development of Pan-Africanism are also aware of why and on what premises the latter originated; hence this has contributed not to the creation of 'more' otherness, but rather to an understanding of why these developments and processes occurred. African nationalism (and its intellectual legitimization) is, nevertheless, something that should be addressed seriously, since many of these ideologies may also contain problematic premises and perspectives. Second, those who are not familiar with this history are unlikely to hold images of Africa and perceptions of African 'otherness' that have been shaped either by Pan-Africanism as an ideology or by other African intellectuals. It is much more likely that the images of Africa stem from superficial visualizations and presentations in the media outside Africa.

Images of Africa – In Media and Development Discourses

The picture of Africa in the Western media is one of catastrophes and wars, implicitly and explicitly telling the audience that the solutions come through aid and various external interventions. This so-called 'Biafra' syndrome originated in 1967–70, when reports from the civil war in Nigeria showed starving children staring into the camera (Palmberg 2001: 205). The crises, droughts and famines that hit the world headlines contribute to the image of a continent in despair and of poverty that cries out for aid, and create negative perceptions of this 'other' continent.

In recent years, this 'afro-pessimism' has partly turned to 'afro-optimism'. In December 2011, *The Economist* apologized for having called Africa a 'hopeless' continent a decade earlier and emphasized that Africa now has some of the fastest-growing economies in the world (*Economist* 2011). Although there are sound reasons to challenge the underlying assumptions and the prospects for this economic growth, it does represent another image of Africa. Still, it is only occasionally that optimistic and positive stories about Africa and elsewhere hit the headlines; and these stories require more in-depth analysis, which is rarely forthcoming in the mainstream and tabloid media. Catastrophes still sell well; and the stories and pictures of the 2011 drought in the Horn of Africa were much the same as those of the drought in Ethiopia in 1984–85. Only Bob Geldof's Live Aid concert was missing.

Development aid is dependent on these images of Africa – the starving and catastrophic continent, rather than the rising economic star. There is, however, no doubt that Africa does face huge challenges, and that poverty is widespread. The point here is whether these images of Africa in the West serve other roles and purposes than merely to depict the African 'otherness'.

Year after year, Norway is ranked the best country in the world to live in. Norway also gives most development aid per capita, and is proud of it. Since the 1980s, its government and parliament have had an official policy that Norway should be a humanitarian superpower on the global scene. The country actively participates throughout the world in peace-keeping operations and (more importantly) peace talks – and it provides humanitarian aid. Creating and preserving this position – and stereotype – necessitates certain perceptions and stereotypes of 'us' and the 'other' (Tvedt 1990; 2002; 2003).

This switches the focus from the 'other' to 'us'. But the images of the 'other' in Africa also have another function in practice. They reinforce the images of 'us' – the donors, and in this case the Norwegians. Being best at peace and development has become a Norwegian 'brand' – it defines what it is to be a Norwegian: being good and possessing a moral good. Norway is literally capitalizing globally on the image of possessing a moral good. One premise for this reasoning is the perception that development in the West took place at the expense of development elsewhere. Although this is partly correct, given colonial history, it also frames an understanding that overlooks autonomous development in Africa and in countries without a colonial history, e.g. Norway. Another reason is humanitarian: the rich should give to the poor, which again strengthens belief in the Norwegian moral good (Tvedt 1990; 2002).

Norway has a unique collective and national ritual in a global development perspective. Once a year since 1974, the state-funded Norwegian Broadcasting Company (NRK) has organized a national collection of money for humanitarian aid. Each year the whole sum of money goes to one selected organization, e.g. the Red Cross, Amnesty International or Doctors without Borders. This initiative engages the whole country. Prior to the main television show, women knit socks that are sold at bazaars, children collect money, and business enterprises organize activities to whip up support. On the Big Day, each household in Norway is visited by volunteers collecting money. When the television show starts, settlements across the country – large and small – are visited, to show the enthusiasm and the engagement of people as they collect money for the poor. All this is accompanied by stories of the work done by that particular year's chosen organization. As the show progresses, statistics are presented for each and every municipality – which has given the most money? Which is the best? Did Norwegians as a whole, nationally, collect more this year than last year? The show is a collective ritual that manifests the Norwegians' moral good and their willingness to help the poor (Tvedt 1995).

Whether the money collected is actually used for the purposes shown on TV is another matter, as indeed is the question of whether the projects have been successful. But that need not concern us here; rather our focus is on what kind of images are presented of the 'other'.

The narcissism of the ritual became even more evident in 2009. That year the selected organization was CARE Norway. As usual, prior to the main television event, pictures showing poor and proud African women with posters supporting CARE and the work of the organization were on display all over Norway. There was only one problem: they had not been taken in Africa. It had all been staged. The photos had been taken by a fashion photographer in a hip area of downtown Oslo. The reality in Africa was not real enough – reality had lost its importance. Even Africa's poverty could be staged and represented as a theatre for the sake of helping the 'other' (Tvedt 2009).

Thus, in the post-colonial discourse, the emphasis has been on the images of the African 'others', shaping and structuring the real lives of real people. The other side of the coin is what the images of the 'others' do to the images of the donors. As we have just seen, the reality may be irrelevant, and the images of the 'others' can be staged. Reality may thus be shaped and adapted to the perceptions and the prejudices of the donors. This maintains the system – or, in this case, the image of Norwegians as the world's 'best' at possessing a moral good that can be spread across the globe. In this process, it is important to draw a distinction between 'us' and 'them', regardless of whether this distinction reflects reality. The 'development industry' is dependent upon a distinct 'other', in whatever terms and forms it is created and whatever content it has.

Discussion – the 'other'

Theoretically and philosophically, the Other is as fundamental as the self – in fact, the synthesis of the Self and the Other is necessary for any communication and engagement in the world. In the afore-mentioned academic dispute between Sahlins and Obeyesekere, Sahlins quoted Benveniste, who had been eloquent on this point:

> Consciousness of self is only possible if it is experienced by contrast. I use *I* only when I am speaking to someone who will be *you* in my address. It is this condition of dialogue that is constitutive of *person*, for it implies reciprocally *I* becomes *you* in the address of the one who in turn designates himself as *I* … Language is possible only because each speaker sets himself up as a *subject* by referring to himself as *I* in his discourse… This polarity does not mean either equality or symmetry: 'ego' always has a position of transcendence with regard to *you*. Nevertheless, neither of these terms can be conceived of without the other… The condition of man in language is unique.
>
> BENVENISTE 1971: 224–225, *quoted in Sahlins 1997: 275*

In a discussion of the Other, since we are all *I* and *you* – being a Self and another – in any social interaction *per se*, one may emphasize some of the structures at work by looking at power relations in this polarity, which Benveniste said mean neither equality nor symmetry. A short description of identification processes may illuminate some aspects. Identity is a fundamental aspect of being human, and 'identification can be defined minimally as the ways in which individuals and collectives are distinguished in their social relations with other individuals and collectives. Identity is a matter of knowing who's who (without which we can't know what's what)' (Jenkins 2004: 5). With regards to ethnicity (and the same goes on a personal level), ethnic classification implies stereotypes like *us* and *them*. Belonging to a group is not merely a personal choice: such belonging and identity may be imposed from outside by dominant groups. Consequently, a person may be assigned an identity or membership of a group that he or she does not want. External definitions are embedded within social relationships between groups, and external groups may define others as groups by virtue of either power or authority relations, whether those others like it or not. People in power with authority, by virtue of their superior status, can categorize others in different groups, upholding the status of both groups in asymmetrical relations (Jenkins 1994: 199).

Such processes are, to a great extent, at work in the development discourse regarding relations between donors and recipients. Added to this is the dependency created by the social relations embedded in receiving. This was first elaborated by Mauss (1990) in his seminal work *The Gift* – there are no free gifts, and to be a receiver is to be inferior. The gift must be reciprocated at some time, in one way or another. If it is not, most likely the stream of money will dry up. Since the gift cannot be paid back economically, the reciprocity often involves humble gratitude to the donors – a position that reinforces the recipient's inferiority.

Returning to Sahlins and Obeyesekere, is it possible to combine essentialism/universalism and relativism in the developing discourse? To say that basically all humans are the same, although there are cultural differences? To a great extent, it would seem that the majority of development actors are rooted in the essential/universal position, backed by humanitarianism and human rights: we are all the same. The important differences are seen primarily as economic; and since we are all the same, it is a moral good or imperative for the rich to help the poor. However, even if this is the case, this perception is deeply rooted in an *a priori* understanding (whether explicit or not) that the Africans are the 'others'. The whole development system is dependent upon this 'other': aid creates asymmetrical power relations and the images of the Africans may also strengthen and contrast with the images of the donors, particularly in the West.

Moreover, whereas both Sahlins and Obeyesekere agreed that it is presumptuous, epistemologically madness and morally repugnant to speak for others, not only is this very much the aim within the development discourse, but it is also the aim to change *them* (the designation of the Other is intentional) – and in these processes the voices of the concerned are often marginalized. To quote Sahlins again, the problem is not 'whether they – the so-called...subalterns can speak. The problem is whether they can be heard and understood' (Sahlins 1997: 273).

Thus, in practice it would seem that universalism and relativism are to a large extent uncritically combined in the development discourse. Whereas this is academically a difficult position to hold, by bypassing such theoretical discussion it is possible to maintain certain images of the Other – with consequences for those concerned.

Conclusion

The history of the ideas and conceptions of Africans as the 'other' is long, stretching back to before the colonial era. Although few will advocate such racial perceptions of Africans today, the shadows of a murky past are present whether deliberate and intentional or not. Hence, awareness of the colonial past is of importance in understanding the future and the premises for engaging with others. In practice, it would seem that concepts of the 'others' (of Africans in particular) are most often unconscious and subject to limited critical reflection – distinctions between 'them' and 'us' just 'exist'. This uncritical conceptualization is not, however, a 'natural' categorization, but rather an expression of highly asymmetrical power relations, often perceived and expressed with derogatory undertones. Although we are all the 'other' from a theoretical perspective when we interact as humans, this social relationship is most often asymmetrical and unequal. African history – in the past and present – has innumerable factors and actors that could have created positive and constructive images of the African 'other'. More often than not, however, the images and concepts of the African 'other' have consistently been to the disadvantage of the Africans. If the image of the African 'other' was equal or superior to the image of the West as an 'other', there would be nothing to develop. Thus, the notion of developing the 'other' necessitates an ideological understanding of the existence of 'another', which it is possible to develop. This 'other' will, of necessity, be inferior from the outset. Despite this 'other' being framed in terms of universalism and humanitarianism, in fact it is deeply rooted in cultural differences: Africans are different, and these differences do Africa no favours. These asymmetrical perceptions and power relations are what Africans oppose: is it possible to have equality and symmetry between and among different groups of 'others'?

References

Ba, D. (2007). 'Africans still seething over Sarkozy speech', Reuters, 5 September, at http://uk.reuters.com/article/2007/09/05/uk-africa-sarkozy-idUKL0513034620070905.

Baaz, M.E. (2001). 'Introduction – African identity and the postcolonial' in M.E. Baaz and M. Palmberg (eds), *Same and Other: Negotiating African identity in cultural production*. Nordic Africa Institute, Uppsala.

Benveniste, E. (1971). *Problems in General Linguistics*. University of Miami Press, Coral Gables.

Bernal, M. (1987). *Black Athena: Afroasiatic roots of classical civilization*, Vol. I, *The Fabrication of Ancient Greece, 1785–1985*. Rutgers University Press, New York.

Bernal, M. (1991). *Black Athena: Afroasiatic Roots of Classical Civilization*, Vol. II, *The Archaeological and Documentary Evidence*. Rutgers University Press, New York.

Borofsky, R. (1997). 'Cook, Lono, Obeyesekere, and Sahlins', *Current Anthropology*, 38:2, pp. 255–82.

Chami, F. (2002). 'The Swahili world' in F. Chami and G. Pwiti (eds), *Southern Africa and the Swahili World*, Studies in the African Past 2. Dar es Salaam University Press.

Childe, V.G. (1934). *New Light on the Most Ancient East: The oriental prelude to European history*. Kegan Paul, London.

Díaz-Andreu, M. (1996). 'Islamic archaeology and the origin of the Spanish nation' in M. Díaz-Andreu and T. Champion (eds), *Nationalism and Archaeology in Europe*. University College London Press, London.

Dietz, V., M.M.A. Kaag, K. Havnevik and T. Oestigaard (eds) (2011). *African Engagements: Africa negotiating an emerging multi-polar world*. Brill, Leiden and Boston.

Diop, C.A. (1974). *The African Origin of Civilization: Myth and Reality*. Lawrence Hill, Westport, CT.

Economist (2011). 'The sun shines bright', 3 December.

Eriksen, T.H.E. (1995). *Small Places, Large Issues: An introduction to social and cultural anthropology*. Pluto Press, London.

Frankfort, H. (1956). *The Birth of Civilization in the Near East*. Doubleday, New York.

Geertz, C. (1995). 'Culture war', *New York Review of Books*, 30 November.

Hall, M. (1986). *Archaeology of Africa*. David Philip, Cape Town.

Hegel, G.W.F. (2007 [1899]). *The Philosophy of History*. Cosimo, New York.

Howe, K.R. (1996). 'The making of Cook's death', *Pacific Studies*, 31, pp. 108–18.

Jenkins, R. (1994). 'Rethinking ethnicity: Identity, categorization and power', *Ethnic and Racial Studies*, 17:2, pp. 197–223.

Jenkins, R. (2004). *Social Identities*. Routledge, London.

Kaiser, T. (1995). 'Archaeology and ideology in southeast Europe' in P.L. Kohl and C. Fawcett (eds), *Nationalism, Politics, and the Practice of Archaeology*. Cambridge University Press.

Mamdani M. (2001). *When Victims Become Killers: Colonialism, Nativism, and the Genocide in Rwanda*. Fountain Publishers, Kampala.

Mauss, M. (1990). *The Gift*. Routledge, London.

Miller, D. (1991). 'Primitive art and the necessity of primitivism to art' in S. Hiller (ed.), *The Myth of Primitivism: Perspectives on art*. Routledge, London.

Mudimbe, V.Y. (1994). *The Idea of Africa*. Indiana University Press, Bloomington.

Obeyesekere, G. (1981). *Medusa's Hair*. University of Chicago Press, Chicago.

Obeyesekere, G. (1992). *The Apotheosis of Captain Cook: European mythmaking in the Pacific*. Princeton University Press, Princeton.

Obeyesekere, G. (1997). 'Comments to Borofsky, R. Cook, Lono, Obeyesekere, and Sahlins', *Current Anthropology*, 38:2, pp. 267–72.

Obeyesekere, G. (2002). *Imagining Karma: Ethical transformations in Amerindian, Buddhist, and Greek Rebirth*. University of California Press, Berkeley.

Oestigaard, T. (2001). *Norge uten nordmenn: En antinasjonalistisk arkeologi*. Spartacus, Oslo.

Oestigaard, T. (2007). *Political Archaeology and Holy Nationalism: Archaeological battles over the Bible and land in Israel and Palestine from 1967–2000*. Gotark Series C No. 67. Göteborg University, Gothenburg.

Palmberg, M. (2001). 'A continent without culture?' in M.E. Baaz and M. Palmberg (eds), *Same and Other: Negotiating African identity in cultural production*. Nordic Africa Institute, Uppsala.

Sahlins, M. (1985). *Islands of History*. University of Chicago Press, Chicago.

Sahlins, M. (1995). *How 'Natives' Think: About Captain Cook, for example*. University of Chicago Press, Chicago.

Sahlins, M. (1997). 'Comments to Borofsky, R. Cook, Lono, Obeyesekere, and Sahlins', *Current Anthropology*, 38:2, pp. 272–76.

Trigger, B. (1984). 'Archaeologies: Nationalist, colonialist, imperialist', *Man*, 19:3, pp. 355–70.

Trigger, B. (1994). *A History of Archaeological Thought*. Cambridge University Press, Cambridge.

Trigger, B. (1995). 'Romanticism, nationalism, and archaeology' in P.L. Kohl and C. Fawcett (eds), *Nationalism, Politics, and the Practice of Archaeology*. Cambridge University Press, Cambridge.

Trigger, B. (2003). *Understanding Early Civilizations: A comparative study*. Cambridge University Press, Cambridge.

Tvedt, T. (1990). *Bilder av 'de andre': Om utviklingslandene i bistandsepoken.* Universitetsforlaget, Oslo.

Tvedt, T. (1995). *Den norske Samaritan: Ritualer, selvbilder og utviklingshjelp.* Gyldendals Pamfletter, Oslo.

Tvedt, T. (2002). *Verdenbilder og selvbilder: En humanitær stormakts intellektuelle historie.* Universitetsforlaget, Oslo.

Tvedt, T. (2003). *Utviklingshjelp, utenrikspolitikk og makt: Den norske modellen.* Gyldendal Norsk Forlag, Oslo.

Tvedt, T. (2009). 'Tid for en annerledes historie', *Dagbladet*, 15 October, at: http://www.dagbladet.no/2009/10/25/nyheter/debatt/tv-aksjonen/nrk/tv_og_medier/8724801/.

Ugwuanyi, L.O. (2011). 'Aligning and harnessing the gains of globalisation to an African advantage: Towards "glo-fricanisation"' in V. Dietz, M.M.A. Kaag, K. Havnevik and T. Oestigaard (eds), *African Engagements: Africa negotiating an emerging multi-polar world.* Brill, Leiden and Boston.

CHAPTER 3

Misconceptions and Poor Understanding – The Debate on Poverty

Mats Hårsmar

Introduction

Most people would claim to know what poverty is. Furthermore, they would regard it as something to avoid. Yet, poverty is widespread. The rapid reductions that have occurred have not reached all. Is this purely a matter of a lack of will and capacity to eradicate poverty? Or is it also a result of limited knowledge and conflicting views on what poverty is?

Currently, the highest shares of poverty are found in a number of sub-Saharan African (SSA) countries and in a few countries in South Asia.

Share of Population Living on Less Than USD 1.25/Day (%), 2012

Despite rapid economic growth in many of its countries, and a continental average growth in GDP of over 5 per cent sustained over the last decade, SSA is still the region with the highest incidence of poverty. According to a recent projection, 41 per cent of its inhabitants will live below the poverty threshold of USD 1.25/day by 2015, i.e. this year (World Bank 2015). The first millennium development goal (MDG) of reducing this level to 29 per cent by 2015 will remain a distant objective. Furthermore, the average income level of those living below the threshold in SSA is a mere 101 cents/day – making the poverty gap larger than anywhere else in the world as shown in figure 3.1 (WDI 2015).

African poverty continues to be primarily a rural phenomenon – despite rapid urbanization. The share of rural poverty declined only slightly from 64 per cent in 1998 to 62 per cent in 2008. Lack of progress in agricultural and rural development is an important part of this story. Another aspect of the same harsh reality is that the share of the population suffering from hunger in SSA declined only modestly, from 25.3 per cent in 1990 to 18.2 per cent in 2014 – a slower reduction than in any other part of the world (von Grebmer et al. 2014). SSA is far from reaching the MDG objective of halving hunger by 2015 (reaching 12.5 per cent). Mainly on account of the 2007–09 financial and food crises, SSA reverted to a situation similar to that of 2002 in terms of the population share

 | DOI 10.1163/9789004305465_004

FIGURE 3.1 *Poverty headcount 2012 map*
SOURCE: MAP BASED ON WORLD DEVELOPMENT INDICATORS, THE WORLD BANK

living on too little dietary energy. In other words, the most recent experience is a lost decade for 250 million malnourished Africans (UN 2011).

Against such a backdrop, it is natural that poverty should have been a prevalent theme in many African studies. Some studies have focused on how the concept is being used locally, underlining the importance of local people defining themselves (Anderson and Broch-Due 1999). However, there is nothing especially "African" about poverty, and there is no particular "culture of poverty" on this continent (Lewis 1971). Reasons why poverty is especially widespread in SSA are to be sought primarily in the political and economic structures. Nevertheless, for descriptions and explanations to be accurate, and for strategies aimed at rooting out poverty to be efficient, a conscious use of the concept is mandatory.

Poverty is, on the one hand, context bound and displays many particularities in its multidimensionality (Addison et al. 2008; Alkire and Foster 2008). On the other hand, it is still possible to find common descriptions and language for a comparison of poverty across individuals and countries. However, this requires that comparisons should not be based on simplistic indicators, such as the USD 1.25/day threshold used above. As will be explained, this misses out on some of the most important aspects and on the more relevant understanding of what poverty is. The objective of this chapter is to dwell on what poverty is and how it can be understood, and to discuss some of the limits of the concept.

Some Roots of the Poverty Concept

> You will always have the poor with you.
>
> MATTHEW 26:11

This quote from the Bible is meant to illustrate that poverty has been discussed and written about throughout human history, as far as we can judge from written documents.[1] Our aim here is not to make any full historical review of how the concept has emerged, but rather to discuss some of its more recent applications. As a simple contextual illustration, a quantitative overview of the English language literature from the year 1500 onwards indicates that the use of the poverty concept during this period first peaked in this literature around 1640 – at the time when the first British civil war occurred – and again around the time of the French revolution in 1789 (Google n-gram 2011).[2] A similar pattern is found in French literature, but with use of the word *pauvrété* lacking the first peak.

The next peak in the use of the concept in English-language literature was not reached until around the year 2000, after a period of increased use from 1950 onwards. This was the period of decolonization and of nation building in a number of the poorest countries in the world. It was also the period of increasing development cooperation driven by the objective of reducing poverty. Immediately after taking office in 1964, US President Lyndon B. Johnson initiated legislation aimed at reducing domestic poverty in the US from its 19 per cent level. This was labelled the "war on poverty", following the title of the president's speech (Johnson 1964). The World Bank president, Robert McNamara enlarged this into a global war on poverty in 1973, when he first used the concept of "absolute poverty" (Loungani 2003). Writings and discussions about poverty have continued ever since, culminating around the millennium with a decade that, among other things, included public campaigning in the Anglophone part of the world on the theme of "making poverty history".

One interpretation of the historical peaks in the literature is that the concept has been in wider use during periods when it has been seen as possible to deal with problems of poverty, when there has been some form of "poverty enlightenment" implying an increased awareness about what to do about poverty (Ravallion 2011).

A more detailed look shows that the way "poverty" has been discussed has changed considerably over the last 50 years. This is illustrated in figure 3.2 where

1 Poverty and riches were themes in Plato's work in ancient Greece (Fuks 1984). The Dead Sea Scrolls contained discussions on poverty (Goff 2003: 129) to mention another example.

2 Statistics from Google Books n-gram viewer, where 500 billion words from 5.2 million books have been scanned and stored electronically.

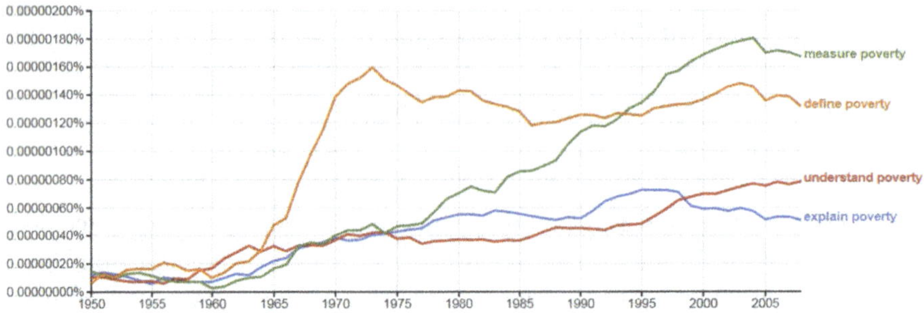

FIGURE 3.2 *Relative use of "poverty" in English language literature.*
SOURCE: GOOGLE N-GRAM VIEWER

the prevalence in English language literature of various uses of the poverty concept is shown. To "define" poverty was the dominant discourse from the mid-1960s to the mid-1980s, with a peak around 1971. From 1980 onwards, the "measuring" of poverty has gained ground, whereas "understanding" or "explaining" poverty has been less common throughout the period.

Such shifts in the discourse on poverty are clearly influenced by the development jargon, the fads of development, which in turn are linked to different development strategies.

For instance, when the World Bank during the 1990s decided to gradually abandon "structural adjustment" as its main approach to working in low-income countries, and to focus more on "poverty reduction strategies", this was reflected in a shift between these concepts in the wider literature. "Poverty reduction" became more cited than "structural adjustment" in 2003.[3] Likewise, as the World Bank, together with a host of bilateral aid agencies and poor-country governments, more recently gradually tried to move away from the poverty focus, this has also been reflected in declining use of "poverty" in the literature. Various policy documents centred on economic growth – "inclusive growth", "vision" documents, "growth strategies" – are replacing poverty reduction strategy papers.

A parallel shift in the development discourse is an increasing focus by many donors on issues that may be classified as Global Public Goods, i.e. climate change, cross-boundary issues relating to security, health, natural resources, knowledge and financial stability. This implies an evolution where development

3 The poverty focus formed an important part of the debt reduction framework for poor countries. When debt reductions were introduced for highly indebted poor countries (HIPC), a concern was that they should not start to build up new unsustainable debts. Therefore the poverty reduction strategy papers were introduced in order for HIPC governments to show that the debt dividends were not used for corruption, but rather for productive spending, particularly in the social sectors (ref. UNCTAD 2011).

dynamics are seen as increasingly regional and global in their character. Even though regional and global forces also impact on poverty, the concept is most often treated as a national or local phenomenon. Hence, it tends to be de-emphasized in more global discourses.

How Has the Poverty Debate Evolved?

The broader policy-oriented thinking about poverty has evolved in close relationship with the academic debate. The most influential scientific discipline has been development economics. Its focus has generally been on measuring levels of poverty. Hence, this research has largely been driven by a functional objective: by a search for policy relevance at an instrumental level. In order to measure poverty levels, descriptions of poverty have been a necessary complement. A "head-count" has been the central component, and static descriptions of poverty levels have been the default position. Increasingly, however, there has been a move towards dynamic perspectives. This move has been driven by methodological advances in econometrics and by improved data. In particular, increased use of panel data and improved modelling have played a role. Conceptual advances have also played a part (Addison et al. 2008; Ehrenpreis 2009).

In poverty studies, both theoretical and methodological positions differ, but with the theoretical differences being more fundamental. Hence, the following description is mainly structured by theoretical perspectives, rather than methodological. Criteria used for selecting positions to describe are:

(a) they have resulted in a substantial amount of academic work;
(b) they have been used in applied analysis of poverty;
(c) they have relevance for a more general public discussion of poverty.

The theoretical lines of division we will use to structure our material emerge from different epistemological positions. Epistemology deals with the question of knowledge: what can we know, and how do we know what we know? These questions lead on to a discussion of what scientific knowledge is. Von Wright (1971) distinguishes two major approaches towards the conditions that an explanation has to fulfil in order to be considered scientific. These two approaches are often referred to as "Aristotelian" and "Galilean", indicating leading proponents of the two traditions. The Aristotelian approach proposes that a scientific explanation shall be understandable in a teleological perspective, i.e. explanations of the character where means are applied to work towards specific ends or objectives. Hence, this approach deals with issues of motivation, action and intention. The Galilean approach promotes a causal-mechanistic type of explanation, subsuming individual causes under assumed general laws of nature. It focuses on cause and effect. Droysen (1858) introduced the labels "understanding and explanation" ("erklären und verstehen" in German) when referring to natural sciences and human sciences ("Geisteswissenschaften"). The concept "verstehen" was then, during the 19th and 20th centuries, further elaborated in the context of a hermeneutic discourse (Dilthey 1991; Lübcke 1988). We will, in the following, use the label "hermeneutic" (interpretive) for the Aristotelian approach and the label "naturalistic" or "empirical" for the Galilean approach.[4]

The naturalistic position – the Galilean approach – builds on research methods developed by natural sciences, later adapted to social sciences. It searches for causal laws through the gathering of data by observation and experiment. The unit of knowledge is "sense-datum", a concept that is described as having no "element in it of reading, or interpretation" but rather being a "brute datum" (Taylor 1985: 19).

Hermeneutics – dominating in the Aristotelian approach – deals on the other hand with the interpretation of social meaning. Hermeneutics was originally a method for the analysis of texts, in particular biblical texts, but was broadened during the early 19th century to deal with all forms of communication and social phenomena. With this, hermeneutics lost its relationship to sacred texts as conveyors of truth. In modern hermeneutics, the concept of truth has been regained. Through a historic process of understanding, it is possible to present, correct and reveal truth (Lübcke 1988: 227). However, hermeneutics does not necessarily apply the same notion of truth as the naturalistic position with its correspondence criteria (Shaffer 1996: 28). Furthermore, hermeneutics claims that scientific inquiry is always interpretive. Even more, it has been argued that social science must deal with a "double hermeneutics", where scientific and research paradigms must be interpreted at the theoretical level and conceptual schemes and meaning structures must be interpreted at the level of data collection (Giddens 1976: 158, 162).

4 The Galilean approach is further characterized by its methodological monism, which implies that the same basic scientific method shall be used regardless of scientific inquiry. It is also characterized by its view that mathematical physics constitutes a methodological ideal for all disciplines and that causal explanations assuming general laws of nature should be used. Positivism forms one part of this tradition. The Aristotelian approach is, on the other hand, characterized by rejecting methodological monism and instead promoting a distinction between nomothetic and ideographic science. This approach has been shaped by its reaction to positivism from a hermeneutic standpoint where understanding is key and the intentionality of agents is seen as a central component for studies in the social and humanistic fields.

The tension between the naturalistic and the hermeneutic positions has influenced various positions in the poverty debate. Can such dividing lines be overcome? This is an essential question for any discussion on poverty. We will in the following describe how the poverty concept has evolved. A discussion on dividing lines will follow.

Income and Consumption as a Base

Historically, the first definition of poverty to emerge was the **subsistence approach**, which arose in 19th century Victorian England. This was a perspective developed by nutritionists and centred on physiological or material needs. According to the subsistence approach, poverty was defined as "the minimum necessaries for maintaining merely physical efficiency". This included clothing, fuel, housing and, first and foremost, food. The approach saw human needs as mainly physical, but not social, and has great similarities to what nowadays is labelled **material approaches** to poverty. One extended version of the latter is the **monetary approach**, in which indicators for the measurement of poverty have been both income and consumption levels, although there may be variation in what assets are included in material or monetary poverty definitions. A common thread is that all these approaches are based on utility theory and placed in the naturalistic camp (Townsend 2006; Chambers 2006).

On the surface of it, measuring poverty in money metrics might seem straightforward, and comparability assured through the use of the same currency across countries. This is the logic behind the USD 1.25/day measure, which is widely used and applied as an international standard by the World Bank. However, there are complications. The currently used level (USD 1.25/day/person) is calculated on the basis of the mean of national poverty lines in low-income countries. This implies that whenever a new calculation is made, comparability with previous poverty lines is lost. More specifically, the current "dollar-a-day" line corresponds to the value of goods and services that USD 1.25 could buy in the US in 2011 prices. The value of these goods is then calculated for each and every country (purchasing power parity). A previously used poverty line was calculated as the value that USD 1.08 could buy in the US in 1993 prices, which corresponded to the mean of poor-country poverty lines in that year (Ravallion et al. 2009).[5]

5 A further complication is that the set of poor countries on which the poverty line is based may have changed. At the recalculation in 2005, some low-income countries had matured

If one were to compare different poverty lines over time, inflation in the US would have to be taken into consideration. A 1993 poverty line, corrected for US inflation, would have meant a 2005 poverty line of USD 1.45/day. Hence, a comparison between the two lines would underestimate the current number of poor people in the world. It turns out that a previous adjustment of the dollar-a-day poverty line (from USD 1/day in 1985 prices) also went in the same direction. An inflation-corrected poverty line from 1985 would have meant a poverty line of USD 1.81/day in 2005. These different poverty lines are not meant to be compared (ibid.). However, the popularity and seeming simplicity of the lines make such comparisons almost unavoidable. The consequence is that reductions in global poverty become seriously overestimated.

In addition to problems related to fluctuating exchange rates and inflation levels, the issue of what goods to base the purchasing power calculation on also complicates the measuring. Should basic goods consumed by the total population, or goods primarily consumed by the poor, be included? And what if poor people consume different goods in different countries? The USD 1/day measure includes all goods and services in relation to how much they are consumed on average internationally. Prices of basic necessities play a minor role in this measure, while they are of great importance to poor people (Robeyns 2005: 31ff).

In the context of material approaches to poverty, mention should also be made of **pro-poor economic growth.** This approach emerged in the 1990s, based on the finding that economic growth impacts poverty reduction differently in different societies because *poverty elasticity* differs. Obviously, this approach makes the assumption that economic growth leads to poverty reduction. The question is how to make economic growth as beneficial to the poor as possible.

There is a debate about how pro-poor growth should be defined. The *absolute* definition looks solely at the effect of economic growth on the poor. When economic growth leads to increasing incomes among the poor, growth is said to be pro-poor. By contrast, the *relative* definition claims that growth is pro-poor only if growth benefits poor people and inequalities simultaneously decrease. The absolute definition is more commonly used. To measure pro-poor growth, the Rate of Pro-Poor Growth (RPPG) is used. This refers to the mean growth rate of consumption by households situated below a certain poverty line, defined in terms of income. However, the underlying assumption that economic growth leads to poverty reduction has been questioned on

into middle-income countries and the relatively lower poverty level of India had a relatively higher influence on the mean (Ravallion et al. 2008).

empirical grounds. A study undertaken by the UNDP International Poverty Centre looked at cases of economic growth in 80 countries during the period 1984–2001. In total, 237 spells of growth were studied. Only 55 of these – some 23 per cent – were found to have been pro-poor. The others either did not result in per capita consumption growth (economic growth lower than population growth – 45 per cent) or were outright cases of anti-poor growth (32 per cent) (Son and Kakwani 2006).

Material approaches to poverty such as the above, focusing exclusively on individuals, have not gone unchallenged. An initial critique came in the 1970s, when the **basic needs approach** was developed by the International Labour Organization (ILO). It emulated the subsistence approach, in that it built on what was perceived as the minimum needs of a family. However, the basic needs approach extended this group of needs to include essential services that were provided not only by the market, but also by and for the community at large, such as safe water, sanitation, public healthcare, education and cultural activities. Needs were extended from the individual level to include things required by local communities and populations more widely in the form of public goods. "Needs" were seen as different from "wants", and the concept of basic needs was used to prioritize among wants. Not all wants are of equal importance. Some goods are necessary in order for people to reproduce, to function in and contribute to their societies. In other words, the basic needs discourse rejected the market as the sole and optimal provider of goods and services (Gasper 1996: 3). Obviously, this approach carried within itself a strong critique of economic policies that prioritized pure market-based solutions.

A debate followed about the distinction between felt needs and justified needs. The basis for this debate was the difficulty in distinguishing between the positive (factual) use of the term and the normative (ibid.: 5). Another debated point concerned what basis to use in determining which needs are more fundamental than others. In other words, it was not really clear what "basic" in the term "basic needs" should refer to. Three distinct starting points were discernible: (i) *Positive* theories that explain behaviour as driven by "needs". Abraham Maslow's hierarchy of needs is perhaps the most famous theory in this category; (ii) Theories that identify prerequisites for various levels and types of functioning, such as physical and mental health. These theories try to explain what makes people happy or content, and they focus on the *instrumental* needs for fulfilling such ends; (iii) theories that are based on *normative* statements that prioritize some prerequisites, and thus are ethical theories of needs (ibid.: 9f).

All the above positions – from the subsistence approach to the basic needs approach – may be classified as belonging to an "income/consumption" (I/C) approach to poverty. These positions adhere to the naturalistic or empiricist tradition. They also have a shared normative underpinning in utilitarianism. There are direct historical links between the naturalist normative theory based on utilitarianism and the I/C position (Kanbur and Shaffer 2005). In its original version, utilitarianism stresses that utility or "happiness" should be maximized across individuals, and that this social outcome is the benchmark against which social states should be evaluated. Bentham called this the "greatest happiness principle" (Bentham 1789). Despite Bentham's claim that pleasure and pain are directly measurable, the problem of measuring utility or happiness in an inter-personal way led to a shift towards the revealed preferences approach. In the latter, the maximal satisfaction of preferences – revealed by consumer choice – is the ultimate benchmark. It was further claimed that this is measurable through a money metric (Samuelson 1966; Kanbur and Shaffer 2005: 16).

Social Relations and Poverty

In contrast to the above, a number of poverty approaches focus on social relations, rather than on consumption. The discussion about how to define justifiable basic needs opened the way for this. During the 1990s, it was increasingly stressed that poverty is based on **relative deprivation** and that both material and social conditions matter to poverty. Poor people are those that are denied resources to fulfil social demands and observe the customs and laws of society. Hence, deprivations may take multiple forms, and are fundamentally described in relation to what is seen as normal or median in society. Things regarded as necessities are, in every society, to some extent defined by custom. For instance, even in the subsistence approach some aspects were defined by custom (e.g. the need for a white shirt for Sunday worship in Victorian England, where the concept of material poverty had its roots). However, seeing poverty as a relative phenomenon leads to the need to differentiate between inequality and poverty. Inequality is linked to poverty, but is not the same phenomenon.

Variations on this theme put emphasis either on **social exclusion** as the active component in the production of poverty, or stress the deprivation[6] of

6 Several authors have worked on what dimensions deprivation consists of, and what the causes and dynamics of deprivation are. Tilly (2007) in particular points to the formation of dual and unequal categories with asymmetrical relations (male-female, black-white, etc.). Such dualities may lead to *exploitation* and to *opportunity hoarding*, which are two main causes of deprivation. Effects from these two are further reinforced by *emulation* and *adaptation*.

various capabilities as the source of poverty. The **capability approach** more clearly than other perspectives shifts the emphasis away from resources and means towards ends that people have reason to value and pursue – and correspondingly, to the freedom they have to reach these ends. It is the deprivation of capabilities, rather than the deprivation of assets or resources, that constitutes poverty. It follows that the opposite of poverty is the freedom to satisfy the valued ends, according to Amartya Sen, who during the 1990s developed this position together with Martha S. Nussbaum (Sen 1999).

Sen makes the distinction between a person's actual achievements, and her or his freedom to achieve. The former represents the combination of established functioning, whereas the latter represents the combination of functionings, from which he or she can choose. With poverty viewed as capability deprivation, focus should be on capabilities with intrinsic value, rather than on income deprivation, which is of instrumental value. Income is one among a number of factors that influence capabilities. Furthermore, the extent to which income affects capabilities varies between different communities, families and individuals. With this shift from material resources to capabilities, social relations are fully brought into the understanding of poverty, while the possibility of observing distinct aspects of poverty is retained. The capability approach still allows for measuring poverty, but moves away from its narrow material definition.

Still another shift places the emphasis on the agents, rather than the observers, as the ones establishing what poverty is and how it should be interpreted. The multiple meanings of poverty stem from the **participatory approach**, which claims that ultimately it is only poor people themselves who can establish the meaning of poverty and assess who the poor are. Such a position implies that possibilities of comparing different communities are lost. However, a deeper understanding of the subjectivity of poverty and the way people define and look upon themselves is gained (Chambers 2006). At the turn of the century, a major debate played out within the World Bank around these issues. Political pressure concerning formulations in the World Development Report 2000 made the lead author leave.[7] As a background study to the Report, the World Bank had commissioned the "Voices of the Poor" study (Narajan et al. 1999). In this study participatory methods were combined with quantitative methods to improve understanding of poverty, instigating intense debates.

7 Ravi Kanbur, now professor at Cornell University, and his team were criticized primarily by US representatives for not putting enough emphasis on economic growth in their analysis of poverty and poverty reduction. This made Kanbur leave before the report was finished (personal communication).

One major advantage of participatory approaches is that they are able to deal with situations where commonly used concepts of poverty do not correspond with local people's perceptions of who is poor. For instance, among pastoralist groups in East Africa, "the poor" are seen as not belonging to their society, since those who own cattle are perceived as not being poor. Persons who are deprived of their cattle are placed in the category of the poor, but they are simultaneously excluded from the pastoralist society. Hence, the poor are defined away as pastoralists, since pastoralists don't allow themselves to be regarded as poor. Such practice becomes increasingly problematic when the pastoralists are facing growing problems of feeding themselves or earning monetary income, despite the fact that they still control cattle (Anderson and Broch-Due 1999). Descriptions of pastoralist societies also indicate that material approaches to poverty may be misleading, since pastoralists migrating to urban areas suddenly become much more dependent on material goods and monetary income in order to fulfil identical basic human functions than they were in rural areas. Food, clothing, shelter and a long list of other things suddenly cost money. This makes comparisons between people from the same society, but living in different localities, impossible if monetary measures are used (Lesamana 2009: 68f).

Furthermore, in certain societies people use goods to build social relations rather than for consumption. For instance, poor people may provide gifts to rich people who have fallen ill, rather than consume extremely scarce resources themselves: they invest in social relations (Berry 1985; 1993). In such a case, the object (the poor person) personifies him or herself through redistribution. This is quite distinct from situations where people are objectified through production and/or consumption, and where social relationships are used to produce commodities for consumption. When the focus is – as in the former situation – on the distribution and exchange of things, the aim is to establish and maintain social relationships. Mention is sometimes made of being "rich in people". In such situations, disposability, rather than possession or property, is central. What people then strive for is not primarily their own consumption – even if they live in what might be described as poverty – but social relationships. Whether or not these relationships are nurtured with the long-term objective of maximizing or smoothing consumption over time is less relevant for the immediate study of poverty. In situations such as these, it would still be more relevant to measure access to relations rather than access to consumption goods, since this would be closer to how people themselves define poverty and who the poor are.

Following Shaffer (1996; 1998), approaches that stress social relations – such as relative poverty, deprivation and capabilities – are grouped together with self-defining approaches under the label the Participatory Approach (PA). The stylized PA position differs from the I/C position on aspects related to epistemology and normative theory.

In PA, the definition of who is poor builds on an interactive process, a participatory poverty assessment (PPA), which involves both the population and the researcher. The data used may be both quantitative (most often of ordinal character, rather than cardinal) and qualitative. Data are generated in a communicative or discursive way, and include local conceptual categories. The individual's preferences are not taken at face value, as in the I/C approach, but are criticized both by participants and outside observers in a dialogue. Poverty concepts within PA tend to be broader than those in the I/C position, and include "physical, social, political, psychological/spiritual elements" (Chambers 1995: 2). Most approaches within PA belong to the hermeneutic philosophical tradition. The normative theory underpinning PA is discursive normative theory or discourse ethics. This is a procedural theory, since the central element is that normative conclusions can only be reached if an actual dialogue takes place. There are a number of conditions regarding the forms of this process relating to the character of speech. First, for any norm to be valid "...all affected can accept the consequences and side effects its general observance can be anticipated to have for the satisfaction of everyone's interests" (Habermas 1990: 65). If this is the case, what Habermas labels an "Ideal Speech Situation" (ISS) is achieved, something which is seen as a necessary condition for producing valid process outcomes.

We will in addition to this make an important adjustment to Shaffer's dichotomic categorization. The capability approach takes a middle position regarding many of the divergent issues. Hence, we treat Shaffer's two opposing positions (I/C and PA) as poles on an axis along which intermediate positions are possible.

Poverty Concepts Compared

Shaffer identifies fundamental differences in the following parameters of the I/C and the PA positions: (i) definition of poverty; (ii) measurement of poverty; (iii) position on consumer preferences; (iv) sources of data; and (v) research objectives and sources of poverty. It is in relation to these aspects that various epistemological and normative positions are influential and become explicit.

The definition of poverty in the I/C position is done by external agents, using "objective" criteria and applying a deductive approach. Poverty is limited to the sphere of material elements that seemingly lend themselves to quantification, and concerns consumption of goods deemed necessary for survival or a minimum level of existence. By contrast, the PA position applies a process in which both internal and external actors take active part and in which more inductive methods are used.

Moving even further towards critical hermeneutics, external perspectives are used very actively in the process of interpretation. The "objective" understanding of poverty should be made an explicit part of the interpretative process. There is currently continuous work occurring regarding the definition and redefinition of poverty, much of which might be happening at the crossroads of the two epistemological positions that Kanbur and Shaffer (2005) and Shaffer (1996) discuss.

The measurement of poverty within the naturalistic I/C position is based on brute (supposedly value-free) data. The definition of poverty in terms of consumption levels makes it possible to measure poverty quantitatively. Quantification is a logical, but not necessary, consequence of using brute data that are verifiable in an "objective" way. In the PA position, both qualitative and quantitative measures are possible, insofar as certain interpretations of meaning structures have to be qualitative in character. The main point is that in the PA position, poverty should not be reduced only to its quantitative dimensions, since that would deprive the poverty concept of meaning. Typically, this implies that the population coverage is more specific than in the I/C approach.

Again, it looks as though the PA position might be slightly more open to interdisciplinary dialogue than the I/C position. The latter would have neoclassical economy at least as a central reference point. However, going back to the utility theory that underpins the I/C position, we may note that Bentham, in the original version of this normative theory, worked with the concept of utility and happiness – concepts that are not measurable inter-subjectively. The option that the revealed preferences theory provided made it necessary to move from the cardinal to the ordinal representation of utility. Further, this shift gave impetus to a host of critical reactions which argued that inter-personal comparisons are not possible (utility is an internal concept, which cannot be observed objectively outside the individual, except through indicators) (Sen 1987: 7ff). In other words, the problem that revealed preference theory set out to resolve is not really solved.

Based on the observed tensions in the problem of defining and measuring poverty, one may infer a trade-off between making inter-subjective measurements versus providing understanding of what poverty means in the individual case. Rather than pitting one against the other, we conclude that both the I/C and the PA positions share this dual challenge: the search for inter-subjectivity and the simultaneous search for understanding of meaning.

In this context, the naturalist normative theory, which is connected to the I/C position, is not at all equipped to discuss or criticize **preferences**, attitudes and beliefs, since these are taken as given. What makes this position problematic is that preferences are generally not at all exogenous, but shaped through social processes. Hermeneutics, and especially critical hermeneutics, on the other hand, aims at moving beyond faulty preferences, attitudes and beliefs through self-reflection among agents and dialogue. By showing that preferences were formed in a process that did not meet the conditions for an ISS, a more mature understanding may be reached (Habermas 1971: 310).

The main **sources of data** in the I/C approaches are direct observation of revealed preferences through the registration of actual expenditure or an individual's responses gathered through questionnaires. In practice, expenditure necessary to satisfy the minimum needs of dietary energy is estimated in order to arrive at the poverty level. In PA, the hermeneutic approach demands data gathered through dialogue, such as the PPA, where poor people themselves participate. This is necessary for the interpretation and understanding of what poverty means. Hence, the kind of data used is typically more non-numeric.

During the last 10 to 15 years, particularly the I/C approaches have been met with increasing doubt and criticism. This is not least due to the increased availability of improved data. Panel data allowing for more dynamic studies, as well an improved knowledge of the dimensions of ill-being other than low consumption, have contributed to an intensified conceptual evolution regarding poverty. Within the discipline of economics, there has been a clear move towards dynamic rather than static models and analyses. This shift has been motivated in part by the empirical fact that changes in poverty levels are usually net changes. As people move out of poverty, a counter-flow of people moving into poverty is taking place simultaneously. These dual moves may often be much larger than the net effect of the movement out of poverty. Hence, there is a need to understand both the dynamics of moving out of, into and further away from poverty (Krishna 2007; Shepherd et al. 2014).[8]

The **objective** of the naturalist position is to describe and explain social reality in correct ways. Both descriptions and explanations should be value neutral: descriptions must not prescribe what ought to be, explanations must not evaluate social phenomena. Hence, it is important in this position to respect consumer preferences as given, and to keep factual descriptions unbiased. The sources of ill-being or poverty are inadequate private consumption of

8 The fact that people move in and out of poverty simultaneously in most cases implies as well that the assumption made in the pro-poor growth discussion that poverty reduction follows from economic growth may need to be questioned.

essential goods and services. Hence, explanations of poverty centre on the reasons for this missing consumption. In the PA, on the other hand, the objective of research is to understand the meaning of poverty. False consciousness should be revealed through self-reflection and dialogue. This should lead to emancipation. Explanations are helpful, but will necessarily include evaluation. In particular, any claim of validity should be evaluated. According to this position, the sources of poverty go well beyond the individual's lack of means for consumption. Typical explanations of poverty would instead include income and non-income sources of entitlements, social relations of reproduction, production and exchange, employment conditions, autonomy, self-respect among others.

Even if there is an essential tension between these two objectives – to describe or to understand – we may see openings for work that transcends the I/C and PA positions on epistemology, normative theory and methods.

Emerging Perspectives

Shaffer (1996) and Kanbur and Shaffer (2005) argue that differences at the level of epistemology and normative theory are essential in every discussion of poverty concepts, measurement, understanding and explanation. However, the conclusion they draw regarding how these differences might influence the prospects for cross-disciplinary poverty studies needs to be questioned. As we have briefly mentioned in relation to all the points discussed above, there are possibilities to move beyond the differences and bridge the philosophical divides. These are by no means simple tasks, but there are promising openings that Kanbur and Shaffer have not emphasized enough.

A route that is increasingly being taken is one that moves from the unidimensionality of poverty towards multidimensionality. The material poverty concept was already in the 1970s partly broadened and complemented through the introduction of the basic needs concept. However, it was during the 1990s and beyond that multidimensionality more thoroughly gained ground (Sen 1999). Important proposals for additional poverty dimensions include informal employment, agency and empowerment, physical safety, or the ability to go without shame (OPHI 2007). Increased insights into situations of multiple deprivations have driven this shift. Deprivation in terms of health or disempowerment or other important aspects of poverty may have different impacts from deprivation in terms of income or consumption (Alkire and Foster 2008: 1).

Hence, the awareness that cross-disciplinary research is needed has grown. This has been accompanied by a discussion of the limitations of aggregated quantitative methods, such as cross-country regressions, and the need to establish clearer links between macro- and micro theory and analysis (Besley and Burgess 2002; Jerven 2011). Thus, leading economists have, over the last decade, involved themselves in discussions about methodological cross-fertilization and multidisciplinary collaboration.[9]

Alkire and Foster (2008), leading the Oxford Poverty and Human Development Initiative (OPHI), have started to develop tools that make the capability approach inter-subjectively measurable, while at the same time capturing the meaning of poverty. They work with quantitative methods and econometric tools, but even if they start from a naturalist or empiricist perspective, they try to bridge to other perspectives as well. What they have initially focused on are the missing dimensions in the poverty concept, and developing tools for measuring many dimensions simultaneously. The tools they have constructed make it possible to use both ordinal and cardinal data (Alkire and Foster 2008: 10). This is important, since it allows for working with data that are more readily available, and even allows for measuring dimensions that are more difficult to operationalize. The Alkire-Foster (A-F) tool for measuring multidimensional poverty operates in 12 separate steps. An underlying idea is to separate the process of identifying who is poor from the process of aggregating the measures into an overall indicator of poverty. Furthermore, the purpose is to avoid a measure that either portrays people as poor if they are deprived in only one dimension, or portrays them as poor only if they are deprived in all dimensions.

The 12-step tool can briefly be described as follows. When the dimensions and indicators of poverty are chosen, separate poverty lines are set out for each dimension. These are used as cut-offs, according to agreed criteria. People can be poor in one dimension or more. Different dimensions can then be given various weights when the deprivations are added together. Following this, a second cut-off level is set, referring to the number of dimensions on which a person needs to be deprived in order to be classified as multidimensionally poor. On the basis of this poverty headcount, the average poverty gap, as well as the adjusted headcount, can be calculated (Alkire and Foster 2008: 4f). The measure can then be disaggregated again, either by group or by each different dimension. This makes the method useful as an analytical planning and policy tool.

9 The prime example is the Q-Squared project, which combines qualitative and quantitative methods and is hosted by the University of Toronto. This has resulted in numerous seminars and working papers on methodological and multidisciplinary issues related to research on poverty: http://www.q-squared.ca/.

Already, this brief summary of the A-F tool indicates that there are a number of steps that potentially involve dialogue and interpretation in the definition of what poverty is, and who is poor. Even if the multidimensional poverty measurement works primarily with quantitative data, and comes from an empiricist tradition, this tool makes bridges to hermeneutics and the participatory approach possible, since the tool is used for the operationalization and measurement of aspects that are relevant for the latter approach. The PPA and other methods that are preferred by PA may hence also be used at various stages in the process of defining and measuring multidimensional poverty.

The participatory approach has made many important contributions. It provides for the inclusion of context as well as meaning – both essential elements for deeper understanding. However, one basic weakness with PA is that inter-subjectivity tends to get lost in the process. This implies that comparisons across societies and countries are rendered difficult and potentially misleading. Cross-country and cross-society comparisons are, after all, essential for policy relevance, and for putting knowledge to practical use. Potentially, however, there is another and possibly more serious problem with participatory methods, which is particularly problematic in relation to processes of deprivation. People may exhibit "adaptive preferences" (Nussbaum 2006: 73), which implies that the preferences they hold have already been shaped and curbed by deprivations they are subject to. If something is perceived as not being within reach, or possible to achieve for a person who finds her or himself in a particular category or position, preferences are regularly adjusted to be in the realm of the realistic. Simply put, people adjust their preferences to what they think they can achieve. Such processes of self-censorship are often practised, for instance by women, who due to social conventions, may have lower aspirations than their male counterparts. It is difficult to get information on the prevalence of adaptive preferences through participatory research methods, because these methods explicitly aim at mapping expressed preferences.

Comparison across Individuals and Societies

In an attempt to move beyond this weakness of participatory methods, Martha Nussbaum's version of the capability approach (ibid. 76ff) reintroduces intersubjectivity in a way that aims at capturing a more basic human level. This is done in a way that does not necessarily exclude the possibility of understanding poverty in a contextual way. Nussbaum describes an open-ended list of ten central human capabilities. This list is not exhaustive and can be changed, but it is an attempt at summarizing what human life is about. When people are deprived of one or more of these capabilities, they will be characterized as poor:

(1) Life – being able to live a worthy life of normal length;
(2) Bodily health – to be adequately nourished, sheltered and have good health, including reproductive;
(3) Bodily integrity – being able to move around freely and securely, having choice in matters of reproduction and sexual satisfaction;
(4) Senses, imagination and thought – to be able to use the senses, imagine, think and reason in a truly human way based on education; using imagination and thought in producing work and events of one's own choice; using one's mind in ways protected by freedom of expression;
(5) Emotions – to be able to attach to things and people, to love, to grieve, to experience longing, gratitude and justified anger;
(6) Practical reason – to be able to form a conception of the good and to critically reflect on the planning of one's own life;
(7) Affiliation – being able to live with and towards others, recognize and show concern for other human beings and engage in various forms of social interaction; having the social bases of self-respect and non-humiliation; being able to be treated as a dignified being whose worth is equal to that of others, which includes non-discrimination;
(8) Other species – being able to live with concern for and in relation to animals, plants and the world of nature;
(9) Play – being able to laugh, to play and enjoy recreational activities; and
(10) Control over one's environment – being able to participate in political choices that govern one's life; to hold property and have property rights on an equal basis with others; have the right to seek employment on an equal basis with others and to work as a human being.

To move from this list to a definition and measure of poverty, the 12-step measuring tool developed by Alkire and Foster is useful. This implies that the definition of what poverty is would be open to dialogue, and that deprivation in more than one of the proposed dimensions above would have to be weighed against the others.

Nussbaum's main argument is that a list is needed to make sure that the wrong capabilities are not prioritized. Some freedoms limit others, some freedoms are bad and some freedoms are more important than others, she argues. Hence commitments about substance are necessary (Nussbaum 2003). Lists such as this may always be criticized for not capturing what is particular to some societies, or for presenting central capabilities in ways that turn out to be unbalanced in relation to actual situations. Therefore, she explicitly welcomes criticism and presents her list as a proposal. And criticism is exactly what has met her list. As Amartya Sen writes: "The problem is not with listing important capabilities, but with insisting on one predetermined canonical list of capabilities, chosen by theorists without any general social discussion or public reasoning" (Sen 2004: 77). To Sen, the lack of capabilities can never be the same in all societies all the time. Furthermore, the capabilities need also to be understood, formulated and valued by citizens. Anything else would be a denial of democracy and a misunderstanding of what pure theory might do, he claims (ibid.: 78ff). Another of Sen's arguments against a canonical list is that one and the same list cannot be used for all different evaluative purposes that occur in practice. The selection of capabilities must be tailored to the task at hand. Taking such positions, Sen aligns himself with the position taken by hermeneutics, with its emphasis on deliberative processes and discursive normative theory.[10]

A more fundamental approach to the choice of capabilities for the poverty definition is taken by Sabina Alkire (2008). She refers to Ingrid Robeyns in suggesting four principles for the selection of capabilities: (i) Explicit formulation of and argumentation for the selection; (ii) Justification of the method used in generating the list of capabilities; (iii) A two-stage process that differentiates between the ideal and the feasible; and (iv) The inclusion of all dimensions that are important. In applying criteria that require the researcher to formulate a list of capabilities through a process that is open to questioning, Alkire and Robeyns place themselves in between the positions taken by Nussbaum and Sen. This position also lies in between the naturalistic and the hermeneutic positions, in the sense that it opens up the possibility to combine brute data with deliberative processes. In this sense, it provides an opening for a middle way.

A Third Way

The capability approach (CA) is in itself a normative framework, evaluating social situations according to the amount of freedom people have to promote the functionings they value and have reason to value. The CA may utilize

10 Nussbaum's counter-argument is that some canonical list is necessary in order to promote justice. If all capabilties were of equal value and if no capability could be curtailed, justice would be made impossible (Nussbaum 2011).

methodologies and analytical techniques of all kinds, and it may use both quantitative and qualitative data gathered from the full range of sources. It is described as a "…framework that researchers can draw on in order to utilize diverse approaches to multidimensional poverty and well-being in a concerted and conceptually coherent fashion" (Alkire 2008: 2).

In describing the theoretical underpinnings of the approach, Nussbaum and Sen are in agreement that the capability approach has been developed as an alternative to utilitarianism (Nussbaum 2006: 408f; Sen 2009: 19, 69f). While utilitarianism focuses on the satisfaction of various goals, it misses the central role of agency, which occurs on Nussbaum's list above. In Nussbaum's view, it is not enough to achieve satisfaction without choice and activity. In this way, utilitarianism might play down the importance of democratic choice, as well as agency.

The CA has its roots in social contract theory,[11] but differs in certain aspects. When contract theories tend to discuss general social institutional and procedural approaches to justice, the CA focuses on social outcomes at the level of individuals. In the words of John Rawls, "there is a correct or fair procedure such that the outcome is likewise correct or fair, whatever it is, provided that the procedure has been properly followed" (Rawls 1971: 86). In contrast, the CA assesses justice from the outcome, and then seeks procedures that will come as close as possible to that outcome (Nussbaum 2006: 82). As well, when it comes to the principle of mutual advantage as the basis for social cooperation, CA is not fully in line with social contract theory. The CA presupposes more of moral sentiments than contractual theory does. Where contractual theories are parsimonious, in claiming that collaboration in society is possible not because of people's benevolence, but because everyone benefits from cooperation, the capability approach demands more from human beings (ibid.: 408f). This is a potential weakness of the CA as a comprehensive social theory. Nussbaum herself also admits that the CA has yet to provide answers to the range of issues that the Rawlsian version of contract theory raises (Nussbaum 2011: 93ff).

Despite its shortcomings, the CA has clear advantages for the purpose of analysing poverty. By focusing on outcomes, and through the process it uses, the CA provides a way forward by opening up perspectives that include both qualitative understanding and inter-subjectivity. The CA in Nussbaum's

11 Social contract theory was developed by Thomas Hobbes, John Locke, Immanuel Kant and others. Its best-known current version is probably the theory of justice developed by Rawls (1971). The basic idea is that individuals agree to be part of a society and to collaborate with a state on the basis of an implicit agreement that they will in some way gain from this.

version aims at establishing functions of human life that are valid across cultures and societies. This process of establishing key capabilities may utilize and build on all different kinds of methodologies, from both the naturalistic and the hermeneutic traditions. Its universalistic ambition allows at the same time for the CA to serve as a basis for cross-societal and cross-individual comparisons and assessments.

Even if the CA is correctly described as a normative *framework*, it is possible to take different positions within the CA in relation to normative *theory*. This conclusion may be drawn from the debate between Nussbaum and Sen referred to above over the list of capabilities. While Nussbaum takes an inter-subjective and unitary normative position, Sen aligns himself with the position of discursive normative theory, with its emphasis on deliberative participation. Still, both are applying the same normative framework to the study of poverty.

If the CA, in combination with the evolution of multidimensional measuring of poverty, now provides avenues for the transgression of divides between the naturalist and the hermeneutic positions, what might this lead to? The largest gain is arguably that there is now a debate where both the issue of inter-subjective comparison and the issue of the understanding of the meaning of poverty are seen as real problems, at the same level of importance. Regardless of position, everyone must today deal with these challenges and the trade-off between them. Another important gain is that within the CA tradition all kinds of methods and data can be used interchangeably, depending on what issues are raised and what questions asked.

What about the utilitarian tradition, with its revealed preference theory and its naturalist position, then? Both Nussbaum and Sen take the explicit position that the CA was developed as an alternative to utilitarianism. Hence, the CA can hardly be a bridge to utilitarian positions. This being so, one might still recall that in the earlier version of utilitarian theory, Bentham and others worked with the "happiness" concept, which is not inter-subjectively quantifiable. As well, when the revealed preference theory with the money metric was developed as a means for inter-subjective comparisons, even this met critique that inter-personal comparisons of well-being were not possible (Sen 1987: 7ff). This criticism is further strengthened when adaptive preferences are taken into consideration. Whatever preferences are revealed may already have been adapted to what individuals perceive as realistic for them to achieve. In other words: the utilitarian tradition faces the same challenges of inter-subjective comparison as other approaches do. Against this backdrop, it is the CA that has moved the issue of inter-personal comparison forward. The open discussion between Sen and Nussbaum on the usefulness of canonical lists of capabilities indicates the opportunities and limitations of such comparison.

As we have reported, there has over recent years been a continuing debate about the need for multidimensionality and cross-disciplinary approaches to poverty studies. Many economists, coming from the utilitarian and naturalist tradition, have taken an active part in this, and have been among the key driving forces behind it. Hence, even if not all will choose to take part, the emergence of the CA in the study of well-being and poverty provides a common framework and arena. This makes it possible to find common epistemological ground and to work with possible trade-offs between inter-subjective comparisons and the understanding of meaning; to find common normative positions; to combine all sorts of methodologies; and to utilize different sets of data.

Conclusion

This chapter has described the conceptual debate about poverty and how poverty should be defined and measured. This description builds on two major philosophical traditions, which have resulted in two distinct approaches to the definition and measurement of poverty: the income/consumption approach and the participatory approach. We have argued that the emergence of the capability approach to the understanding and study of poverty provides middle ground between these two positions. Furthermore, the capability approach makes it possible to use a multitude of methods and data. It is thus a useful platform for moving in the warranted direction of further multidisciplinary, multidimensional and dynamic approaches to the study of poverty.

What such shifts will imply in terms of alternative and more accurate measures of poverty, and improved strategies for the reduction of poverty largely remains to be seen. Investments in new data are costly and take time. However, attempts at its implementation are under way. The increased focus during recent years on measuring poverty that we noted through the scanning of English language literature seemingly indicates a turn towards the I/C approach. However, even this opens up opportunities for a transgression of the I/C and the PA approaches. By increasingly measuring poverty multidimensionally and dynamically, such a trend may bring with it deepened analysis and understanding of what poverty is.

We agree with Kanbur and Shaffer (2005) that differences of epistemology and normative theory are of fundamental importance in describing and analysing what separates various positions on the definition, measurement and explanation of poverty. We further agree that these differences have not been highlighted enough in the past. However, there is no reason why such differences need to remain. The evolution of the capability approach opens up possibilities to bridge the epistemological and normative barriers. This will not happen in a way that abandons the differences once and for all. Rather, the capability approach provides an arena where such differences can be discussed. Instead of perceiving them as fundamental lines of division, tensions between inter-subjective measurement and contextual understanding, as well as between externally justified and internally adaptive preferences may be treated as the trade-offs that they are. No one can escape such difficulties any longer by hiding away in any single epistemological corner.

References

Addison, T., D Hulme and R. Kanbur (2008): "Poverty Dynamics: Measurement and Understanding from an Interdisciplinary Perspective", *BWPI Working Paper 19*, Manchester: University of Manchester.

Alkire, S. (2008): "Choosing Dimensions; The Capability Approach and multidimensional Poverty", *Munich Personal RePEc Archive Paper No 8862,* Munich: MPRA.

Alkire, S. and J. Foster (2008): "Counting and Multidimensional Poverty", *Working Paper 7, Oxford Poverty and Human Development Initiative,* Oxford: Queen Elisabeth House, Oxford University.

Anderson, D. and V. Broch-Due, (1999): *The Poor are not Us – Poverty and Pastoralism*, Oxford: James Currey; Nairobi: EAEP; and Athens: Ohio University Press.

Bentham, J. (1789 (1948)): *The Principles of Morals and Legislation*, New York: Haffner Press.

Berry, S. (1985): *Fathers Work for their Sons.* Berkeley: University of California Press.

———. (1993): *No Condition is Permanent.* Madison: University of Wisconsin Press.

Besley, T. and R. Burgess (2002): "Redistribution, Growth and Poverty Reduction", (mimeo), London: London School of Economics.

Chambers, R. (2006): "What is Poverty? Who asks? Who answers?", *Poverty in Focus*, UNDP, Brasilia: International Poverty Centre, December.

———. (1995): "Poverty and livelihoods: whose reality counts?." *Environment and urbanization* 7.1: 173-204.

Dilthey, W. (1991): *Introduction to the Human Sciences.* Princeton: Princeton University Press.

Droysen, J.G. (1858, 1977): *Historik: Vorlesungen über Enzyklopädie und Methodologie der Geschichte.* Stuttgart: Fromann-Holzboog.

Ehrenpreis, D. (2009): "Poverty – What it is and what to do about it – Ideas and Policies in the International Community and in Swedish Development Cooperation", in Wohlgemuth, L. and B Odén (eds): *Where is Swedish Aid Heading?*, School of Global Studies, Gothenburg: University of Gothenburg.

Fuks, A. (1984): *Social Conflict in Ancient Greece*, Leiden, the Netherlands: E.J. Brill Publishers.

Gasper, D.R. (1996): "Needs and Basic Needs: A Clarification of Meanings, Levels and Different Streams of Work", *Working Paper 210*, The Hague: Institute of Social Studies.

Giddens, A. (1976): *New Rules of Sociological Method*, London: Hutchinson.

Goff, M.J. (2003): *The Worldly and Heavenly Wisdom of 4Q Instruction*, Leiden, the Netherlands: E.J. Brill Publishers.

Google n-gram, 2011: http://books.google.com/ngrams, accessed on 2011-11-15.

Habermas, J. (1971): *Knowledge and Human Interest*. Boston: Beacon.

———. (1990): *Moral Consciousness and Communicative Action*. Cambridge MA: MIT Press.

Jerven, M. (2011): "The Quest for the African Dummy: Explaining African Post-Colonial Economic Performance Revisited" *Journal of International Development*, 23.2: 288–307.

Johnson L.B., (1964): "Proposal for A Nationwide War on The Sources of Poverty", *Special Message to Congress*, March 16, Washington D.C.

Kanbur, R. and P. Shaffer (2005): "Epistemology, Normative Theory and Poverty Analysis: Implications for Q-Squared in Practice", *Working Paper 2, Q-Squared*, Toronto: University of Toronto.

Krishna, A. (2007): "Escaping Poverty and Becoming Poor in Three States of India, with additional evidence from Kenya, Uganda, Peru", in Narayan. D. and P. Patesch (eds): *Moving Out of Poverty – Cross-Disciplinary Perspectives on Mobility*, London: Palgrave, Washington D.C: World Bank.

Lesamana, J.A.M. (2009): "Transition from Subsistence to Monetary Economy – A Counter Discourse to Mainstream Development Strategies" Master's Thesis, Development Management, Kristiansand, Norway: University of Agder.

Lewis, O. 1971: "The Culture of Poverty" in Pilisuk, M and P. Pilisuk (eds): Poor Americans: How the White Poor Live, Transaction Publishers.

Loungani, P. (2003): "The Global War on Poverty – Who's Winning?", Finance & Development, December, Washington: IMF.

Lübcke, P. (1988): *Filosofilexikonet*, Stockholm: Forum.

Narajan, D., R. Patel, K. Schafft, A. Rademacher, S. Koch-Schulte (1999): "Can Anyone Hear Us? – Voices from 47 Countries", *Voices of the Poor, volume 1*, Washington D.C.: World Bank.

Nussbaum, M.C. (2003): "Capabilities as Fundamental Entitlements: Sen and Social Justice", *Feminist Economics*, Vol 9.2–3: 35–59.

———. (2006): *Frontiers of Justice – Disability, Nationality, Species Membership*, Cambridge, MA: Belknap/ Harvard University Press.

———. (2011): *Creating Capabilities*, Cambridge, MA: Harvard University Press.

OPHI (2007): "Annex: OPHI Research Agenda Details", (mimeo), Oxford: Queen Elisabeth House, Oxford University.

Ravallion, M. (2011): "On Multidimensional Dimensions of Poverty", *Policy Research Working Papers 5580*, Washington D.C: World Bank.

Ravallion, M. and S. Chen (2008): "The Developing World is Poorer than We Thought, But No Less Successful in the Fight Against Poverty", *World Bank Policy Research Working Papers 4703*, Washington D.C: World Bank.

Ravallion, M., S. Chen and P. Sangraula (2009): "Dollar a Day Revisited" The World Bank Economic Review, Washington D.C: World Bank.

Rawls, J. (1971): *A Theory of Justice*. Cambridge MA: Harvard University Press.

Robeyns, I. (2005): "Assessing Global Poverty and Inequality: Income Resources and Capability" in C. Barry and T. Pogge (eds): *Global Institutions and Responsibilities – Achieving Global Justice*. Oxford: Blackwell.

Samuelson, P.A. (1966): *The collected scientific papers of Paul A. Samuelson* (Vol. 2), Cambridge, MA: MIT press.

Sen, A.K. (1987): *The Standard of Living*. Cambridge: Cambridge University Press.

———. (1999): *Development as Freedom.* Oxford/ New York: Oxford University Press.

———. (2004): "Capabilities, Lists and Public Reasoning: Continuing the Conversation", *Feminist Economics* 10:3.

———. (2009): *The Idea of Justice*. London: Allen Lane.

Shaffer, P. (1996): "Beneath the Poverty Debate – Some Issues", IDS Bulletin 27:1, Brighton: IDS, University of Sussex.

Shaffer, P. (1998): "Gender, Poverty and Deprivation: Evidence from the Republic of Guinea", *World Development* 26.12: 2119–35.

Shepherd, A., L. Scott, C. Mariotti, F. Kessy, R Gaiha, L. da Corta, K. Hanifnia, N. Kaicker, A. Lenhardt, C. Lwanga-Ntale, B. Sen, B. Sijapati, T. Strawson, G. Thapa, H. Underhill and L. Wild (2014): *The Chronic Poverty Report 2014-2015: The Road to Zero Extreme Poverty*, London: ODI.

Son, H. and N. Kakwani (2006): "Global Estimates of Pro-Poor Growth", *IPC Working Paper Series 31*, Brasilia: IPC.

Taylor, C. (1985): *Philosophy and the Human Sciences: Philosophical Papers*, vol II, Cambridge: Cambridge University Press.

Tilly, C. (2007): "Poverty and the Politics of Exclusion", in Narayan, D and P Patesch (eds): *Moving Out of Poverty – Cross-Disciplinary Perspectives on Mobility*, London: Palgrave, Washington D.C.: World Bank.

Townsend, P. (2006): "Poverty and Human Rights", Paper presented at IPC and UNDP Conference on "The Many Dimensions of Poverty"; Brasilia, August 29–31.

UN, 2011: "Assessing Progress in Africa toward the Millennium Development Goals – MDG Report 2011", UNDP, AfDB, UNECA, AU, Addis Abeba/New York.

UNCTAD, (2011): *World Investment Report 2011 – Non-Equity Modes of International Production and Development*. New York and Geneva: UNCTAD.

von Grebmer, K., A. Saltzman, E. Birol, D. Wiesmann, N. Prasai, S. Yin, Y. Yohannes, P. Menon, J. Thompson, A Sonntag (2014): *"2014 Global Hunger Index: The Challenge of Hidden Hunger"*, Bonn: Welthungerhilfe / Wahington D.C.: IFPRI / Dublin: Concern Worldwide.

von Wright G.H. (1971): *Explanation and Understanding*, London: Routledge and Kegan Paul.

WDI (2015): World Development Indicators, *http://data.worldbank.org/* accessed on 2015-02-13.

World Bank (2015): *Global Monitoring Report 2014/2015 – Ending Poverty and Sharing Prosperity*, Washington D.C.: World Bank.

CHAPTER 4

Debating Empowerment: A Case Study of Knowledge Practices in the Development Assistance Committee

Rosalind Eyben

Introduction

'Perhaps never before has so much been made of the power of ideas, right theory or good policy in solving the problems of global poverty', observes David Mosse in his edited collection (2011a: 3). Anthropologists, he suggests, have either analysed the material effects of these ideas as weapons in the battlefields of knowledge in development programming, or, from a Foucauldian perspective, have examined how discourses create development subjects. But until recently there has been little interest in 'knowledge practices at the top' (ibid.: 2) – head offices of development organizations with a global reach. One can offer various explanations for this. Arguably what goes on at the top is less interesting to study. The tedious nature of what happens in committee rooms – admirably described by Green (2011) – compares unfavourably with the excitement and colour found at the interface of international development professionals, government officials and citizen groups in an aid-recipient country. Compared to what happens in the process of programme implementation, policy texts are constructed with relative ease (Bebbington et al. 2007). Furthermore, access to the top is difficult and it is hard to protect anonymity in analyses that describe what people do and say (Bebbington et al. 2004). Notwithstanding this, the last decade has seen the publication of several insider accounts of knowledge practices at the top, including in the World Bank (Bebbington et al. 2004; Broad 2007; Mosse 2011b) and in government aid agencies (Eyben 2004; Gastel and Nuijten 2005; Green 2011). All of these analyse the recursive connections between discourses, politics and practices, and render visible the actors and the spaces in which discourses of aid are constructed and contested.

This chapter offers a case from a rather different organizational context, the Development Assistance Committee (DAC).[1] Unlike the World Bank or

1 This chapter is based on material gathered while under contract to the OECD, and I am grateful for authorization to use it for the present academic purpose. An early version of this paper was presented in 2011 at a seminar in the Nordic Africa Institute, Uppsala, and the resultant

 | DOI 10.1163/9789004305465_005

the Dutch or British aid ministries, the DAC – the donors' club – is not an implementing agency. As a constituent part of the Organisation of Economic Co-operation and Development (OECD), it seeks to influence how the world thinks and acts by identifying and finding 'good practice' solutions to problems; these become standards against which member states' actions are scrutinized through peer review processes (Mahon and McBride 2009). Whether this influence happens depends on the wider political environment in the member state's agency and on the skills of those using DAC guidance to exert pressure on their own management. Overall, the DAC has reflected the mainstream thinking of its time – for example, as one of the sites that produced the Washington Consensus (Zimmerman and Smith 2011). Because OECD staff – the Secretariat that supports the work of the DAC committees – broadly see their task as securing agreement, they worry if the group they are shepherding strays too far from what the Secretariat perceives to be the mainstream. This risk has been greatest among the policy thematic networks in the DAC's subsidiary bodies – governance (GOVNET), gender (GENDERNET) and poverty (POVNET). Because such spaces have attracted the radical fringe of non-economists, struggling for a voice in their own organizations and finding strength in numbers in the DAC, Ruckert (2008: 111) suggests that the DAC should be conceived of as 'a condensation of antagonistic social forces'.[2] The present paper is an ethnographic observation of one such ideological struggle that occurred in a sub-committee – a 'task team' – composed of some 15 officials from the head offices of bilateral and multilateral agencies that met at regular intervals between 2008 and 2011 to produce three sets of texts, advised by the author in the role of 'expert' consultant. Our task was to produce guidance on the link between poor people's empowerment and pro-poor growth.

Batliwala (2007: 557) proposes that, of all the development buzzwords, 'empowerment is probably the most widely used and abused…coined to represent a clearly political concept, it has been "mainstreamed" in a manner that has virtually robbed it of its original meaning and strategic value'. Initially taken up by the social movements of the second half of the last century, empowerment was co-opted by mainstream development practitioners and converted into a neo-liberal and consumerist discourse that, Batliwala argues,

---

lively discussion very usefully guided my thoughts in producing a fuller draft. I am also grateful for comments on a further version from colleagues in the IDS Participation Team and for feedback received from four members of the task team that forms the subject of this paper. Every effort has been made to protect their anonymity. I take sole responsibility for the content.

2 See Eyben (2012) for further elaboration of these points.

took 'power' out of empowerment. Could the task team, I wondered, be persuaded to put it back in and to reflect this in the texts we produced? The DAC had long served as a space in which staff from head offices could construct guidelines and principles that they hoped subsequently to use in order to influence policy discourse back home. Among my motives for accepting the consultancy was loyalty to an increasingly marginalized epistemic community in Aidland,[3] commonly referred to as 'social development specialists' – that is, agency staff responsible for the social and political analysis of aid programmes and policies. Social developers have a concern for process and relationships; an appreciation of diversity and difference, even at the most local level; an awareness of the operations of power; a continuing engagement with understanding and addressing the causes and consequences of inequalities; sensitivity to their own positionality; and, lastly, an interest in making visible those social realities that are not easily apparent to busy policy-makers. In the early 1990s, when employed by the UK development ministry, I had co-founded with Dutch and Swedish social developers an informal international forum that met regularly to share ideas and strategies for participatory approaches and poverty reduction (Eyben 2003).

Although we gained some traction, by the mid-2000s social developers were losing the discursive battle to a managerial mainstream that was reviving economic growth as the development goal. It was within this increasingly challenging environment that social developers in POVNET had been trying to get agreement for the Network to produce policy guidance on empowerment. Feeling that I should support these efforts, I sought to discover how far and in what ways the social developers in the task team could endow empowerment with a more transformative cluster of meanings than had so far been the case in DAC publications. Conscious of not being a neutral party, I was alert to the risk of not establishing good relations with those I saw as non-social developers on the task team. Thus I sought to provide my advice in a technical and balanced 'expert' manner, often cheerfully agreeing to textual changes that I disliked, while with my social development hat on, seeking and testing the available room for manoeuvre. I shared an earlier draft of this paper with four members of the task team, three of whom broadly agreed with my interpretation and analysis; the fourth objected, did not recognize much of what I had described and pointed out issues and perspectives I had overlooked. I have revised the text in response to this critical feedback, clarifying misconceptions

3 See Raymond Apthorpe's discussion of the coining of this term (2011) and Mosse's definition of Aidland as 'the aggregate effect of expert thought and planning which is the virtual world of aid professionals' (2011a: vii).

and rectifying factual errors. Most importantly, I have nuanced my analysis and made it less of a 'black and white' struggle between the social developers and the rest.

Distinct from disagreements over interpretation, a further serious objection relates to whether, having been employed to work as a consultant to the task team, it is appropriate for me thereafter to write in a critical academic vein about the process. I have previously discussed (Eyben 2009) the case of David Mosse's former colleagues objecting to his anthropological account (Mosse 2005) of a project in which he and they had worked together as team mates. This resulted in a lively debate in *Anthropology Today* about the ethics and politics of multi-positionality (Sridhar 2005) and became the subject of a detailed analysis by Mosse himself (2006). I suggested then that the moral issue might be whether the consultant anthropologist accepted the assignment in good faith and satisfactorily fulfilled his or her terms of reference – or in bad faith, accepting the job primarily for academic research purposes. In this present case, I took the job in good faith and delivered what was required of me. At the same time, as an anthropologist interested in power and relations in international aid, I was curious about the processes that I was observing and of which I was part. Nevertheless, ethnographically, the study has its limitations. First, because of the care I have taken to protect individuals' anonymity, I have deliberately avoided much of the 'thick detail' that a good ethnography requires. Second, as with the other members of the task team, my perspective is not omniscient: I was only partially aware of the relationships and conversations associated with the task team's work, and my analysis and interpretation necessarily reflect those limitations.

With these caveats in mind, the present paper analyses how points of view shifted over time and examines why and how the task team succeeded in constructing an official policy text that ran counter to Aidland's mainstream neoliberal environment. I note the irony that, within months of our work being concluded, POVNET was abolished. Can our success be explained, I ask, by the fact that it posed no threat? Was it just a small rear-guard victory within Aidland's major retreat from a battlefield of knowledge, where previously the people-centred and transformative discourses of development had carried some weight?

To answer these questions, I first look at empowerment's history in Aidland – and more specifically in the DAC. The paper then explores sequentially two key issues that were contested in the production of the three sets of texts for which the task team was responsible. The first issue was about making donors visible by including a reflexive analysis of their behaviour and practices; the second concerned putting power back into the concept of empowerment. I look at how these issues played out in two of the three products of the task team. The task team generated 'Stories of Empowerment' as a new genre for the DAC, with the aim of revealing the complex processes and relationships involved in donor efforts to facilitate empowerment. The subsequent controversy over the methodology for collecting and narrating these Stories revealed the task team's disagreement over the meaning of empowerment and the implications for practice. The second product was a Policy Guidance Note (PGN) – a more conventional genre. By the time the PGN was drafted in the second phase of the task team's work, a gradual shift had occurred in recognizing power and positionality as issues for consideration. This paved the way for consensus about content and language that is surprisingly radical for the present era. In the present chapter's conclusion I discuss the dissonance between this radicalism and the broader institutional and discursive trends in Aidland, of which the demise of POVNET is just one illustration.[4]

Empowerment in Aidland: Its Roots, Growth and Contested Status

Empowerment entered development discourse in the 1970s, when the radical edge of aid practice was reading Freire (1970) and regarding empowerment as a process of liberation from structural oppression, through collective critical awareness or 'conscientization'. As Goulet (1979: 536) put it, empowerment was about 'hitherto passive human beings transformed into active subjects creating their own history'. By the following decade,[5] many of the themes we were subsequently to tackle in our POVNET discussions were already present in the literature, including the empowerment of different categories of people, such as peasants (Cohen and Uphoff 1980), the disabled (Miles 1989) and women (Sen and Grown 1988); empowerment was also linked to topics of indigenous technical knowledge (Thrupp 1989), participatory research (Tandon 1981), people-centred development (Thomas 1983; Korten and Klauss 1984) and rights-based approaches (Brodhead 1987). By this time, however, 'empowerment' as a set of meanings associated with liberation and critical consciousness was being challenged by another set of non-Freirean meanings, as for example in Bryant's rational actor analysis of USAID support to squatters' empowerment in Zambia (1980). In the 1990s, both sets of meanings became more common. Established people-centred development scholars such as

4 The third product was a collection of Good Practice Notes. All three are available at http://www.oecd.org/dac/povertyreduction/reducingpovertythroughempowerment.htm.

5 From an analysis of Google Scholar.

Chambers (1992) began to use empowerment in their conceptual toolkit as the concept spread widely within development studies, policy and practice and was incorporated into the language of the big United Nations conferences.[6] But as it became a buzzword, so it became the subject of greater scrutiny.

Mohanty (1995) claimed that 'empowerment' had shifted its meaning to signify those in authority giving power to marginalized or discriminated groups. This made it a disabling concept: people's right to struggle is constrained when they are organized from above. Thereafter, top-down empowerment as a means of limiting the scope for bottom-up action continued to be discussed (Craig et al. 2000); this was combined with regret that empowerment's radical and transformative character was being diluted or altogether replaced by meanings that privileged agency as individual consumerist choice (Cleaver 1999). This confusion about empowerment's meaning, suggested Mohan and Stokke (2000), could be attributed to the contradiction between, on the one hand, a higher-level consensus between neo-liberals and post-Marxists about bottom-up empowerment that diminished the overweening power of the state and, on the other hand, a crucial lower-level disagreement over the resultant political agenda. From the neo-liberal perspective, empowerment of the powerless is achieved by integrating them into decision-making processes without changing the societal status quo, whereas the post-Marxist agenda concerns people's organized action to overturn the established order.

At the start of the new millennium, empowerment received the ultimate stamp of mainstream approval when it was privileged as a central concept in the *World Development Report* on Poverty (World Bank 2000). Left undefined in the report, a definition was subsequently provided as 'the expansion of assets and capabilities of poor people to participate in, negotiate with, influence, control and hold accountable institutions that affect their lives' (Narayan 2002: xviii). In a critical commentary on the Bank's emphasis on people's agency, Moore (2001) argued that, rather than seek to support directly organizations of the poor, donors might do better to turn their attention to helping create the broader political conditions in which poor people could organize politically.

6 An analysis of Google Scholar found that, of all references (excluding citations) published between 1990 and 1995 that included the phrase 'international development', 5 per cent included also 'empowerment'; between 1995 and 2000, this increased to 16 per cent. If we replace 'international development' with 'international aid', 'empowerment' appears in 15 per cent of all references published between 1990 and 1995, increasing to 22 per cent in the second half of the decade. The term has since become slightly less common in 'international development' references, but continues to grow in popularity for 'international aid'. In the last full year, 2011, 35 per cent of all 'international aid' references also included the word 'empowerment'.

This would require, he suggested, a subtle and nuanced understanding of politics and political action. In the decade that followed, what came to be called 'political economy' analysis grew increasingly popular among bilateral agencies. However, on the whole, non-governmental organizations (NGOs) and the researcher activists supporting them engaged more centrally with informal 'power' than did the bilateral agencies. Thus, VeneKlasen and Miller (2002) provided empowerment frameworks that built on ideas of collective consciousness-building leading to strong and balanced citizen–state relations. On the other hand, for the World Bank, the DAC and many official donors, the key meanings of empowerment were concerned less with collective action and more with choice, influence and autonomy. Linked increasingly with 'women', empowerment was becoming development's magic bullet, achieved through micro-finance, female education and political quotas (Eyben and Napier-Moore 2009). Empowerment thus stayed extraordinarily fashionable in mainstream discourse, while continuing to be subjected to ever more critical deconstruction (Cornwall and Brock 2005), as well as scrutinized for the dissonance between the text produced at head office and the contingency of practice in the field (Bebbington et al. 2007). This was the backdrop to POVNET's decision in 2008 to build on its earlier work on social protection and empowerment (2006–08) by initiating a new phase of work (2009–10) on empowerment and pro-poor growth.

Empowerment and Poverty Reduction at the DAC

In the mid-1990s, the DAC played an important role in encouraging its membership – bilateral aid agencies – to make poverty reduction a central objective (combined with participatory approaches) that had long interested social developers in the agencies (Eyben 2012). The Working Party on Good Governance (subsequently known as GOVNET) that was established in 1993 included 'Participatory Development' in its title, and human-rights-based approaches were a central theme of its work. 'People-centred' and 'participatory development' were key phrases in the DAC's bold and highly influential *Shaping the 21st Century*, published in 1996, which defined aid's goals as poverty reduction, social development and environmental sustainability (Thérien and Lloyd 2000) and whose 'International Development Targets' were the basis for the Millennium Development Goals (Manning 2009).

POVNET was established in 1998 as part of this trend, and in its early years social developers from the different bilateral agencies (including the author), organized informally through their own inter-agency network, represented the majority perspective in the room. POVNET produced the DAC Guidelines on Poverty Reduction (OECD 2001) – a publication that is still seen by today's social developers as 'a state of the art sourcebook'. In contrast to the *World Development Report*'s three pillars of opportunity, security and empowerment (World Bank 2000) the DAC Guidelines provided a more complex framework that emphasized – at least in the main text, if not in the more mainstream executive summary – human rights and the political and socio-cultural dimensions of poverty reduction.

Meanwhile, social development was losing its dominant position in POVNET. Poverty reduction's centrality in what was broadly a human development approach[7] to the Millennium Development Goals[8] had made it too important a topic to leave to social developers, who, in most aid agencies, had never been more than marginal. Officials from their organizations' mainstream – economists and managers – began to attend the meetings, with the result that POVNET replaced its former concerns (rights-based and participatory perspectives on poverty) with a concern for the kind of economic growth that would reduce poverty. Its guidance on pro-poor growth (OECD 2006) emphasized that, without the additional revenues that growth delivers, direct poverty reduction would not be sustainable, and that what was required was a pace and pattern of growth that enhanced the ability of poor women and men to participate in, contribute to and benefit from this growth. And to achieve this, the poor needed to be informed and empowered to influence a policy-making process that was accountable to their interests (OECD 2006: 35). The chair of the DAC described the guidance as the successful resolution of long-standing arguments between economists and non-economic social scientists (alias social developers) about pro-growth versus pro-poor strategies (Manning 2007). This was an oversimplification: the pro-poor growth consensus was between social developers and *some* economists – those opposed to the neoliberal Washington Consensus (for the sake of brevity, I call them 'human developers'). The guidance was the fruit of an alliance born during the 'social dimensions of structural adjustment' campaign of the late 1980s that shaped the agenda of the 1995 Copenhagen Social Summit (Eyben 2006), which in turn influenced the Millennium Development Goals. Importantly, this alliance did not resolve the paradigmatic differences between the social and human developers that were subsequently exposed in POVNET's work on empowerment.

---

7 Defined as the process of expanding human choices and strengthening human capabilities.

8 See Eyben (2006) and Hulme and Fukuda-Parr (2009) for further discussion of these differences in perspective in the development policy world.

To sum up, there was not just one but two areas of contention in POVNET: the first between the neo-liberal and the human development perspectives; and the second between human development and social development. Neo-liberal and human development approaches are both rooted in methodological individualism. While human developers are concerned with the redistribution of assets, incomes and services among individuals, the social development perspective conceives of poverty as not just a problem of redistribution, but also of collective and individual recognition and of representation (Dahl et al. 2004). This requires attention to be paid to society, culture and power, as forces that shape history and individual lives.

POVNET's decision in 2008 to produce further guidance was a means of continuing the human and social development consensus on the pro-poor growth theme. This was felt by its advocates to be necessary because of the perceived threat of a neo-liberal push-back from representatives of some member states active in the Network who favoured the new concept of 'inclusive growth'. Like pro-poor growth, inclusive growth is subject to various definitions, but (as it is defined by the World Bank) it differs from the DAC's understanding of pro-poor. The latter 'is mainly interested in the welfare of the poor while inclusive growth is concerned with opportunities for the majority of the labor force, poor and middle-class alike' (Ianchovichina and Lundstrom 2009: footnote 1). Inclusive growth is not concerned with reducing inequalities, and nor does the concept recognize that poverty will only be tackled when poor people gain a voice in policy-making. The POVNET delegates from member states and international organizations who volunteered to join the task team were those who objected to the new concept of inclusive growth, which they perceived as undermining the DAC Guidelines (OECD 2001; 2006).

Consequently, because neo-liberalism had only limited influence in the empowerment task team (as distinct from its parent body, POVNET) arguments about the meaning of empowerment mainly reflected disagreement between human and social development perspectives – *not* between these two perspectives and neo-liberalism. At the same time, these ideological/philosophical differences were rarely articulated as distinctly as this in the task team's debates. Meanings and epistemological approaches fractured, combined and re-formed in relation to the subject under discussion and the speaker's positionality. In the heat of the moment, everyone, including the author, shifted un-reflexively between perspectives. Nevertheless, the relatively small group of social developers kept 'on message' about putting power back into empowerment and about its ramifications for donor practices.

Most of the social developers had been members of the previous task team on social protection and pro-poor growth (OECD 2008), where their efforts to put power back into empowerment had been disappointing. Despite frequent references to empowerment, other than in one mention of unequal power relations, 'power' only appears in the text as spending or purchasing power. Hence, while the human developers wanted further work on empowerment on pro-poor growth because they saw it as fundamental to the expansion of choice, social developers hoped this new task team would be more successful than the social protection team had been in reframing empowerment. GENDERNET was also keen to see POVNET take empowerment seriously, and this provided an opportunity for gender equality to be more included in POVNET than had hitherto been the case. POVNET's work depended on additional voluntary contributions from member states – for example to hire consultants like me and to cover publication costs. One of the social developers pledged a substantial contribution from their agency, on the implicit condition that empowerment should be a central element in the 2009–11 work programme. The social developers, however, had to compromise to secure this agreement: the task team would not be concerned with empowerment and poverty reduction as they had hoped, but would focus more explicitly on empowerment and pro-poor growth.

Against this background, and with a provisional budgetary allocation of between 300,000 and 500,000 Euros, it was agreed that a task team would be established from among interested POVNET members. The Secretariat accordingly drafted an outline of purpose:

> The aim…is to help donors better support the capacities and efforts of poor women and men, and their civil society organisations, to be more effectively involved in and benefit from growth and poverty reduction strategies. It will assist donors to work with government and other stakeholders to strengthen political will and the supportive framework to engage in dialogue. This work will also address how donors can support public policies that empower the informal economy and unleash its growth potential.[9]

Worried that this framing of empowerment was not advancing the agenda, the same social developer whose agency was providing one of the biggest voluntary contributions suggested that a background paper on the concept of

9 From the note dated 30 April 2008, drafted by the Secretariat, 'Preparing the 2009–10 POVNET work programme: content and modalities', p. 6.

empowerment be commissioned from the Pathways of Women's Empowerment programme, which was hosted at the UK's Institute of Development Studies. For this background paper, I drew on research that I had undertaken on the shifting meanings of women's empowerment in international development agencies (Eyben and Napier-Moore 2009). I found that instrumentalist meanings of empowerment, associated with efficiency and growth, were crowding out socially transformative meanings of rights and collective action. In an effort to make headway in an unfavourable policy environment – and to keep alive their purpose – officials who favoured these transformative approaches strategically juggled the different sets of meanings of empowerment. Hence they preferred fuzziness over clarity. When there was little chance of securing collective agreement to the desired meaning, such strategic ambiguity provided room for manoeuvre. I had thus assumed that, with the challenges they might face in the task team, the social developers would avoid seeking clarity, and choose rather to focus on the practical details of the kinds of aid instruments and donor behaviour that could support transformative approaches. I thought that, in order to avoid a contest over definitions, it was all to be done by stealth. I also thought the DAC Secretariat – which by virtue of its role always looks for consensus among the membership – would want to avoid divisive debates by opting for a 'fuzzword' (Cornwall 2007). I was proved wrong. From the Secretariat's perspective, empowerment's fuzziness had wasted a lot of time in former POVNET meetings; early agreement on a 'working definition' would help this task team move faster. The social developers agreed.

Instructed that our background paper should propose a definition, we suggested that empowerment happens 'when individuals and organised groups are able to imagine their world differently and to realise that vision by changing the relations of power that have been keeping them in poverty' (Eyben et al. 2008: 3). We argued that empowerment should be understood as the interplay between 'power within', 'power with' and 'power to' (Rowlands 1997); that poverty should not be seen as an absolute state, but as relative and relational; and that empowerment is a process that changes the idea of who one is vis-à-vis the social institutions that shape identity.

In November 2008, I was invited to present the paper at the first of ten meetings of the task team (the last of which took place in February 2011). Most there knew each other reasonably well from previous participation in POVNET meetings, but also from other events and networks. Some of them appeared to be strategically focused. One of them, seated in front of a large white board, tactically took the opportunity to sketch a diagram about how the task team should proceed with its work. My notes from the meeting read:

> thus managing to convince the meeting that the task team would work to collect stories of empowerment amid the faint murmurs from an economist about the value of regression analyses... We all kept staring at the board and it was difficult to escape his framing.

The social developers enthusiastically accepted the proposal that the task team use narratives of empowerment to capture the complexity of the process, and I was asked to develop a methodology for the task team to review. Some were less enthusiastic. One participant with a social development background declared that his agency was in favour of inclusive, not pro-poor growth, that he had little room for manoeuvre, and that it would be difficult for him to justify coming to further meetings. Others appeared to be struggling with the conceptual discussion. One person's remark about seeing little connection between empowerment and human rights elicited audible gasps of shock and surprise from the social developers. I wondered at the time whether some task team members might have felt themselves at a disadvantage in the discussions, uncomfortable with speaking about abstract concepts such as power, thinking that others might disparage their opinions. As a task team member commented on reading a draft of this chapter, non-native English speakers might have been feeling challenged, unaware of the linguistic nuances in relation to these concepts.

That initial meeting was followed by a further two in the first half of 2009, which I did not attend. At these it was agreed to produce 'Good Practice Notes' on empowerment in relation to particular topics, such as natural resources management, monitoring and evaluation, legal empowerment and women's economic empowerment. Task team members volunteered the topic for which they were willing to produce a 'note', in most cases planning to hire a consultant from their own budgets to help them do this. 'Stories of Empowerment', the idea generated at the first meeting and discussed in detail below, were also to be identified and written up by task team members. Material from these two sets of texts would then be drawn upon for the subsequent drafting of the Policy Guidance Note, the most official of the documents. At the third meeting, it was also decided to recruit a consultant to draft the PGN and provide overall intellectual support for the task team's work, including inputs into the drafting of its two other sets of products. Hence, I recommenced my engagement with the task team at its fourth meeting, in autumn 2009.

Debating Empowerment

The paradigmatic division between the social and human development perspectives discussed earlier played out in the two longest and most contested debates about empowerment at the task team meetings. These concerned the positionality of the donors (which I discuss in relation to the task team's unconventional product, 'Stories of Empowerment') and the centrality of power in empowerment (which I look at in the context of the production of the Policy Guidance Note).[10]

Meetings lasted from one and a half to two days (occasionally interspersed with tele-conferences) when participants reviewed and provided feedback on draft texts. Mostly we met in the OECD complex in Paris, where the arrangements and lay-out of the meeting rooms reminded one (female) social developer of 'yesterday's male boardrooms'. Sometimes we met at the head office of a task team member. These meetings tended to be more relaxed and informal, with the Secretariat participants – away from their home base – less obviously in charge. In these more familiar surroundings of an agency head office, we hunted for power outlets for our laptops, lent each other adaptors and listened to our hosts' latest gossip about the goings on in their organization. But regardless of location – and unlike meetings in a typical aid bureaucracy – there was no explicit formal hierarchy among those present. However, privately comments were made that some voices appeared to carry more weight than others, and that only some participants (not all) were allowed to speak as long and as frequently as they desired.[11]

Everyone felt the meetings could be managed better. The order of business was shuffled around to accommodate travel plans – 'I'm sorry, I have to leave for Hong Kong in half an hour' – and the last item of business was often rushed, much to the vexation of one participant: 'We need to make sure we leave enough time for planning! We always rush off to airports just when we get to this item.' There was suspicion among some that the rush at the end was a deliberate tactic, allowing decisions to be made in the interim and presenting these at the next meeting as *faits accomplis*.

Early on, the task team agreed to a proposal to allow Southern participation in the meetings 'to help…ground concepts, analysis and conclusions in the

10 These debates also featured in the discussions about the draft Good Practice Notes that, for reasons of brevity, I do not examine.

11 A Secretariat staffer (not involved in POVNET) commented to me that because participants in thematic network meetings were often in marginal positions in their own organizations, they took the opportunity to hog the limelight when they came to the DAC.

realities and livelihoods of people living in poverty in developing countries'.[12] It was expected that such participation would be from a diversity of regions and backgrounds, including representatives from government, think tanks, the private sector and civil society. Task team members were invited to suggest names. In the event, only three such participants were appointed – all from civil society and two from the same country. Nevertheless, although they participated in less than half of the meetings, and although they admitted to being rather confused about their role, they noticeably added weight to the social development perspective. They even volunteered to draft a Good Practice Note on social movements (OECD 2012) – something one of the social developers had wanted to do but had felt constrained to undertake because (I was told) of 'the neo-liberal atmosphere of the DAC'. The Southerners were, however, agreeably surprised that there did not appear to be any such neo-liberal constraint on what *they* said, and they commented that they could speak freely at the meetings. One of them, however, privately expressed irritation about perceived tokenism, observing that they had been invited to join the task team only after the programme of work and its details had been agreed. I sympathized with their predicament: I had also missed out on influencing the agenda by not being invited to the second and third task team meetings. When I returned to the task team for the fourth meeting, I was dismayed to discover what had happened to the 'Stories of Empowerment', as I now discuss.

Making Donors Visible

Everyone agreed that donors are not central to many of the empowerment processes in aid-recipient countries, but the discussions about the Stories revealed a gap in understanding. Some saw the Stories as a vehicle for donor staff to learn about how and when to support empowerment processes; others, focusing on the self-evident truth that donors often played a minor role, thought the Stories could be about any empowerment process (not necessarily one supported by donors) and should concentrate on explaining the positive outcomes for poor people.

At the first task team meeting, the intention behind the Stories had been to help task team members and their colleagues in country offices become more reflexive practitioners. The purpose was for them to learn about the power effects of donor action and to capture these effects in narratives about process

12 'Terms of Reference on Participation of Development Partners in Meetings of the DAC Network on Poverty Reduction (POVNET)', 2009, p.1.

and relationships – narratives in which multiple points of view (including that of the explicit donor) were represented, rather than synthesized into a single account. Ideally, task team members were to be involved in the collection of these Stories to learn what donors can and cannot usefully do and to incorporate their findings into the Policy Guidance Note. The methodology also stressed that the process should be empowering for all those involved, enabling people – including task team members and their colleagues – to imagine new possibilities for action. It was emphasized that we were *not* looking for stories of 'best practice', but should rather focus on the donors learning about how other project stakeholders interpreted and viewed donor behaviour.

Although the proposed methodology was formally approved at the April 2009 meeting of the task team, the minutes of the meeting contradicted that approval by also recording:

> Discussion clarified that the role of the [Stories] is to provide narratives of processes where empowerment has occurred and led to more beneficial involvement of poor people in economic activity. Donor involvement in or support of these processes is not a prerequisite for the relevance or adoption of a story.

Among the early ideas for the Stories put forward by task team members were: educating girls in Tanzania; the struggles of indigenous people in Nepal; and support for micro-finance in the Congo. Eventually, over twenty Stories were collected, in most cases with help from consultants or journalists. Most first drafts ignored the guidelines about multiple perspectives – particularly those commissioned from journalists, who wrote good news stories ('sunshine stories', as one social developer put it) about the transformed lives of 'the poor'. As one of the Southern participants commented: 'Being poor is having other people write about you.' Thus, what we had thought to be a good and innovative idea became everything that the methodology sought to avoid. 'The poor' and their 'voices' were being extracted to tell de-contextualized stories (Cornwall and Fujita 2007). As one disgruntled social developer put it, we had ended up with stories for ministerial speeches. All intermediary actors, particularly the donors, had become invisible. As I argued when I returned to the task team in October, by rendering the donors invisible, the task team was blocking any chance of learning about the role that donors could play in facilitating empowerment. The intentions of establishing a new genre in support of a transformative understanding of empowerment were beginning to unravel.

Only in one instance did a task team member (a social anthropologist with a background in participatory monitoring and evaluation) choose to follow the methodological guidelines and be the principal investigator. This person was subsequently to wonder whether one perhaps needed to be an anthropologist to understand the methodological point about different perspectives. Another social developer noted that it required constant effort to encourage the task team to focus on donor behaviour in supporting or constraining empowerment processes. Yet rendering donors invisible contradicted the task team's terms of reference, which stipulated that the aim was to improve donor practice. Contrary to these terms of reference, some members insisted that the team's task was to communicate good practice about empowerment to a much broader audience, including aid-recipient governments and civil society. This insistence was based on the tradition of most previous DAC guidance, which explained to everyone (not just the DAC's own membership) how development should be done. The reluctance to focus on donor behaviour was justified 'because we are not doing things ourselves but allying ourselves with people who are doing'.

Arguing that it was inappropriate to put donors into the frame, some in the task team were initially impervious to the counter argument that they *were* in the frame, and that by lurking in the shadows they were exercising hidden power (Gaventa 2006). If they did not make themselves visible, they could neither be held accountable nor learn how to be more effective. By choosing to see empowerment entirely from a single perspective – what happens to poor people, as interpreted by the omniscient voice of a consultant – and by ignoring the broader structures, relations and institutional actors involved, they were keeping shut the black box about how aid happens. Furthermore, bearing in mind the existence of the vast scholarly literature about empowerment, what was the added value of the DAC's contribution to this literature, other than to investigate and critically reflect on its own practices?

Nevertheless, and despite this setback, the social developers did secure some early discursive wins. The minutes of the second meeting of the task team record that

> The language of the document needs to be sensitive to the subject matter, and the term 'the poor' should be replaced by 'poor people', 'people living in poverty', or 'poor women and men'. This will help signify awareness that 'the poor' is a restraining category which does not recognise men and women living in poverty as people in their heterogeneity.

The task team also agreed to switch from passive to active voice. 'The poor' could no longer 'be empowered' (as in an initial draft text that mentioned how 'the World Bank reported that 25,000 out of 30,000 beneficiaries were empowered'). And as discussion about the Stories continued, so the social developers began to make gradual progress. On my return in October 2009, the Secretariat took the lead in reminding the task team of the methodological guidelines by asking me to present a summary of the key criteria against which the texts should be drafted. This included: (i) recognizing that donors may be very distant from the primary stakeholders, and thus acknowledging the need to capture the relational links through other actors, e.g. government ministries or NGOs; (ii) recognizing the possibility of challenge and conflict in empowerment processes; and (iii) looking at donors' discourses and procedures and how these affected empowerment, including capturing what the other stakeholders thought about these discourses and procedures.

When the next meeting reviewed revised versions of the Stories, there had been a significant shift in understanding the purpose of them. Comments from different task team members were made about 'respecting different realities' and 'the need for edge – not just the normal blah-blah'. It was agreed that some Stories would require further work (in one case, obliging the agency concerned to send its consultant back to the field to conduct further interviews). Other Stories were rejected as beyond redemption: their whole basis was now appreciated as inappropriate. In one such instance, the task team decided that 'the story is too short; there are only the voices of the ultimate beneficiaries; local conflicts are under-explored; most of the voices are men and local officials; the process was extractive; there is no information about the empowerment process'. And an outlier: 'What has the story got to do with pro-poor growth?'

By June 2010, the work on the Stories had been completed. Some of the social developers – and the author – had invested much emotional effort and energy in the process. I felt the eventual products were very different from the original intention, but were better than it had seemed they might be at one point. The arguments about the Stories – along with the conversations about the Good Practice Notes not examined in this chapter – meant that, for a whole year, we had been debating what empowerment meant for donors' practices. This laid the groundwork for the task team's final and most important textual product – the Policy Guidance Note. Once approved by the DAC High-Level Meeting of development cooperation ministers, the PGN would become official DAC policy, against which – in theory – the performance of member states could be assessed as part of the regular DAC peer review process.

Keeping Power on the Agenda

The main sensitivity that I now discuss concerned the treatment of 'power' in the drafting of the Policy Guidance Note (OECD 2012)[13] and in last-minute efforts to remove 'power' as a concept both from the overall definition of empowerment and from the policy statement to be approved by the DAC High-Level Meeting.

An initial attempt to structure the note in terms of *power to* (productive assets, the market and care economies and human capabilities), *power with* (democratic governance, collective action) and *power within* (critical consciousness, inclusion) was rejected for having 'too much power'. Without significant change to the content, the sections were accordingly relabelled as economic, political and social empowerment. Following the previous year's discussion about the Stories and the Good Practice Notes and the eventual agreement that empowerment was a process that donors could either support or hinder, the final and most important part of the PGN – 'Implications for Donor Practice' – was readily agreed. This distinguished it from its immediate POVNET predecessor, the PGN on social protection, which included the role of governments and other actors, in addition to recommendations for donors.

Although donors had now become the focus of the PGN, other fault lines emerged. The first concerned economic empowerment. Early on, some task team members had wanted to restrict the PGN to just this issue. Although persuaded to broaden it out (provided I could demonstrate the linkages with pro-poor growth), they still saw the economic as the most important section, requiring the greatest care. In the second draft of the PGN, I had included a definition of economic empowerment drawn directly from the earlier background paper:

> Economic empowerment is the capacity of women and men to participate in, contribute to and benefit from growth processes in ways which recognize the value of their contributions, respect their dignity and make it possible to negotiate a fairer distribution of the benefits of growth.
>
> EYBEN ET AL. 2008: 9

13 Although reviewed by the task team as a whole, ultimate responsibility for the stories and the Good Practice Notes lay with the individuals who commissioned them using their organizations' resources. The PGN, however, was a DAC official document and had to follow a format and standard developed in previous publications. I was also asked to draft the note by drawing on the relevant academic literature, as well as on the material from the stories and Good Practice Notes, submitting successive versions of the PGN to the task team for its consideration and amendment.

Neo-liberal perspectives were manifesting their influence, and these references to 'distribution' and 'value' created some anxiety. It was decided that some task team members would, with support from the Secretariat, assume responsibility for re-drafting this part of the note, so that it better reflected the DAC position on pro-poor growth, as understood to be articulated in the 2006 PGN on this subject.[14] Accordingly, a revised draft stated:

> Economic empowerment is the capacity of women and men to exercise control over their livelihoods through being able to make choices on what productive activities to invest in, to decide how and when to engage in markets and to influence the terms on which they do so.

Social developers did not demur at this change, deciding to invest their own efforts in getting the right language into the *overall* definition of empowerment. The task team had accepted the background paper's working definition, and most members had assumed that, as such, it would be included in the final draft of the Policy Guidance Note. Hence, there was surprise and annoyance when, at the task team's penultimate meeting, an alternative definition was proposed – one from which 'power' had been removed:

> People are empowered when individually or together they are able to conceive of and define better lives for themselves and set and pursue targets for achieving them by changing political, economic and social institutions.

In a subsequent email exchange, encouraged by this almost last-minute act of resistance to the inclusion of 'power' another task team member offered a more neo-liberal perspective:

> People are empowered when they gain and exert influence in political, social, legal and economic decision-making processes and institutions and as a result of it their living standards improve (at least at the same pace as average income growth).[15]

---

14 In fact, the 2006 text makes frequent reference to distributional issues, but the wider political environment had meanwhile become less sympathetic.

15 Thus taking an 'inclusive' rather than 'pro-poor growth' line.

Yet another proposed:

> From a pro-poor growth perspective, empowerment is about poor women and men and their representatives gaining and exercising influence on decisions and processes that will improve their livelihoods. To lead to desired results, individuals and their representatives need the capacity and opportunity to influence such decisions and processes while those taking such decisions need to be accountable to the interests of poor people.

These alternative definitions ran counter to the general tenor of what was otherwise an agreed document. The social developers were worried. They emailed and phoned each other to discuss how to retrieve the situation. It looked as if they were losing the definitional battle just when they thought it had been won. They circulated among the task team alternatives that brought 'power' back into the definition. One proposal was more radical than the original working definition. It had a Marxist ring when referring to changing the structures, as well as the relations of power that keep people in poverty.

Alarmed by the split within the task team at this late stage, the Secretariat proposed a compromise definition that everyone reluctantly accepted:

> Empowerment happens when people, individually or collectively, conceive of, define and pursue better lives for themselves. From a Pro-Poor Growth perspective, poor women and men need to change existing power relations and gain and exert influence over the political, economic and social processes that determine and, all too often, constrain their livelihood opportunities.

The Final Contest

There was one final contest over 'power'. I was surprised at how easy it had been to include among the PGN's five priority messages the statement that 'Donors need to pay attention to the inequitable power relations, including their own behaviour, which keep people in poverty.' However, I had not realized that it was not the PGN that would be approved by ministers at the DAC High-Level Meeting, but rather a two-page policy statement serving as the note's preamble or executive summary. Just before the last meeting, in early 2011, task team members received a draft of this statement, along with the meeting agenda, wherein discussion of the draft was placed as the last item to be considered, when everyone would be rushing to catch trains and planes. The policy statement had quite a different tone from the PGN, and all references to power had disappeared. An alarmed social developer emailed me:

> I am delighted with the PGN, but rather shocked by some of the statements in the first page of the policy statement…may be I am an old fashioned nostalgic leftist…but it sounds sometimes like a manifesto for neo liberalism.

As a result of this social developer's intervention, discussion of the policy statement was moved up the agenda, and on the insistence of most task team members the draft was changed to reflect more faithfully the priority messages in the PGN. Thereafter this statement took a year to be approved through a 'no objections' procedure.[16] This was followed in April 2012 by the publication of the Policy Guidance Note in a volume that also included the Good Practice Notes (OECD 2012).

At the start of a two-and-a-half-year debate about its meaning, the task team had agreed a working definition of 'empowerment' that recognized both agency and structural power relations that can constrain or support autonomy and choice. The resistance within the task team to this definition centred on a refusal to recognize structure and power, combined with a dislike of notions of 'power within' and processes of conscientization. Interestingly, in arguing about empowerment, no one, including me, openly suggested that these were ideological debates. Instead, everything that was openly said was kept at the level of the technical. In drafting the Policy Guidance Note, this technical approach allowed me to cite selectively the 'evidence' in support of a transformative approach, without danger of being openly accused of bias (other than in one instance, when – to my gratification – I was accused of being a 'feminist'). I could use my position as technical expert – including being the only person in the task team with easy access to the academic literature – to make ex-cathedra statements. This strategy worked well in relation to discussions of social and political empowerment, especially as the social developers in the task team were happy with the claims I was making. However, as non-economists, they and I were on weaker ground when it came to what mattered most to the Secretariat: namely the need to frame economic empowerment in a manner that would not contradict the overall OECD position.

---

16 www.oecd.org/officialdocuments/publicdisplaydocumentpdf/?cote=DCD/DAC(2012)5/FINAL&docLanguage=En.

Conclusion: Possibilities and Limitations

This chapter's objective was to examine a micro-level process, in order to make visible the actors and the spaces in which discourses of aid are constructed and contested. It has revealed both the possibility of agency and the limitations of structure. By successfully incorporating power into the much-abused concept of empowerment, a group of middle-ranking bureaucrats was able to think reflexively about themselves as politically positioned actors. They produced guidance that, if followed, would enhance the capacity of donors to support, rather than undermine, processes of social transformation. It had not been a foregone conclusion. There was a sustained and lively debate within the task team about meanings and audience. We – the social developers – were more successful than I had at first thought possible. The individuals involved were able to make a difference to the outcome. Micro-level action matters. Nevertheless, there were self-imposed invisible boundaries to our discussions.

The first of these surfaced briefly at the penultimate meeting of the task team. Rather mischievously, I mentioned how the arguments about the effects of donor practices on the empowerment of people in poverty were limited to what donors did or did not do within aid-recipient countries, ignoring the effects on people in poverty of donor governments' actions in other policy spheres. We agreed to recognize this limitation and a paragraph was accordingly drafted:

> The present Guidance has not considered the potential empowering or disempowering effects of action by donor governments in relation to global financial, trade, climate change and other international policy areas. Still today people living in poverty in developing countries have the least voice and influence on the decisions of global institutions.

There was another invisible boundary to our discussion. I stayed silent about Mohanty's (1995) proposition, discussed earlier, that empowerment becomes a disabling concept when people are organized from above. In our debates about how donors should support empowerment, we never asked ourselves whether we could most usefully do this by closing our programmes down, thus ceasing to be 'progressive patrons' (De Wit and Berner 2009).

Finally – and particularly worth considering with respect to the argumentative construction of text and genre in the task team's work – is why and how it was possible to produce a surprisingly radical text in the current global political environment of development cooperation. Was it because the task team's product would not have any material effect? The passion and enthusiasm of the social developers reflected their efforts to keep burning the dying flame of people-centred and rights-based development. It may be just because that flame is dying that the wider donor community remained indifferent to what POVNET was doing. Many of the most influential bilateral and multilateral agencies were either not represented in the task team or rarely attended POVNET meetings. Poverty reduction was once again becoming a niche activity. The Secretariat had tried to keep POVNET alive through the focus on 'pro-poor growth', but even that was becoming a *démodé* idea, as the more neo-liberal 'inclusive growth' took hold. The member states and international organizations supporting this new line – and not represented in the task team – simply stopped coming to POVNET.

The subsequent low level of attendance at its meetings led the Secretariat to suggest the closure of POVNET, as part of a general review of the DAC's architecture. Within a few months of the task team's final meeting, POVNET was abolished. The official record of the meeting that agreed its closure recorded (in terms familiar to feminist bureaucrats who find that gender disappears once it is mainstreamed):

> Poverty reduction was highlighted as a key mandate of the DAC. As such, it should be an objective in all areas of DAC work, rather than being seen as a mere part of its institutional structure.[17]

For a knowledge product to be legitimate, it requires an audience (McNeill and St Clair 2011), otherwise its subsequent discursive or operational influence may be minimal. If they judge there will not be such an audience, people will not contribute to its production. The low level of attendance at POVNET meetings appears to confirm the PGN's lack of legitimacy. Although published by the OECD in a glossy cover, the Policy Guidance Note is likely to have little material effect.

The success in securing this text – and the wider indifference to its publication – must be understood in the context of a major geo-political shift in development cooperation. In an environment in which many of the traditional donors are becoming reluctant to maintain large aid programmes in these times of austerity and in the face of challenges from rising powers such as China, increasingly influential Aidland actors, it is unfashionable to conceive of aid as a potential instrument for social transformation. The month after POVNET was closed down, the DAC organized the Fourth High-Level Forum on

17 Letter from the chair of DAC 'Outcome of the discussion on AC Architecture, AC Meeting of 3 November 2011', OECD BA (2011) 58: 1.

Aid Effectiveness (HLF4), whose negotiated outcome document refers to 'inclusive growth'; 'empowerment' features in the outcome document only as it relates to women, explained as 'a pre-requisite for sustainable and inclusive growth'. There are no references to power relations in the HLF4 outcome document.

The task team's work is available in a single document online and in hard copy from the OECD bookshop (OECD 2012). Nevertheless, in the absence of a strong constituency in the bilateral aid agencies to urge that the document be distributed to country programme offices and be mentioned favourably by senior officials and ministers, that work is likely to stay unnoticed and disregarded. The last of the five priority messages in the PGN states 'Empowerment takes time, sustained engagement and the ability to balance short-term results and long-term impact.' The message most OECD donors are highlighting is very different and concerns the delivery of aid packages for tangible, quick and quantifiable results, whose achievement is attributed entirely to the donor intervention. Of course, the situation may change again – and certainly many in Aidland are pushing back against the current trend. However, for the time being, the task team's work on empowerment is likely to stay largely unnoticed.

References

Apthorpe, R. (2011). 'With Alice in Aidland: A seriously satirical allegory' in D. Mosse (ed.), *Adventures in Aidland: The anthropology of professionals in international development*. Berghahn Books, New York.

Batliwala, S. (2007). 'Taking the power out of empowerment – an experiential account', *Development in Practice*, 17:4–5, pp. 557–65.

Bebbington, A., S. Guggenheim, E. Olson and M. Woolcock (2004). 'Exploring social capital debates at the World Bank', *Journal of Development Studies*, 40:5, pp. 33–64.

Bebbington, A., D. Lewis, S. Batterbury, E. Olson and M.S. Siddiqi (2007). 'Of texts and practices: Empowerment and organisational cultures in World Bank-funded rural development programmes', *Journal of Development Studies*, 43:4, pp. 597–621.

Broad, R. (2007). '"Knowledge management": a case study of the World Bank's research department', *Development in Practice*, 17:4–5, pp. 700–08.

Brodhead, T. (1987). 'NGOs: In one year, out the other?', *World Development*, 15, pp. 1–6.

Bryant, C. (1980). 'Squatters, collective action, and participation: Learning from Lusaka', *World Development*, 8:1, pp. 73–85.

Chambers, R. (1992). 'Participatory rural appraisals: Past, present and future', *Forests, Trees and People Newsletter*, 15/16, pp. 4–9.

Cleaver, F. (1999). 'Paradoxes of participation: Questioning participatory approaches to development', *Journal of International Development*, 11:4, pp. 597–612.

Cohen, J.M. and N.T. Uphoff (1980). 'Participation's place in rural development: Seeking clarity through specificity', *World Development*, 8:3, pp. 213–35.

Cornwall, A. (2007). 'Buzzwords and fuzzwords: Deconstructing development discourse', *Development in Practice*, 17:4–5, pp. 471–84.

Cornwall, A. and K. Brock (2005). 'What do buzzwords do for development policy? A critical look at "participation", "empowerment" and "poverty reduction"', *Third World Quarterly*, 26:7, pp. 1043–60.

Cornwall, A. and M. Fujita (2007). 'The politics of representing "the poor"' in Joy Moncrieffe and Rosalind Eyben (eds), *The Power of Labelling: How people Are categorized and why it matters*. Earthscan, London.

Craig, G., M. Mayo and M. Taylor (2000). 'Globalization from below: Implications for the Community Development Journal', *Community Development Journal*, 35:4, pp. 323–35.

Dahl, H.M., P. Stoltz and R. Willig (2004). 'Recognition, redistribution and representation in capitalist global society. An interview with Nancy Fraser', *Acta Sociologica*, 47:4, pp. 374–82.

De Wit, J. and E. Berner (2009). 'Progressive patronage? Municipalities, NGOs, CBOs and the limits to slum dwellers' empowerment', *Development and Change*, 40:5, pp. 927–47.

Eyben, R. (2003). 'Mainstreaming the social dimension into the overseas development administration: A partial history', *Journal of International Development*, 15:7, pp. 879–92.

Eyben, R. (2004). 'Battles over booklets: Gender myths in the British aid programme', *IDS Bulletin*, 35:4, pp. 73–81.

Eyben, R. (2006). 'The road not taken: International aid's choice of Copenhagen over Beijing', *Third World Quarterly*, 27:4, pp. 595–608.

Eyben, R. (2009). 'Hovering on the threshold: Challenges and opportunities for critical and reflexive ethnographic research in support of international aid practice' in S. Hagberg and C. Widmark (eds), *Ethnographic Practice and Public Aid: Methods and meanings in development cooperation*. University of Uppsala.

Eyben, R. (2012). 'Struggles in Paris: The DAC and the purposes of development aid', *European Journal of Development Research*, 25:1, pp. 78–91.

Eyben, R. and R. Napier-Moore (2009). 'Choosing words with care? Shifting meanings of women's empowerment in international development', *Third World Quarterly*, 30:2, pp. 285–300.

Eyben, R., N. Kabeer and A. Cornwall (2008). 'Conceptualising empowerment and the implications for pro poor growth', IDS paper, available at: http://www.ids.ac.uk/files/dmfile/conceptualisingempowermentpaperforPOVNET.pdf.

Freire, P. (1970). *Pedagogy of the Oppressed*, trans. Myra Bergman Ramos. Continuum, New York.

Gastel, J. Van and M. Nuijten (2005). 'The genealogy of the "good governance" and "ownership" agenda at the Dutch Ministry of Development Cooperation' in David Mosse and David Lewis (eds), *The Aid Effect: Giving and Governing in International Development.* London, Pluto Press.

Gaventa, J. (2006). 'Finding the spaces for change: A power analysis', *IDS Bulletin*, 37:6, pp. 23–33.

Goulet, D. (1979). 'Development as liberation: Policy lessons from case studies', *World Development*, 7:6, pp. 555–66.

Green, M. (2011). 'Calculating compassion' in David Mosse (ed.), *Adventures in Aidland: The anthropology of professionals in international development.* Berghahn Books, New York.

Hulme, D. and S. Fukuda-Parr (2009). 'International norm dynamics and "the end of poverty": Understanding the Millennium Development Goals (MDGs)', Brooks World Poverty Institute Working Paper 9609.

Ianchovichina, E. and S. Lundstrom (2009). 'Inclusive growth analytics: Framework and application', World Bank Policy Research Working Paper 4851.

Korten, D.C. and R. Klauss (1984). *People Centred Development: Contributions toward theory and planning frameworks.* Kumarian Press, West Hartford.

Mahon, R. and S. McBride (2009). 'Standardizing and disseminating knowledge: The role of the OECD in global governance', *European Political Science Review*, 1:1, pp. 83–101.

Manning, R. (2007). 'Pro-poor growth: Negotiating consensus on a contentious issue', *Development*, 50:2, pp. 42–47.

Manning, R. (2009). 'Using indicators to encourage development: Lessons from the millennium development goals', Danish Institute for International Studies Report No. 2009:01.

McNeill, D. and A.L. St Clair (2011). 'The World Bank's expertise' in D. Mosse (ed.), *Adventures in Aidland: The anthropology of professionals in international development.* Berghahn Books, New York.

Miles, M. (1989). 'Information-based rehabilitation for Third World disability', *Social Science and Medicine*, 28:3, pp. 207–10.

Mohan, G. and K. Stokke (2000). 'Participatory development and empowerment: The dangers of localism', *Third World Quarterly*, 21(2), pp. 247–68.

Mohanty, M. (1995). 'On the concept of "empowerment"', *Economic and Political Weekly*, 30:24, pp. 1434–36.

Moore, M. (2001). 'Empowerment at last?', *Journal of International Development*, 13:3, pp. 321–29.

Mosse, D. (2005). *Cultivating Development: An ethnography of aid policy and practice.* Pluto, London.

Mosse, D. (2006). 'Anti-social anthropology? Objectivity, objection, and the ethnography of public policy and professional communities', *Journal of the Royal Anthropological Institute*, 12:4, pp. 935–56.

Mosse, D. (2011a). 'Introduction: The anthropology of expertise and professionals in international development' in D. Mosse (ed.), *Adventures in Aidland: The anthropology of professionals in international development*. Berghahn Books, New York.

Mosse, D. (2011b). 'Social analysis as corporate product: Non-economists/anthropologists at work in the World Bank in Washington DC' in D. Mosse (ed.), *Adventures in Aidland: The anthropology of professionals in international development*. Berghahn Books, New York.

Narayan, D. (2002). *Empowerment and poverty reduction: A sourcebook*. World Bank Publications, Washington DC.

Organisation for Economic Cooperation and Development (OECD) (1996). *Shaping the 21st Century*. OECD, Paris.

Organisation for Economic Cooperation and Development (OECD) (2001). *The Ac Guidelines for Poverty Reduction*. OECD, Paris.

Organisation for Economic Cooperation and Development (OECD) (2006). *Promoting Pro-Poor Growth: Key policy messages*. OECD, Paris.

Organisation for Economic Cooperation and Development (OECD) (2008). *Social Protection, Poverty Reduction and Pro-Poor Growth: A Policy Guidance Note*. OECD, Paris.

Organisation for Economic Cooperation and Development (OECD) (2012). *Poverty Reduction and Pro-Poor Growth: The role of empowerment*. OECD, Paris.

Rowlands, J. (1997). *Questioning Empowerment: Working with women in Honduras*. Oxfam Publications, Oxford.

Ruckert, A. (2008). 'Making neo-Gramscian sense of the Development Assistance Committee: Towards an inclusive neoliberal world development order' in R. Mahon and S. McBride (eds), *The OECD and Transnational Governance*. University of British Colombia, Vancouver.

Sen, G. and C. Grown (1988). *Development, Crises and Alternative Visions: Third World women's perspectives*. Earthscan, London.

Sridhar, D. (2005). 'Ethics and development: Some concerns with David Mosse's *Cultivating Development*', *Anthropology Today*, 21:6, pp. 17–19.

Tandon, R. (1981). 'Participatory research in the empowerment of people', *Convergence: An International Journal of Adult Education*, 14:3, pp. 20–29.

Thérien, J.P. and C. Lloyd (2000). 'Development assistance on the brink', *Third World Quarterly*, 21:1, pp. 21–38.

Thomas, T. (1983). 'Reorienting bureaucratic performance: A social learning approach to development action', NASPAA Working Paper 8.

Thrupp, L. (1989). 'Legitimizing local knowledge: From displacement to empowerment for Third World people', *Agriculture and Human Values*, 6:3, pp 13–24.

VeneKlasen, L. and V. Miller (eds) (2002). *A New Weave of Power: People and politics*. Practical Action Publishing, Rugby.

World Bank (2000). *World Development Report on Poverty*. World Bank, Washington DC.

Zimmermann, F. and K. Smith (2011). 'More actors, more money, more ideas for international development co-operation', *Journal of International Development*, 23:5, pp. 722–38.

CHAPTER 5

Beyond Livelihoods: Occupationality and Career Formation in African Artisanal Mining

Deborah Fahy Bryceson

Introduction

The livelihoods concept has been central to development thinking and projects in African countries for over twenty years. The examination of household livelihood diversity in relation to household assets has become a standard approach for rural and urban livelihood projects in many development agencies. These exercises have been supplemented with a proliferation of detailed academic studies of livelihood change in rural communities dotted throughout Sub-Saharan Africa, and a burgeoning number of Masters and PhD theses emanating from African and Western academia. However, few studies have attempted to review the findings and to question the approach's utility in terms of what it has revealed. What is its theoretical contribution and track record in providing useful insights? How can the body of applied research it has spawned be assessed? What are the approach's limitations? And indeed does it now, and will it in the future, have any relevance for researchers and development practitioners?

In this chapter, I consider how the livelihoods concept was conceived, look at its analytical accomplishments and investigate its utility to donors' efforts to achieve poverty reduction. In critiquing its limitations, I introduce the concept of 'occupationality'; I define this and discuss its potential to probe the decision-making dilemmas and moral underpinnings of livelihood diversification. Furthermore, it affords a means of tracing how livelihood diversification can eventually lead to work specialization. This transition is illustrated by a recent case study of Tanzanian artisanal gold miners. I will conclude by juxtaposing the livelihoods concept with the concept of 'occupationality' and career formation.

Rural Poverty Discourse in Sub-Saharan Africa: Challenging the World Bank Discourse

The goal of poverty alleviation has dominated development studies and donor agency work for decades. The World Bank's *World Development Report* (WDR)

 | DOI 10.1163/9789004305465_006

on poverty in 1990 was a trend-setting document in a burgeoning field of poverty research led by the World Bank and development economists who were intent on developing an array of poverty indicators and measures to monitor the effects of the implementation of structural adjustment programmes and economic liberalization (World Bank 1990). Meanwhile, many anthropologists and sociologists defended the utility of qualitative research over the positivist social science emphasis on quantitative analysis. The theme of the 2000/01 WDR (World Bank 2000a) was again poverty; this report was accompanied by another publication, entitled *Voices of the Poor*, based on the personal testimony of vast numbers of poor people around the world (World Bank 2000b).

Certain logical discrepancies surfaced when the World Bank's conception of poverty was viewed alongside its neo-liberal policy agenda. The Bank's efforts to expand global market liberalization were far more dominant and, in effect, sidetracked its poverty-reduction goals. The contradictory juxtaposing of market liberalization with poverty alleviation began to be explained in the 2008 WDR, which argued that certain rural smallholders could not compete in the world market and should therefore not only diversify away from agriculture, but leave their rural homes and migrate elsewhere to maximize their income-earning potential (World Bank 2008). This document was historic in terms of donor agency literature, breaking away as it did from a long line of colonial and postcolonial thinking, which stressed that poverty alleviation was best served by agricultural investment in rural smallholder peasant producers (Havnevik et al. 2007).

The following year the 2009 WDR report proceeded further, suggesting that uncompetitive rural producers should seek to move to more productive regions and urban areas, where levels of productivity are deemed to be higher (World Bank 2009). In essence, the 2009 report attempts to reconcile global market liberalization with labour displacement and poverty alleviation along the theme of the poor physically distancing themselves from poverty. Narayan et al.'s (2009) supplement to the 2009 WDR – entitled *Moving Out of Poverty* – cites qualitative interviews with large numbers of migrants. Highlighting migration success stories, this document is a landmark in donor thinking, since previously urban migration was seen as counterproductive, rather than as capable of absorbing labour.

But clearly, there is a danger in confusing movement with the idea of improvement and opportunity. Movement may just as likely be downward degradation as upward economic success. The World Bank discourse continually skirts around the fundamental problem of global labour displacement of peasantries and others engaged in manual labour, glibly shifting the issue from what they do to where they do it. The inference is that they will find work in the right place, which may entail migration.

Origins, Conceptual Content and Systemization of Livelihood Studies

The livelihoods concept emerged in the development studies literature of the early 1990s, after what is often referred to, in the context of Africa, as the 'lost decade' of the 1980s. The setbacks of the late 1970s global oil crises continued to reverberate. African exports, notably peasant agricultural exports, were in steep decline. The sheer size of the continent, the widely dispersed nature of peasant agriculture and the high cost of petrol were all impediments to African peasant farmers' competition in the world market. A period of severe drought and crop failure in the Sahel and East and Southern Africa during the 1980s compounded the situation for agricultural producers. In this context, farming households increasingly engaged in a search for alternative non-agricultural income-earning opportunities (Bryceson 1999; 2002a).

Documenting these trends, the themes of 'survival strategies' (Dessalegn Rahmato 1991; Taylor and Mackenzie 1992; Bangura 1994) and 'coping strategies' (Corbett 1988; Maxwell 1996; Adams, Cekan and Sauerborn 1998) eventually led to 'livelihood studies' (Ellis 1998; Barrett, Reardon and Webb 2001), a progression in the literature that reflected the growing ubiquity of economic diversification among smallholder farmers at all income levels (Bryceson 1996). Livelihood studies had its antecedents in the early 1970s work on non-farm diversification, initiated by agricultural economists from Michigan State University (Byerlee and Eicher 1972; Liedholm 1973), and in later work on non-farm linkages (Haggblade, Hazell and Brown 1989). These authors were exceptionally upbeat about the prospects of non-agricultural activity becoming a spur to productivity improvement in peasant agriculture. While their work stressed the economic stimulus of household economic diversification on agriculture (Reardon, Delgado and Matlon 1992), livelihood studies were more multidisciplinary in orientation, and perversely situated in the context of agricultural involution.

In the scramble to find alternative livelihoods, rural peasant communities and local economies experienced profound change. The oil crisis and food insecurity accelerated an underlying process of de-agrarianization within the African countryside that involved: (i) occupational adjustment, (ii) income-earning reorientation, (iii) social re-identification, and (iv) spatial relocation away from strictly agriculture-based modes of livelihood (Bryceson 1996). Alternatives to commercial agriculture were various: trade, services, alcohol production, handicrafts, small-scale mining (to list the most salient directions). Amid deepening de-agrarianization, social re-identification was accompanied by a process of 'de-peasantization', which I define as the gradual movement away from farm-based, peasant family production units to other

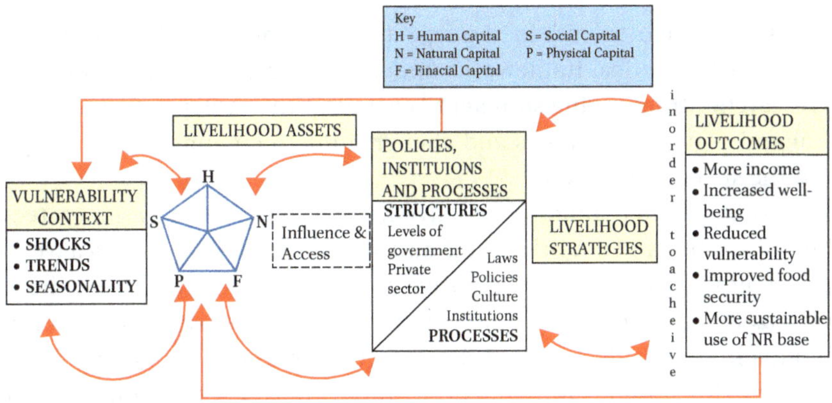

FIGURE 5.1 *The sustainable livelihoods framework.*
SOURCE: CARNEY (1998: 5)

forms of social organization associated with non-agricultural work activities (Bryceson 2000a). This had erosive consequences for rural communities – and for peasants as a social class.

Several international development agencies were quick to sense the structural changes and to embrace the livelihoods concept as a way of aligning their development outreach with the new demands for external assistance. They were in the front line of the 1980s humanitarian responses to drought in the Horn of Africa and the appearance of HIV/AIDS. These disasters overlapped with the continuing downturn in peasant commercial agriculture. Rural inhabitants' survival and coping strategies were observed by donors, who then devised the livelihoods approach as a constructive way of confronting the confluence of forces that were acting on rural households.

The United Kingdom's Department for International Development (DfID) (Carney 1998) was instrumental in the systematization of livelihood studies with its 'sustainable livelihoods approach', which provided a schematic household decision-making model and community-based framework of analysis (diagrammatically presented above) that centred on a pentagon of five types of household assets (human capital, natural capital, financial capital, social capital and physical capital).

There are, of course, advantages and disadvantages to summarizing the complex processes of de-agarianization and de-peasantization diagrammatically (Figure 5.1). By instrumentally facilitating the rapid collection of data on changing work patterns in various areas, the sustainable livelihoods approach and its flow diagrams assisted with field reconnaissance and the design of broad-based development agency interventions. However, reducing the complexity of the gradual erosion of African peasantries to an inventory checklist approach seems, in retrospect, overly mechanistic. Recourse to ready-made theoretical frameworks undermines original thought, diverting the researcher from taking sufficient account of the in-depth history, wider global and regional dynamics and changing micro circumstances that prevail at the specific study site.

Nonetheless, this standardized livelihoods approach has generated a deluge of studies and countless PhD and Masters theses, providing a wealth of case study material for comparative research. Surprisingly, few scholars have seized the opportunity, and work that synthesizes the findings of different livelihood studies over a broad range of areas does not figure prominently in the literature. However, there have been some notable multi-country livelihood studies, which have cast light on spatial variation in livelihood patterns continentally. These will be reviewed in the next section.

There are five main limitations to the livelihoods concept. First, in terms of location: most livelihood studies have had a household or village focus – 'bite-sized' case studies that are ideal for students, but are rarely accompanied by indications of how they fit into national and international trends. Second, the livelihoods approach has generally been limited to contemporary studies, which have been ahistorical in terms of their wider context. The backdrop to most livelihood studies has tacitly been the de-agrarianization process, but few researchers have stood back and attempted to ask why this should be so. Their studies have largely described the contemporary situation. Third, the narrow analytical scope of the studies has lacked theoretical richness. The livelihoods approach has been deployed more as a research technique to investigate the who, the what, the when, the where and the how – but not the why. Finally, there has been a strong economic bias, with recognition of the operation of various institutions, which has nonetheless remained unanalysed. While the household has been the focus of study, other social and economic institutions have been treated basically as collective decision-making production units, regardless of internal dissension within.

Comparative Findings from Livelihoods studies in Africa

Multi-country livelihood studies deploying consistent methodologies across countries provide the strongest basis for comparison. The UK DfID-funded Livelihoods and Diversification Directions Explored by Research (LADDER) research programme (run by Frank Ellis and his colleagues) produced a rich corpus of publications that compared rural livelihoods in Kenya, Uganda, Tanzania and Malawi (Ellis 1998; 2000; Ellis and Bahiigwa 2003; Ellis and Mdoe 2003; Ellis, Kutengule and Nyasulu 2003; Ellis and Freeman 2005). The LADDER village-level surveys investigated household livelihoods and asset holdings using participatory wealth-ranking exercises to identify three wealth groups that were used as the basis for a stratified random sample survey. The LADDER findings revealed increasing economic differentiation between households that was associated with rising market activity. Asset inequalities were graphically depicted in livelihood asset pentagons to summarize the findings and make them readily accessible to policy-makers and other researchers. The LADDER analysis extended to discussions of household income groups' circumstances within the institutional context of the settlements.

The Dutch Ministry of Foreign Affairs-funded De-agrarianization and Rural Employment (DARE) research programme conducted surveys and qualitative interviews that compared pairs of commercially oriented (as opposed to more subsistence-based) agricultural villages in geographically contrasting regions of Tanzania, Nigeria, Ethiopia, Malawi and South Africa. The stratified random sample survey centred on household members' agricultural and non-agricultural income-generating activities over time. The data indicated a trend towards a rising incidence of non-agricultural income earning in a proliferation of forms, as well as a changing intra-household division of labour. Male heads were increasingly no longer the sole cash earners within the household unit, as youth and women became more involved in earning money (Bryceson 1999; 2000b; 2002a; 2002b; Meagher 2001). In the process, the power balance in the household was shifting away from male patriarchy. As rural householders became more involved in non-agricultural income earning, there was nonetheless a ubiquitous retention of the agricultural subsistence fall back, offering a degree of insurance against failure of the experimental non-agricultural activities.

The DARE intra-household study revealed that along the path of non-agricultural income diversification tensions arose between people's sense of family and community on the one hand, and their individual earnings and achievement on the other. Tendencies towards individual autonomy challenged the economic pooling of income by household members, notably by young people and women. As patriarchal power within the household weakened, so young people tended to gain discretionary decision-making powers over their earnings. Generational divides surfaced as rural youth became income earners in their own right. While continuing to live *in situ* in villages, they gained more mobility and displayed a preference for more urbanized modes and mannerisms.

Findings from the LADDER and the DARE research programmes, along with work by Elke Grawert (1998) on rural Sudan and by Elizabeth Francis (2000) on Kenya and South Africa, pointed to the proliferation of relatively low-earning income-generating activities on the part of rural householders. Furthermore, there was little evidence to support the views of the non-farm diversification theorists Byerlee and Eicher (1972) and Liedholm (1973), who had predicted forward and backward linkages between non-agricultural and agricultural activities that would boost the productivity of farming. Such linkages were generally not in evidence, as commercial agricultural production continued to decline. Above all, what one saw was experimental livelihood diversification, composed of multiple income flows, frequent cross-subsidization of activities, a great deal of discontinuity through trial and error plagued by unpredictable markets, and, most strikingly, a trend towards labour diversification rather than specialization.

Moving beyond Livelihood Studies to Occupationality

During the 1990s and 2000s, the livelihoods approach gained sway in development thinking because it was so logical, so comprehensive and so purposeful in its aim of poverty reduction through the facilitation of work opportunities, and also because attention started to be paid by many donors to environmental sustainability and human rights. But the question of whether it has made a difference to welfare and to our understanding of developmental processes must be posed.

Certainly it has made matters clearer by revealing changing work patterns; but there is a tacit recognition that the pursuit of viable work activities, improvement in household asset holdings and the achievement of sustainable livelihoods are less in evidence. This is indicated by the expanding formulation of social protection and social safety-net policies for those who cannot find viable alternatives to peasant agriculture – though the programmes do tend to assume that this is a temporary rather than a permanent structural constraint (Devereux 2001; 2010).

In this context, there is a strong case for pushing rural research beyond livelihood studies. For the last thirty years, Tanzanian rural dwellers have endeavoured to diversify into non-agricultural production in the direction of trade, the provision of local services, alcohol production, handicrafts and a welter of activities too numerous to list here. Kjell Havnevik's (1993) early work documenting rural diversification in Tanzania's Rufiji river valley was a landmark study, detailing an impressive range of rural work activities. This was followed by Pekka Seppälä's (1998) and Seppälä and Bertha Koda's (1998) studies, in which they documented both the cultural and the economic dimensions of income diversification in Tanzania's Lindi region. Findings from these studies converged on the central fact that the broad masses engaged in these new non-agricultural activities were earning vital, but monetarily quite small, returns. Furthermore, the activities were generally quite makeshift in nature, with very little in the way of a clear specialized career pattern.

Small-scale mining, however, is distinct from most other non-agricultural activities, given the higher value of its output, the possibility of handsome monetary returns and a career trajectory for many miners (Chachage 1995; Bryceson and Jønsson 2010). Over the past two decades, it has been of growing economic importance in Tanzania and several other African countries (Bryceson and MacKinnon 2012). Here, I use an empirical case study of Tanzanian artisanal miners to illustrate the significant theoretical implications of artisanal mining for development discourse on poverty alleviation and mobility. A close examination of artisanal mining in Tanzania necessarily takes one beyond the concept of livelihoods formulated in the 1990s.

Before turning to the case study, it is helpful to map the analytical direction to be traversed in moving away from the livelihoods concept. First, I propose to 'scale up' – to abandon the livelihoods approach's focus on the village and the household – and instead to concentrate attention on broad sectoral change processes linked to fluctuations in the world economy with respect to de-agrarianization, de-peasantization (Bryceson 2000a) and 'mineralization' of African economies. By 'mineralization', I mean the increasing reliance on mineral production for national, regional and local African economies (Bryceson et al. 2014).

Second, there is also a need to 'scale down' to the individual actor's work motivation – to think through what cognitive changes are taking place in the individual's consciousness as he or she experiments with specific forms of work (Bryceson 2010a). Some of the questions to be posed are: how is the individual's sense of identity affected (Bryceson 2010b; Jua 2010)? How is trust configured at the new workplaces? Can trust travel over long distances (Dijkstra 2010)? How are changing family ties, social networks and gender differentiation negotiated (Lindell 2010; Mbilinyi 2010; Meagher 2010; Simone 2010)? Under what circumstances do notions of professionalism arise (Seppälä 2010)?

Interrogating these processes of change and attempting to mould the meaning of their various facets into an identifiable work trajectory, I use the term 'occupationality' to stress how an individual's livelihood search is a process both of finding viable work and of acquiring an identity as an economically active member of society (Bryceson 2010b: 5).

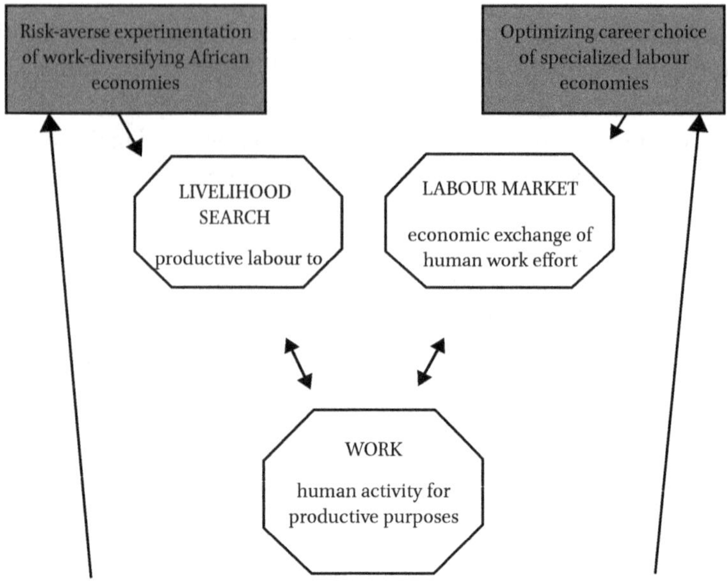

FIGURE 5.2 *African diversified occupationality versus specialized occupational work context.*
SOURCE: BRYCESON (2010b: 7)

The concept is aimed at probing individual psycho-social adjustments to changing work circumstances. 'Occupationality' encompasses a process of 'skill acquisition, economic exchange, psychological adjustment and social positioning through which an individual becomes actively engaged in specific work and identifies with it as an extension of his or her social being' (Bryceson 2010b: 4). It is remarkable that over recent decades so much attention has been paid in social science literature to gender, ethnic and religious identities, while occupational identities have been ignored.

Having criticized the oversimplicity of the livelihoods diagram, I hasten to explain that Figure 5.2 is not intended to convey the essence of a universal approach or research methodology. Rather it is simply a flow diagram of interrelationships, contrasting the livelihoods approach on the left-hand (light grey) circuit with the specialized work career (dark grey) circuit on the right. Both circuits converge in the work sphere – with the livelihoods circuit encompassing the additional consideration of occupationality. While the livelihoods approach focuses on labour diversification, denoted by the realms of risk-averse experimentation and livelihood search boxes, I would argue that it is important also to consider the psycho-social realm of individuals and collectivities of workers to gain an understanding of the viability (or indeed unviability) of the work they are doing.

Individuals engaged in livelihood diversification look for a source of economic sustenance and simultaneously quest for a socially acceptable work identity. There is continual tension between seeking work with social status and finding work that provides adequate sustenance. Many (if not most) are forced to give priority to the latter, but even so their efforts may fall far short of economic adequacy. These personal calculations and decision-making dilemmas represent entangled political, social and cultural dimensions of identity and affiliation that are not adequately considered in the livelihoods approach.

In the following case study of Tanzanian artisanal gold miners, the possibility of a crossover from a livelihood to a specialized work career is suggested in the embryonic formation of an informal, but nonetheless increasingly professional, cadre of Tanzanian artisanal gold miners.

Artisanal Gold Mining in Tanzania

Gold mining has been one of many labour responses to ongoing de-agrarianization in Tanzania. Seen as a relatively lucrative alternative to agriculture and trade activities because of its potentially higher earnings, artisanal gold mining attracts the more adventurous in spirit, who are willing to leave the security of their home areas and make the effort to gain new work skills and spend time networking with people from widely different regional backgrounds. This section is based on research detailed in Jønsson and Bryceson (2009) and Bryceson and Jønsson (2010).

Sectoral Development

Gold mining's attractiveness arises from the more lucrative market that it enjoys both nationally and internationally, compared with other commodities produced in the Tanzanian countryside. Surprisingly, it is a relatively easy field to enter, in the sense that it requires little start-up capital. On the other hand, artisanal gold mining is demanding: it tests miners' physical endurance and their willingness to be mobile. Miners face daunting risks, including economic failure, mining accidents and personal insecurity. Success requires an ability to enter into trusting cooperative relationships with other miners and a readiness to work long hours; it is also helped along by sobriety, thrift and large measures of good luck. The chances of success are boosted by geographical mobility, which involves frequent movement from one speculative gold-rush site to another (Jønsson and Bryceson 2009). A mobile, multi-ethnic workforce with a high turnover of people characterizes such mining locations.

In Sub-Saharan Africa, Tanzania is one of a cluster of countries that are transforming rapidly from being primarily agriculture exporting to being mineral exporting. In 2005, mineral exports exceeded agricultural exports for the first time. More than ten big gold strikes and scores of other more minor strikes have occurred since 2000, particularly in the country's 'ring of gold', which extends in a large circle south of Lake Victoria, along the contours of the bifurcated East African Rift Valley (Bryceson et al. 2012).

It is estimated that there are 685,000 artisanal miners in Tanzania (out of a population of 40 million); of these, roughly two-thirds (approximately 450,000) are gold miners (Bryceson et al. 2012). This is regarded as a conservative estimate by many observers (Bryceson and Jønsson 2010). Ongoing processes of de-agrarianization and legalization of artisanal small-scale mining in the late 1990s has opened the floodgates to artisanal mining (Bryceson 1999; Jønsson and Bryceson 2009). The search by artisanal miners for mineral riches propels many to move on when they get to an extraction depth of about 50 metres – generally the depth at which artisanal miners' basic technology is insurmountably challenged by the constraints of water drainage and potential cave-ins, especially during the rainy season (personal communication with Jesper Bosse Jønsson 2013).

The proliferation of artisanal mining sites has been very rapid over the last thirty years. Artisanal mining sites arise spontaneously and vary organizationally from place to place in terms of their labour composition, productivity and payment systems. However, it is clear to even a casual observer that artisanal mining work lives and lifestyles represent a very different occupational trajectory from what exists in Tanzania's agricultural settlements.

Occupational Division of Labour

Tanzania's artisanal gold mining has evolved into a hierarchical division of labour. At the top of the pyramid is a primary mining licence (PML) owner who has the 'claim', i.e. the purchased legal right to exploit an area for five years (Bryceson and Jønsson 2010). PML claim owners are frequently educated people working in white-collar occupations, or even in the government bureaucracy, who are strategically placed to hear of claim availability from Tanzanian state sources. As claim owners, they are legally responsible for mining activities carried out on their stake. This includes all aspects of mining site operations, labour management and ensuring that safety and environmental regulations are followed (Fisher 2007; 2008; Mwaipopo et al. 2004). However, many PML owners are infrequent visitors to the mine site and leave site management to a 'pit holder'.

The 'pit holders' informally lease the mine site from the PML claim owner. In so doing, they take charge of mobilizing the workforce, sourcing and procuring all the necessary capital inputs and managing the day-to-day digging activities in the pit. They are the ones who shoulder most of the burden of working capital investments, as well as the risks and costs related to periods when digging yields no gold output. The informality of their agreement with the claim owner does not protect them from the possibility of a claim owner selling the claim to a third party, thereby jeopardizing the pit holder's labour and investments (Fisher 2007; Jønsson and Fold 2011). They tend to be highly experienced miners with extensive work contacts, who started their working lives as diggers but, thanks to skill and shrewdness, have gradually become people of substance and influence, who can readily source labour and the necessary capital inputs through patron–client networking. Their continuation as pit holders rests on continually finding more gold. If they do not strike gold, or otherwise encounter serious production impediments, they may drop down the mining hierarchy to become diggers once again. To avoid this, they often seek to carry out their pit management activities in partnership with other pit holders, in order to spread the risk.

The 'diggers' are the most numerous members of the mining fraternity. They also face material risks, and in periods of no mineral output their daily labour goes unrewarded (except for the provision of food and medicine). While their labour spans a number of activities, the division of labour among them is primarily between *waponjaji*, the drillers who chip away at the rock (mainly with hammers and chisels, but sometimes with power drills), and *vutafelo*, who have the task of removing the waste material and gold-bearing rocks from the pit. It should be added that the unpredictability of gold-digging outcomes means there is scope for movement both up and down between these two lower rungs of the hierarchy.

Remuneration in the mining hierarchy centres on the division of gold-bearing rocks. The split between the different categories of people varies, but generally it roughly involves 30 per cent for the claim owner, 40 per cent for the pit holder (who shoulders most risk and actual responsibility) and 30 per cent to be divided among the pit diggers, who usually number about five to six per digging site (Jønsson and Fold 2011).

Dynamics of Artisanal Mining Sites

It should be borne in mind that mine sites vary in composition and organizational structure, and so it is necessary to specify the time and place of artisanal mining work. In order to illustrate career progression, I rely on the survey results of fieldwork at two sites surveyed in central and southern Tanzania, as documented in Jønsson and Bryceson (2009) and Bryceson and Jønsson (2010). The two sites were Matundasi (a mature gold settlement, where gold was first discovered in the 1930s) and Londoni (a recent gold-rush site dating from 2004, where the population has surged from a baseline of 1,600 to approximately 10,000). An age-stratified random sample survey of 108 gold miners was conducted between August 2006 and February 2008. The sampled miners were mostly migrants, representing 15 of Tanzania's 21 regions and 27 of the country's 125 ethnic groups. The most numerous were the Sukuma (constituting 22 per cent of the total sample), who are known for their mining skills thanks to the richness of the gold deposits in their home area. The average age at which these miners had started to mine was 24 years. The average age of the surveyed miners was 36. The objective of the survey was to trace the miners' mobility and career movement.

The Matundasi site represented an income-diversified settlement, with a stable population that displayed a relatively balanced gender and age profile. There were 1,500 active miners hemmed in by large-scale mining interests, and only nine small-scale claim owners. By contrast, the Londoni site had 215 claim owners skewed towards economically active men aged 20–40.

Over a third of those sampled had worked only one site. Almost half (47 per cent) had worked from two to four sites. Another 13 per cent had experience of five or six sites, and a tiny minority (4 per cent) were veterans of various regions. On average, they had stayed at 2.72 sites – 2.4 in Matundasi and 3.1 in Londoni – and on average had spent 3.4 years at each site. Altogether, the 108 miners surveyed had accumulated 293 work sojourns at 70 different mine sites. The majority (77 per cent) were originally from rural areas.

Their original motivation to mine focused on livelihood improvement beyond what agriculture or trade could offer. Most of the respondents had started mining near to their place of birth, or else had moved to a mine in another region where they had relations who were already familiar with the mining site. There is a distinct difference between miners' behaviour at their first mining site and at subsequent sites. At their first site, they generally stayed longer, acquiring mining skills and useful work contacts. In effect, this period served as their apprenticeship. From their second mining site onwards, the miners were driven by opportunities that they became aware of through their collegial networks. These networks facilitated new site information, pit access and loan support and were vital for building a mining career compared to family connections. As they move from site to site, miners tend to end up increasingly far from their natal homes. They are willing to move great distances in their quest for minerals, and are heavily attracted to gold strikes.

Unfolding Career Patterns

To discern career patterns, we categorized the sample survey into four 'site groups': (i) the stationary '1-site group' composed of those who did not move around; (ii) the less mobile '2–3 site group'; (iii) the reasonably mobile '4–5 site group'; and (iv) the highly mobile '6 or more site group'.

Examining the career progression and success of these four groups, the most mobile tended to be farther from their home areas than did the stationary and less mobile miners, as determined by comparing the birthplaces of miners at their first site, relative to those who had visited successive sites. At the first site, people gained practical experience of mining and socially interacted within the mining settlement, gradually coming to identify themselves as miners and becoming part of a miners' network through a process of occupationality (Jønsson and Bryceson 2009; Bryceson 2010b). Significantly, the miners spent more time at their first mining site (on average 59 months for all miners, which included those in the more stationary 1-site mining group) than at subsequent sites (only 32 months on average). The reason for stays at succeeding sites being shorter appeared to be related to a strong focus on the material rewards from mining, which impelled miners to seek another site as the gold became depleted, in the hope of better prospects.

The entwining of career progression with mobility is evidenced by the fact that those in the 1-site group were younger on average (29 years) – many were still doing their informal 'apprenticeship' with the likelihood of a mobile mining career ahead of them. The average age of those in all the multiple-site groups was roughly similar, at 39–41. However, each of the multiple-site groups was distinct in terms of representing a progressively greater number of years in mining: those who had been to the most sites had started mining, on average, at a younger age and had spent less time at each mine site where they worked.

In terms of material success, the average monthly income figures for each site group indicated that mobility and persistence pay off, with progressively higher earnings for those in multiple-site groups. Furthermore, as miners move to additional sites, they are more likely to own a house, which is an economic achievement, as well as an indicator of social status.

It is pertinent to consider whether Tanzanian small-scale artisanal miners exemplify people who are successfully 'moving out of poverty', as termed in the WDR (World Bank 2009). This Tanzanian case study suggests that artisanal miners who are at the peak of their economically active years, and are willing to take the risk of moving from site to site, are most likely to gain higher earnings. Furthermore, the experienced miners who had retired were generally not inclined to farm because they did not see it as sufficiently remunerative – indeed, they often saw a return to agriculture as a sign of economic failure: in other words, a last option. Only 5 per cent expressed a desire to invest in farming. Their efforts to save were primarily aimed at business initiatives, being involved in the financial side of commercial mining, and settling in a regional town with business prospects and improved housing (Jønsson and Bryceson 2009; Bryceson and Jønsson 2010). Most had moved from agrarian backgrounds to a mining career that they hoped would culminate in business success, rather than in a quiet retirement and a return to their rural roots.

From Livelihood Diversification to Occupational Specialization

The emergence of specialized career miners centres on sharing mobility strategies, social aspirations and a collective occupational identity associated with specializing in mine work. This contrasts markedly with the income-diversifying livelihood experimentation that dominated the preceding decade of the 1990s, when individuals and households juggled different livelihood activities, uncertain which might yield adequate returns. Miners' career formation is congealing in the artisanal mining of gold, with the emergence of innovative on-the-ground organizational responses to functional problems of trust and the work effectiveness of mining teams in a period of rapid economic change. I define the term 'career' as an occupational activity that demands the commitment of time for a significant period of one's life in order to acquire skills and to accumulate work experience. In this sense, the pursuit of a mining career at the Matundasi and Londoni sites afforded an opportunity for many miners to improve their economic and social status, as suggested by our study findings. Long-term career commitment is linked to the expectation of eventual reward for sacrificing behaviour in an apprenticeship period, followed by upward progression in a hierarchically ranked pyramid.

Significantly, sustained sectoral growth allows for the expansion of the pyramid. In the case of gold, the exceptionally high (and rising) price that it has commanded on the world market over the past decade has contributed to expansion of the sector. This is the material context in which career formation and progression is possible. In terms of the career pyramid of Tanzanian artisanal mining, it is the (relatively few) pit holders who are the competitive achievers that maintain structural coherence of the work effort and uphold the legitimacy of the production pyramid, both internally and externally. The claim owners are the financiers, who often have political connections – so they represent an elusive rung of the hierarchy. Furthermore, it should be noted that career progression is rarely a straight line upwards from digger to pit holder. The unpredictability and the hazards of finding gold lead many pit holders to have to rejoin the ranks of diggers (though their skills and social networks may, in due course, help to propel them upwards again).

Returning to the issue of poverty alleviation, do mining careers offer a way for large numbers of the rural poor to escape poverty? This is a question that needs to be answered on a case-by-case basis. In Tanzanian artisanal mining, those who succeed and become successful high-earning miners are in a minority.

These Tanzanian findings are based on a survey sample that was biased towards success. Interviews took place among miners who were persisting with a mining career; but large numbers of miners leave for various reasons: uncertain pay, dangerous working conditions, disease, lack of security, homesickness, lack of money, etc. The available data does not provide any means of knowing what percentage of miners leave. But the majority of the sample – which covered all ages, from teens through to people in their fifties, on an age-stratified basis – consisted of 1-site miners with under six years' experience; this suggests that probably most small-scale miners do not persist with mining into old age.

Furthermore, miners' working lives are short. They peak in their thirties and have to start winding down in their forties; so those who do succeed tend to have been early starters (in their teens). In any case, Tanzanian artisanal miners' days on any particular site are numbered, given the technical limitations of their gold-extraction activities: the tools and limits on capital investment that restrict them to a depth of about 30–60 metres. Almost inevitably, then, in Tanzania the long-term future lies in large-scale mining, rather than small-scale. This trajectory is reinforced by the World Bank's pressure for African national governments to seek the direct foreign investment of large-scale mining companies (Bourgouin 2014).

Conclusion

In summary, the livelihoods concept revolves around economic diversification at the local level, and reveals little about broader cultural and sectoral changes. Livelihood analysis provides a descriptive synchronic snapshot of what is happening to specific households. The addition of the concept of occupationality, as argued in this chapter, allows examination of the nature of the change in people's identity as they experiment with new forms of livelihood. It entails a consideration of the dynamism of collective groups of people engaged in livelihood searches, and enables deeper consideration of their new identity formation. So, too, during individuals' livelihood diversification searches, occupationality serves as a vital provisional step towards the formation of occupational careers. Occupational careers coalesce around an enhanced specialization in work activities that afford incentivized income earning and social status enhancement. As a growing number of people are attracted to occupational specialization, sectoral development takes place. In Tanzania, the outstanding economic opportunity offered by the rise in the international gold price, combined with the occupationality of increasing numbers of miners, has generated a collective identity that has paved the way for occupational specialization and career formation.

Nonetheless, the price of gold can fluctuate wildly over time, and the mode of operation and underlying principles of economic gain in the global economy, combined with the dominant power of international banking and the money markets, are not likely to afford African workers the scope for enduring occupational career formation in artisanal mining. Large corporate mining interests are lurking in the wings, waiting for willing African governments to let them do deals by which the labour-absorbing work of artisanal mining will almost inevitably be marginalized or outlawed. So artisanal mining is not a panacea for poverty reduction. Rather it demonstrates that there are little niches of possibility in certain places and for specific durations of time. No amount of rose-tinted discussion about livelihood diversification and sustainability can hide the fact that the chances of the poor earning a viable income for themselves and their children are contracting, not expanding. We are not witnessing a sustainable career trajectory. Some miners do succeed in tunnelling out of poverty, but not very many. And the question is how long these tunnels will remain passable before they finally cave in on artisanal small-scale mining.

References

Adams, A.M., J. Cekan and R. Sauerborn (1998). 'Towards a conceptual framework of household coping: Reflections from rural West Africa', *Africa*, 68:2, pp. 263–83.

Bangura, Y. (1994). 'Economic restructuring, coping strategies and social change: Implications for institutional development in Africa', *Development and Change*, 25:4, pp. 785–827.

Barrett, C.B., T. Reardon and P. Webb (2001). 'Nonfarm income diversification and household livelihood strategies in rural Africa: Concepts, dynamics, and policy implications', *Food Policy*, 26:4, pp. 315–31.

Bourgouin, F. (2014). 'The politics of mining: Foreign direct investment, the state and artisanal mining in Tanzania' in D.F. Bryceson, E. Fisher, J.B. Jønsson and R. Mwaipopo (eds), *Mining and Social Transformation in Africa: Mineralizing and democratizing trends in artisanal production.* Routledge, London, pp. 148–60.

Bryceson, D.F. (1996). 'De-agrarianization and rural employment in Sub-Saharan Africa: A sectoral perspective', *World Development*, 24:1, pp. 97–111.

Bryceson, D.F. (1999). 'African rural labour, income diversification and livelihood approaches: A long-term development perspective', *Review of African Political Economy*, 80, pp. 171–89.

Bryceson, D.F. (2000a). 'Peasant theories and smallholder policies: Past and present' in D.F. Bryceson, C. Kay and J. Mooij (eds), *Disappearing Peasantries? Rural labour in Africa, Asia and Latin America.* Intermediate Technology Publications, London, pp. 1–36.

Bryceson, D.F. (2000b). 'African peasants' centrality and marginality: Rural labour transformations' in D.F. Bryceson, C. Kay and J. Mooij (eds), *Disappearing Peasantries? Rural labour in Africa, Asia and Latin America.* Intermediate Technology Publications, London, pp. 37–63.

Bryceson, D.F. (2002a). 'Multiplex livelihoods in Rural Africa: Recasting the terms and conditions of gainful employment', *Journal of Modern African Studies*, 40:1, pp. 1–28.

Bryceson, D.F. (2002b). 'The scramble in Africa: Reorienting rural livelihoods', *World Development*, 30:5, pp. 725–39.

Bryceson, D.F. (ed.) (2010a). *How Africa Works: Occupational change, identity and morality in Africa.* Practical Action Publishing, London.

Bryceson, D.F. (2010b). 'Africa at work: Transforming occupationality and morality' in D.F. Bryceson (ed.), *How Africa Works: Occupational change, identity and morality in Africa.* Practical Action Publishing, London, pp. 3–26.

Bryceson, D.F. and J.B. Jønsson (2010). 'Gold digging careers in rural Africa: Small-scale miners' livelihood choices', *World Development*, 38:3, pp. 379–93.

Bryceson, D.F. and D. MacKinnon (2012). 'Eureka and beyond: Mining's impact on African urbanisation' in D.F. Bryceson and D MacKinnon (eds), *Mining and Urbanisation in Africa: Population, settlement and welfare*, Special issue of *Journal of Contemporary African Studies*, 30:4, pp. 513–537.

Bryceson, D.F., E. Fisher, J.B. Jønsson and R. Mwaipopo (eds) (2014). *Mining and Social Transformation in Africa: Mineralizing and democratizing trends in artisanal production.* Routledge, London.

Bryceson, D.F, J.B. Jønsson, C. Kinabo and M. Shand (2012). 'Unearthing treasure and trouble: Mining as an impetus to urbanisation in Tanzania' in D.F. Bryceson and D. MacKinnon (eds), *Mining and Urbanisation in Africa: Population, settlement and welfare*, Special issue of *Journal of Contemporary African Studies*, 30:4, pp.631–649.

Byerlee, D. and C. Eicher (1972). 'Rural employment, migration and economic development: Theoretical issues and empirical evidence from Africa', Michigan State University Department of Agricultural Economics Working Paper 20.

Carney, D. (ed.) (1998). *Sustainable Rural Livelihoods: What contribution can we make?* Department of International Development, London.

Chachage, C.S.L. (1995). 'The meek shall inherit the earth but not the mining rights: Mining and accumulation in Tanzania' in P. Gibbon (ed.), *Liberalised Development in Tanzania.* Nordic Africa Institute, Uppsala, pp. 37–108.

Corbett, J. (1988). 'Famine and household coping strategies', *World Development* 16:9, pp. 1099–112.

Dessalegn Rahmato (1991). *Famine and Survival Strategies: A case study of northeast Ethiopia.* Nordic Africa Institute, Uppsala.

Devereux, S. (2001). 'Livelihood insecurity and social protection: Re-emerging issue in rural development', *Development Policy Review*, 19:4, pp. 507–19.

Devereux, S. (2010). 'Social protection in Africa: Evidence, politics and rights', *Poverty and Public Policy*, 2:3, pp. 53–77.

Dijkstra, T. (2010). 'Does trust travel? Horticultural trade in Kenya' in D.F. Bryceson (ed.), *How Africa Works: Occupational change, identity and morality in Africa.* Practical Action Publishing, London, pp. 47–65.

Ellis, F. (1998). 'Household strategies and rural livelihood diversification', *Journal of Development Studies*, 35:1, pp. 1–38.

Ellis, F. (2000). *Rural Livelihood Diversity in Developing Countries.* Oxford University Press.

Ellis, F. and G. Bahiigwa (2003). 'Livelihoods and rural poverty reduction in Uganda', *World Development*, 31:6, pp. 997–1013.

Ellis, F. and H.A. Freeman (2005). 'Comparative evidence from four African countries' in F. Ellis and H.A. Freeman (eds), *Rural Livelihoods and Poverty Reduction Policies.* Routledge, London, pp. 31–47.

Ellis, F. and N. Mdoe (2003). 'Livelihoods and rural poverty reduction in Tanzania', *World Development*, 31:8, pp. 1367–84.

Ellis, F., M. Kutengule and A. Nyasulu (2003). 'Livelihoods and rural poverty reduction in Malawi', *World Development*, 31:9, pp. 1495–510.

Fisher, E. (2007). 'Occupying the margins: Labour integration and social exclusion in artisanal mining in Tanzania', *Development and Change*, 38:4, pp. 735–60.

Fisher, E. (2008). 'Artisanal gold mining at the margins of mineral resource governance: A case from Tanzania', *Development Southern Africa*, 25:2, pp. 199–213.

Francis, E. (2000). *Making a Living: Changing livelihoods in rural Africa.* Routledge, London.

Grawert, E. (1998). *Making a Living in Rural Sudan: Production of women, labour migration of men, and policies for peasants' needs.* Macmillan, London.

Haggblade, S., P. Hazell and J. Brown (1989). 'Non-farm linkages in rural Sub-Saharan Africa', *World Development*, 17:8, pp. 1173–201.

Havnevik, K.J. (1993). *Tanzania: The limits to development from above.* Nordic Africa Institute, Uppsala.

Havnevik, K., D.F. Bryceson, L.-E. Birgegard, P. Matondi and Atakilte Beyene (2007). *African Agriculture and the World Bank: Development or impoverishment?* Nordic Africa Institute, Uppsala.

Jønsson, J.B. and D.F. Bryceson (2009). 'Rushing for gold: Mobility and small-scale mining in East Africa', *Development and Change*, 40:2, pp. 249–79.

Jønsson, J.B. and N. Fold (2011). 'Mining "from below": Taking Africa's artisanal miners seriously', *Geography Compass*, 5:7, pp. 479–93.

Jua, N. (2010). 'Body and soul: Economic space, public morality and social integration of youth in Cameroon' in D.F. Bryceson (ed.), *How Africa Works: Occupational change, identity and morality in Africa.* Practical Action Publishing, London, pp. 129–48.

Leidholm, C. (1973). 'Research on employment in the rural non-farm sector in Africa', Michigan State University paper.

Lindell, I. (2010). 'Between family and market: Urban informal workers' networks and identities in Bissau, Guinea-Bissau' in D.F. Bryceson (ed.), *How Africa Works: Occupational change, identity and morality in Africa.* Practical Action Publishing, London, pp. 149–64.

Maxwell, D. (1996). 'Measuring food insecurity: The frequency and severity of "coping strategies"', *Food Policy*, 21:3, pp. 291–303.

Mbilinyi, M. (2010). 'Sweet and sour: Women working for wages on Tanzania's sugar estates' in D.F. Bryceson (ed.), *How Africa Works: Occupational change, identity and morality in Africa.* Practical Action Publishing, London, pp. 165–84.

Meagher, K. (2001). *The Bargain Sector: Economic restructuring and the non-farm sector in the Nigerian savannah.* African Studies Centre, Leiden, and Ashgate, Aldershot.

Meagher, K. (2010). 'Social capital or social exclusion? Social networks and informal manufacturing in Nigeria' in D.F. Bryceson (ed.), *How Africa Works: Occupational change, identity and morality in Africa.* Practical Action Publishing, London, pp. 105–26.

Mwaipopo, R., W. Mutagwaba, D. Nyanga and E. Fisher (2004). 'Increasing the contribution of artisanal and small-scale mining to poverty reduction in Tanzania'. Department for International Development, London.

Narayan, D., L. Pritchett and S. Kapoor (2009). *Moving Out of Poverty: Success from the bottom up.* Palgrave Macmillan, London.

Reardon, T., C. Delgado and P. Matlon (1992). 'Determinants and effects of income diversification amongst farm households in Burkina Faso', *Journal of Development Studies*, 28:2, pp. 264–96.

Seppälä, P. (1998). *Diversification and Accumulation in Rural Tanzania: Anthropological perspectives on village economics.* Nordic Africa Institute, Uppsala.

Seppälä, P. (2010). 'With or against the odds? Professionalization of the labour force in Tanzania' in D.F. Bryceson (ed.), *How Africa Works: Occupational change, identity and morality in Africa.* Practical Action Publishing, London, pp. 245–61.

Seppälä, P. and B. Koda (eds) (1998). *The Making of a Periphery: Economic development and cultural encounters in southern Tanzania.* Nordic Africa Institute, Uppsala.

Simone, A.M. (2010). 'Linking irregular economies: Remaking trans-urban commercial networks through new forms of social collaboration' in D.F. Bryceson (ed.), *How Africa Works: Occupational change, identity and morality in Africa.* Practical Action Publishing, London, pp. 87–104.

Taylor, D.R.F. and F. Mackenzie (eds) (1992). *Development from Within: Survival in rural Africa.* Routledge, London.

World Bank (1990). *World Development Report: Poverty.* World Bank, Washington, DC.

World Bank (2000a). *World Development Report 2000/2001: Attacking poverty.* Oxford University Press, New York.

World Bank (2000b). *Voices of the Poor: Crying out for change.* World Bank, Washington, DC.

World Bank (2008). *World Development Report 2008: Agriculture for development.* World Bank, Washington, DC.

World Bank (2009). *World Development Report 2009: Reshaping economic geography.* World Bank, Washington, DC.

CHAPTER 6

The Concept and Paradoxes of Displacement[1]

Amanda Hammar

Introduction

In an eloquent TEDtalks presentation in late 2009, the Nigerian fiction writer Chimamanda Adichie spoke of the 'dangers of the single story'.[2] By that she meant the dangers of narrow, singular interpretations or representations of a place or a so-called 'people' or category of people – interpretations that collapse worlds of diversity, complexity and contradictions into stereotypes or oversimplifications. These simplifications, in turn, can reinforce fear, ignorance and arrogance, fuel violence and exclusion, as well as undermine dignity, equality and agency. Adichie's words reinforced my own deep unease with the distorting limitations of mono-dimensional perspectives, fixed standpoints and stale paradigms, and with *overly familiar* ways of thinking and knowing that make us at best complacent, and at worst blind. Radical or 'hyperbolic' doubt is a necessary condition for intellectual pursuit, Pierre Bourdieu (1999) once suggested, with particular reference to studying the state. In other words, we have to be attuned to the cracks and disjunctures we sense but may not yet be able to articulate in relation to the things we think we know well.

Adopting such productive doubt has become intrinsic to my own intellectual practices. One direct prompt in this direction came from working for many years (during the 1980s and part of the 1990s) in the field of development policy and practice in Southern Africa. Here I experienced at first hand the stultifying effects on one's critical thinking of the hegemonic paradigm of a largely unreflective developmentalism that took far too much of its own framing of the world for granted. This kind of critical doubt deepened during the 2000s as I witnessed the severe and sustained political and economic crises in Zimbabwe. This experience necessitated a dramatic re-evaluation of the workings of the Zimbabwean state and of the once-lauded, if always problematic, project of national development and nation-building. But another key factor

1 My appreciation to the Nordic Africa Institute (NAI) and especially Kjell Havnevik for the invitation to present some of these ideas at NAI in November 2011. In addition, my thanks to Tea Virtanen for her helpful editorial comments on an earlier draft of this chapter.

2 See at: http://www.youtube.com/watch?v=D9Ihs241zeg.

 | DOI 10.1163/9789004305465_007

that provoked a re-thinking of the familiar has come from an increasing proximity to, and unavoidable engagement with, the notion and multiple manifestations of *displacement*.

Both prior to the start of the now-chronic Zimbabwe crisis and since it began, my research has been closely related to situations and effects of violent, state-generated or state-sponsored physical and symbolic dislocation of targeted groups of people.[3] Although much of this work was concerned with empirical cases of forced removal – the common assumption of what 'displacement' means – little of the formal 'displacement' literature that I explored reflected or helped to analyse the kinds of complexities and contradictions that I was observing empirically.[4]

Significantly, I was not dealing with the category of formally documented refugees or internally displaced persons (IDPs), for which a large literature and terminological discourse certainly exists. In addition, my framework was self-consciously inclusive of broader questions of belonging, authority and state-making, and was situated in relation to historically and spatially contextual political economies. Clearly, there was something going on related to 'displacement'[5] that was not yet (or not sufficiently) being captured analytically. Specifically, in contexts of displacement, something was being *produced* symbolically and materially and not just lost, and there were both people and practices remaining out of view, intentionally or otherwise.

Displacement, then, is one of the arenas of the social world that calls for a degree of radical rethinking and reconceptualization. The sheer scale and persistence of empirical displacement deserves more extensive and analytically varied scrutiny in itself.[6] In particular, its often invisible or unremarked effects on so many people and processes require more 'nuanced' – i.e. more layered and interconnected – analytical attention than they have to date received.

3 So, for example, my doctoral research focused on the eviction of small-scale migrant farmers by the local state in northwest Zimbabwe in 1997/98 (Hammar 2001). Subsequent work addressed the broader links between state-making and displacement (Hammar 2006; 2008), and a research project during the mid to late 2000s examined the movement of displaced white commercial farmers from Zimbabwe to Mozambique (Hammar 2010).

4 Here meaning either in the realm of Refugee Studies or Migration Studies in general.

5 At times I put displacement in quotation marks; at other times not. Here it is to emphasize the notion of displacement as simultaneously a familiar and yet undefined arena; a notion that evokes naturalized assumptions and images, but in fact begs analytical unpacking.

6 In 2009, the World Bank estimated that up to 42 million people worldwide were affected by forced displacement, involving IDPs or refugees. Within this global context, on its website, UNHCR notes that Africa is the continent most affected by forced displacement. Find UNHCR at: http://www.flickr.com/photos/unhcr/sets/72157622492127591/.

This is especially true of the African continent. Here, the extent, conditions and consequences of diverse forms of displacement, and the ways in which key dimensions of displacement are seen or unseen and understood or misunderstood, have profound implications for the politics and possibilities of social, spatial, political and economic life. Hopefully such implications will become more visible as this chapter unfolds.

Before proceeding, a brief note on the scale and diversity of displacement in Africa is required. Official counts in recent years indicate that in 2009/10, there were in the region of 2.3 million refugees and between 11.1 and 11.6 million IDPs on the continent (IDMC and Norwegian Refugee Council, 2010: 2–3). The countries most affected in the past decades in terms of actual numbers have undoubtedly been Sudan (especially Darfur, and more recently South Sudan), the Democratic Republic of Congo and Somalia. Also important are countries like Angola, Rwanda, Liberia and Burundi, where significant numbers of refugees have returned, even though internal displacement remains substantial. Other countries of note in more recent times include the Central African Republic (CAR), Côte d'Ivoire, Ethiopia, Kenya, Nigeria, Senegal and Zimbabwe (ibid).

Yet in quantifying physical displacement there is a clear acknowledgement of the problem of accurate information. Many of the figures are estimates – even in relation to those who are officially 'countable' through their relationship to formal systems of emergency aid or other forms of humanitarian assistance, such as those registered in IDP or refugee camps. At the same time, there are literally countless 'undocumented' people who – either deliberately or due to the nature of the crises that have affected them – will not or cannot be counted. The causes of displacement – political, economic or environmental – and geographical location not only influence how displacement is experienced (and by how many) and the nature of its effects, but also whether (and if so how) particular populations may be accounted for, accommodated or supported. For example, far less visible to the technocratic eye are IDPs or refugees who settle in urban areas, frequently through self-settling, and who often attempt to make themselves invisible *as* displaced, or misplaced, persons. The latter present administrative, political, economic and social challenges that are different from those presented by rural displacees.

At the same time, while refugee and internal displacement numbers are cumulatively overwhelming, the available figures and any related interventions seldom take account of the complex ways in which host communities are affected. Nor do they capture adequately the significance of those who are forced to remain behind or who are 'displaced-in-place'. Added to this already overcrowded empirical and administrative scenario is a parallel set of hard-to-verify numbers and social conditions related both to those who have been resettled, and to those who have returned or will return to their former places of origin or to alternative locations.[7]

All this raises important questions about the nature of knowledge and knowledge production about African conditions in general, and about African displacement conditions in particular. In addition to the need to understand and address both the immediate and long-term practical needs of forcibly displaced or confined populations, there are also other dimensions of change that displacement produces, and which require in-depth analysis. These include, among others, key shifts in spatial, social, economic and political relations, with consequences at the local, national and often regional levels. Conceptually, displacement provides a critical lens through which to reflect theoretically on some of the unexpected and seemingly contradictory patterns that a disrupted and uncertain world throws up. By investigating displacement empirically in its diverse manifestations, one is compelled to recognize (and then to make theoretical sense of) the paradoxes that conditions of enforced dislocation, relocation and/or confinement inevitably reveal. This in turn requires analytical openness through a more nuanced and expanded – non-technocratic – definition of displacement.

In this chapter I provide some reflections on the meanings of displacement and on why it is important to study it. I also present some elements of an approach to displacement that I have begun to develop and which I find useful in this reflective endeavour. I believe that such an approach might contribute to our understanding of the broader conditions of physical, social, political and economic exclusion and of their diverse effects and responses in African contexts and elsewhere. I would like to start the discussion by acknowledging how common displacement is in human experience. Though always contextually unique, in any analysis of the phenomenon of displacement the very commonality or universality of the experience of it across time and place raises the challenge of *familiarity*. I move on to a brief discussion of various *definitions* of displacement, before discussing three key analytical entry points that I find useful in investigating the multi-dimensional phenomenon of displacement: place, positionality and production. These three dimensions help reveal the *paradoxes* of displacement, which reinforce the need to adopt a more layered,

7 These broad observations refer, in a very general sense, to the technocratic and legal discourses and interventionist practices of the international and national regimes that tackle the problem of displaced persons. There are, of course, many exceptions within particular settings. In addition, scholarship in a range of disciplinary fields provides rich analyses of all these dimensions; however, they are too extensive to refer to here.

multi-sited perspective in its understanding than the more technocratic approaches generally permit.

The Challenges of Familiarity

One way of reinforcing the earlier points of Adichie and Bourdieu with regard to critical blindness is to consider the threat to a more open and nuanced way of seeing that (over)familiarity can pose. As already noted, familiarity can and does collapse worlds of diversity, complexity and contradictions into stereotypes or oversimplifications. There are, however, at least two sides to familiarity: there is the side of it that can blind; but there is also the other (perhaps rarer) side that can sensitize one through resonance and recognition.

In its more commonsense meaning – primarily that of *physical* dislocation – displacement is familiar to most of us on some level. It has been internalized in various ways: perhaps most recognizably through culturally or politically embedded narratives of the formation or destruction of societies, both ancient and still extant. We are surrounded by countless stories of displacement: from the biblical, to the legendary, to the literary, and to the factual. The sources range from oral histories to historical archives, and from scientific journals to policy documents, media reports, fiction and poetry.

For some, displacement has been experienced more immediately, through family histories of dispossession, dislocation and loss, whether some time ago or more recently. For others, it is connected to even more direct personal experience – of being a refugee or of being in exile or confinement. Though a widespread historical and contemporary phenomenon on the continent, this is not specific to Africa: Asia and Latin America are regions that are equally marked. And Europe's own history – from the persecution of the Huguenots in France in the late seventeenth century[8] to the upheavals of the Second World War and beyond – has been profoundly informed by large-scale displacements.

In particular places and times, narratives of displacement are often woven together in complex patterns, so that past displacements may be used – through simplified causal explanations and/or partisan forms of blame – either to produce or to legitimize fresh displacements. This is especially salient in relation to grand historical events of sweeping significance. Through various forms of discursive and cultural reinforcement, they become part of what anthropologist Michael Jackson (2004) would call the *historical* past, as

8 See Barnett (2002) for a discussion of the links between this and the evolution of the broad refugee regime alongside the development of the modern, Westphalian state system.

distinct from a more individualized *biographical* past. Such historical pasts, Jackson suggests, then become available for invocation in the present by various sovereign authorities, as 'legitimating precedents or explanations for actions' (ibid.: 81). We might take, for example, the epic Old Testament story of the exodus of the Jews from Egypt – a symbolic tale of forced flight from intolerable conditions of enslavement – and God's 'promise' of Israel as a Jewish homeland. This particular 'historical past' has been invoked in contemporary political discourse (and reinforced by more recent global tropes of security) to legitimize the continued dispossession of the Palestinians. In turn, this reality has generated political discourse and direct actions by Palestinians and their allies to counter such effects.

In the context of Africa, colonialism's large-scale dispossession of African peasants mobilized large numbers to fight anti-colonial wars of national liberation, particularly in Southern Africa during the 1960s and 1970s. Ironically, such wars themselves generated the displacement of millions. The same anti-colonial, nationalist discourse was used in the 2000s by Zimbabwe's Mugabe regime to justify contemporary forms of violence and the displacement of thousands of white farmers. But this also included the mass displacement of hundreds of thousands of black farmworkers, as well as of opposition supporters more generally in both rural and urban areas.

Yet beyond grand displacement *events* and their legitimizing narratives in an increasing number of settings in Africa, displacement and its uncertainties manifest something of an everyday, chronic presence. This echoes Henrik Vigh's reference to 'crisis *as* context', where crisis 'acquire[s] an air of social and existential constancy' (Vigh 2008: 12). In this sense, displacement paradoxically becomes both a taut thread of normality for large sections of the population (where what is 'normal' and known is also somehow safer) and an ever-present threat that constantly generates uncertainty. But on whichever scale one thinks about displacement, each case and context is empirically specific. This requires us to investigate each on its own terms, while also paying attention to concepts and historical patterns that can help cast light on connections with other times and places. I return to some examples later.

Beyond discursive narratives, specifically in relation to Africa we are possibly even more familiar with the many powerful *visual* images of displacement. One might search for examples on the internet using keywords like 'refugees' or 'IDPs'. Similarly, one can find countless photographs produced by the news media or used by various charities to raise funds for those who endure violence and dislocation either through war or through 'natural' disasters and other kinds of emergency situations. The argument here is not that these images are 'untrue' in themselves or inaccurate *per se*, but rather that they reflect a selective and partial perspective that, in the absence of critical commentary, is implicitly represented as the whole. One of the most striking effects of such images is to reinforce a certain type of 'displaced' person, or rather a *stereo*type that tends to (re)produce ahistorical images of victimhood, passivity and absolute loss, often alongside actual or merely implied images of gratitude for being helped or saved.

Such familiar narratives and images naturalize and oversimplify ways of thinking about 'the displaced' and 'displacement'. This creates ideas or logics of difference that generate particular discursive and practical regimes of recognition of personhood. These in turn (re)produce logics of entitlement and exclusion within and across space and reinforce related regimes of management and control of bodies and borders. There is a need to deepen our ways of seeing and analysing the displaced and the dynamics of displacement that challenge overly narrow representations and interpretations, and that guard against their potential dangers.

Definition(s) of Displacement

I shall now discuss what I mean by displacement and provide a corresponding working definition. I want to emphasize that my understanding of the concept has emerged through empirical research over many years, as well as through personal experience and observation. When I first started working explicitly on questions of displacement in the late 1990s, it was not really intentional, and I had no clear idea at the time of what 'displacement' encapsulated. My initial engagement began when I undertook the first exploratory fieldwork for my doctoral research in late 1997. My original plan was to examine local community land conflicts in northwest Zimbabwe. However, chance exposed me to an evocative hand-drawn image in someone's office that portrayed a group of men in a truck on their way to carry out the eviction of a remotely situated community I had yet to encounter. Following the story behind this compelling image radically altered the focus of my doctoral research, and also my more general intellectual orientation. I ended up investigating close-up the brutal eviction of small-scale migrant farmers by the local district authority in a marginalized rural corner of the country.[9] One of the key insights from this work – and one that informed subsequent research – was the significance of the close relationship between territory, authority and violence, and between

9 This culminated in my PhD thesis entitled '"The day of burning": Land, authority and belonging in Zimbabwe's agrarian margins in the 1990s', 2007, Roskilde University, Denmark.

belonging, displacement and state-making. At the same time, I paid attention to the other side of the coin: namely, questions of displaced citizens' resistance, reinvention and replacement.[10]

All this exposed a range of complexities and paradoxes related to displacement. Through attention to these, there emerged a somewhat organic conceptualization of displacement that retained – but also moved beyond – the element of force or compulsion at its heart. Consequently, I have come to define displacement as:

> enforced changes in interweaving spatial, social and symbolic conditions and relations.

Each of the main words in this definition is, in fact, a key or 'provocation': enforced, spatial, social and symbolic. The notion of *en/forced* necessarily leads one to ask open-ended yet relational questions about who or what has compelled changes affecting whom, and in what ways. It necessarily requires an analytic lens that reflects on relations and practices of power, sovereignty and authority, in terms of the capacities and legitimations underpinning modes of force. In addition, it makes visible the conditions and counter-agency of those being compelled. The *spatial* is a necessary, but not isolated or predictable, element of this process. Space in itself always matters (Massey 2005), in this regard both in terms of actual and symbolic location or place, what it contains, how it is occupied, used, controlled and/or desired, and so on. At the same time, not all displacement involves physical removal or compelled movement away from a particular place. For some, it may mean 'involuntary immobility' (Lubkemann 2008) or forced confinement, such as in the IDP camps of northern Uganda (Finnström 2008), or simply abandonment and/or having no means of moving (Solidarity Peace Trust 2009; Lubkemann 2010; Magaramombe 2010).

The relationship of a given group of people to a familiar place is always internally differentiated and always complex. Both differentiation and complexity *in* place necessarily alter under conditions of crisis. This is even more the case when people are compelled to move to a *new* place, especially under enforced conditions that often combine violence and other kinds of disruption. This profoundly affects both their *social* relationships to place in the very broadest sense – meaning historical, physical, economic, cultural, political relationships – and their *symbolic* relationships at multiple levels.

10 Some of the publications that have resulted from this research include Hammar (2001; 2006; 2008; 2010).

My definition of displacement relates to, but also contrasts with, more standard technocratic and humanitarian definitions. These are the more familiar ways in which displacement and the displaced have been conceptualized and have come to be 'known'. The World Bank, for example, provides this succinct definition:

> forced displacement refers to the situation of persons who are forced to leave or flee their homes due to conflict, violence, and human rights violations.
>
> CHRISTENSEN AND HARILD 2009: 4

The International Organization for Migration uses the term 'forced migration' rather than 'forced displacement'. Similarly acknowledging the dimension of force through threatening political conditions, it expands somewhat on the range of recognized causalities, including, for example, dimensions of environmental and developmental displacement. It defines forced migration as:

> A migratory movement in which an element of coercion exists, including threats to life and livelihood, whether arising from natural or man-made causes (e.g. movements of refugees and internally displaced persons as well as people displaced by natural or environmental disasters, chemical or nuclear disasters, famine, or development projects).[11]

Both definitions largely echo aspects of the original 1951 United Nations Convention Relating to the Status of Refugees, amended by the 1967 Protocol,[12] and the UN's much later 1998 Guiding Principles on Internal Displacement.[13]

---

11 'Key migration terms', International Organization for Migration website, available at: https://www.iom.int/key-migration-terms.

12 The Convention defines a refugee as: 'A person who owing to a well-founded fear of being persecuted for reasons of race, religion, nationality, membership of a particular social group or political opinion, is outside the country of his nationality and is unable or, owing to such fear, is unwilling to avail himself of the protection of that country; or who, not having a nationality and being outside the country of his former habitual residence as a result of such events, is unable or, owing to such fear, is unwilling to return to it.' Available at: http://www.unhcr.org/pages/49da0e466.html.

13 The Guiding Principles (which do not have the same weight as a Convention) define internally displaced persons as 'persons or groups of persons who have been forced or obliged to flee or to leave their homes or places of habitual residence, in particular as a result of or in order to avoid the effects of armed conflict, situations of generalized violence, violations of human rights or natural or human-made disasters, and who have not

Interestingly, in 1969 the Organization of African Unity (OAU) added an *external* dimension to the primarily *internal* threats identified in the UN Convention, reflecting the continental realities and politics of the times. The OAU resolved that the term 'refugee', besides encompassing the Convention definition, should:

> *also* apply to every person who, *owing to external aggression, occupation, foreign domination* or events seriously disturbing public order in either part or the whole of his country of origin or nationality, is compelled to leave his place of habitual residence in order to seek refuge in another place outside his country of origin or nationality.[14] (my emphasis)

All of these technocratic-humanitarian definitions arose out of dramatic conditions of mass displacement and suffering and were prompted by an international ethic of 'the responsibility to protect'.[15] However, at the same time they invoked a whole series of global discourses that, over more than half a century, have created and then calcified formal categories of places and people, at the same time as generating institutions to deal with them. Together, this has constituted a global refugee protection and humanitarian aid regime. While having normatively good intentions, it has produced conceptual, physical and symbolic closures and analytical blind-spots, with negative consequences. Labels such as 'refugees' and 'IDPs', for example, are what David Turton (2003) refers to as 'artefacts of policy concerns rather than of empirical observation and scientific enquiry'.[16] Useful in their own right, such labels nonetheless help

crossed an internationally recognized State border.' Available at: http://www.brookings.edu/~/media/Projects/idp/GPEnglish.pdf.

14 The OAU's 1969 Convention Governing the Specific Aspects of Refugee Problems in Africa is available at: http://www.unhcr-centraleurope.org/pdf/resources/legal-documents/international-refugee-law/1969-organization-of-african-unity-convention-governing-the-specific-aspects-of-refugee-problems-in-africa.html.

15 The 'responsibility to protect' (R2P) was a concept introduced by the International Commission on Intervention and State Sovereignty in 2001, which later became part of a resolution passed by the United Nations General Assembly in October 2005. It established international principles on the responsibility to protect populations from genocide, war crimes, cleansing and crimes against humanity. This includes recognizing the right of the international community to intervene, if considered necessary and approved by the UN Security Council, to protect or halt such acts of mass atrocity within a given state, irrespective of that state's national sovereignty. For a critical discussion of R2P, see Stahn (2007).

16 See also Zetter (2007) on labelling of refugees.

to create further invisibilities and exclusions through what they are *unable to address*, and who and what they are *unable to see*, as well as through certain distorted forms of gate-keeping that they generate.

The Implications of a more Open Approach to Displacement

In my definition of displacement, I deliberately refrain from focusing purely on enforced *movement*; rather, in an inclusive move of my own, I emphasize enforced changes in interweaving spatial, social and symbolic conditions and relations. One key aspect of this, as already indicated, is to incorporate both enforced movement and enforced *confinement*, the latter also being called '*in situ* displacement' or 'displacement-in-place' (Magaramombe 2010), or 'involuntary immobility' (Lubkemann 2008). Often displacement includes elements of both at the same time. So, for example, in the mid-2000s in Zimbabwe, up to three-quarters of a million urban inhabitants had their homes and businesses destroyed by the Zanu (PF) party-state under a campaign dubbed Operation *Murambatsvina*[17] and were forced to relocate, unassisted, to untenable places. But during this campaign, even when homes were not destroyed and people could stay where they were, livelihoods were lost entirely and a sense of the future itself was displaced (Jones 2010). Alternatively, one could think of northern Uganda, which experienced war from the mid-1980s to the mid-1990s, and where, in the following decade, up to 90 per cent of the 1.3 million inhabitants in Acholiland were forced by the Ugandan government to remain in so-called protected camps. These were often just a few kilometres from their original homes and fields, which they were no longer allowed or able to access (Bøås and Bjorkhaug 2014). These examples – and countless others – point to the fact that displacement can be a dramatic, one-off event and be (or become) chronic in nature, routinized through state practices of deliberate political or ethnic forms of selective exclusion, or through sustained structural neglect.

Migration, and mobility more generally, are two powerful tropes used widely and legitimately in the study of African realities and African agency (De Bruijn et al. 2001). Displacement and migration certainly *are* processes that historically and spatially overlay and shape one another in particular contexts. Southern Africa provides rich examples of this in two respects. On the one hand, the region has a long history of labour migration, voluntary and forced. This was largely linked to the mines and commercial farms in South Africa and Zimbabwe that established both routes of survival and rites of passage for millions, precipitated not least by

17 This translates from ChiShona as 'clear out the trash'.

far-reaching colonial dispossessions. On the other hand, the wider region – including neighbouring states in central Africa – is marked by experiences of mass dislocation and relocation. Since the 1960s, national liberation and civil wars have been primary causes, especially in Mozambique, Angola, Zimbabwe and, more recently, the Democratic Republic of the Congo; but also key in precipitating large-scale displacement are post-colonial state projects of political and economic violence, as in Zimbabwe since 2000. In many cases, the older routes of migration have been utilized in newer contexts of displacement.[18]

Yet even though the field of Migration Studies, and the more recently emergent and related Diaspora Studies, demonstrate important links between the core phenomena they investigate and displacement processes, it is crucial to maintain a clear focus on the *enforced* dimension of displacement. This is not central to definitions and studies of migration. The enforced nature of spatial, social and symbolic dynamics and effects that characteristically define displacement necessarily calls for approaches that take into account the multi-dimensional complexities of the phenomenon. First, such inquiries should take account of the politics and political economies that generate particular exclusions, dispossessions, dislocations, relocations or confinements. Second, they should look at the cultural politics that often serve to legitimize and reinforce these practices. Third, they should explore the ways in which different social groups resist, counter or confront such practices and their effects.

With regard to enforcement, inevitably the state is central in most cases, although this is often in alliance with a range of other players who may have their own interests, too, and on occasion may conduct (semi)autonomous acts of displacement. These other actors may include, for example, political parties, traditional leaders, war veterans or local militia. This has certainly been the case in Zimbabwe. They may include domestic and international corporate businesses, as in the case of oil in the Niger Delta and elsewhere (Watts 2004), or in mining (Downing 2002). One also needs to consider the role of international donors in both the physical and the broader social and economic displacement effects of various forms of development.[19] Even local and international non-governmental organizations are significant actors in certain displacement settings, as in the case of various conservation projects (Brockington and Igoe 2006; Hammar 2001).

18 See, for example, Hammar, McGregor and Landau (2010) and the various articles in the special issue of the *Journal of Southern African Studies*, 36:2 (2010), which focused on displacement in Zimbabwe and its relationship to the Southern Africa region.

19 With respect to dam displacements, see, for example, Scudder (1973) and Roy (1999). For a discussion of the destructive effects of World Bank 'advice' and conditionality on Mozambique's cashew nut industry, see Hanlon and Smart (2008).

But whether it entails different forms of forced movement *away* from a place or forced enclosure or immobility *in* place in various ways, displacement includes not only elements of material dispossession and loss, but also – or rather *always* – a range of symbolic and social dislocations. Among other things, this incorporates the experiential loss or dislodging of the familiar conditions of home and social relations – a phenomenon that Finn Stepputat has termed 'domicide'. With this, there is often a radical loss of security – existential and political, as well as physical – producing what Achille Mbembe has called 'a condition of rightlessness'.[20]

A study of displacement in this way thus brings us close to the relationship between power and precariousness. Yet this is never a monolithic or simple story, as Adichie reminds us. It is never just a story of one-sided violence and exclusion on the one hand, and passive victimhood on the other. There are always complex histories and effects associated with different forms of empirical displacement. In addition to institutional and individual cruelties and destruction and loss, there are always stories of courage and generosity, of opportunity and inventiveness, as well as gain.

Perhaps unsurprisingly under such conditions of stress and uncertainty, there are also stories of exclusions within exclusions among the displaced themselves (Hammar 2006), and stories of new gate-keepers and opportunists emerging. Finally, as people struggle to survive in new and precarious conditions, there are stories of evasion and disconnection from kin, just as much as there are tales of efforts to keep families together at all costs. So, for example, Eric Worby (2010) writes of Zimbabweans who have found their way to Johannesburg in search of security and survival. These people, forced by the conditions of their displacement – and consequent illegality in many cases – to live very precarious lives there, deliberately disconnect from families back home, or from relatives who arrive later, by disappearing or not answering calls. This is done either out of shame at the conditions of their lives or because they simply lack the means to take on one more burden. Or we hear from Blair Rutherford (2008), Max Bolt (2010) and others of how Zimbabweans living and working on commercial farms in northern South Africa, close to the Zimbabwe border, work backbreaking hours and save all they can of their meagre wages to send back to their desperate families at home.

---

20 Both terms – Stepputat's 'domicide' and Mbembe's 'condition of rightlessness' – were expressions used in those speakers' keynote presentations made at an international conference in Johannesburg in July 2008 on 'Political Economies of Displacement in Zimbabwe', co-convened by the Nordic Africa Institute and Wits University.

Three Dimensions of Displacement: Place, Positionality and Productivity in Zimbabwe

I would like to turn now to three dimensions that I see as key entry points for thinking more intimately, one might say, about displacement and its paradoxes: place, positionality and production. Illustrations are drawn specifically from Zimbabwe.

Place

Experience has led me to conclude that *each reshaped place bears its own particular scars*, and each in turn bears witness to its befores and afters. Part of the work of research into displacement, I argue, is to engage as closely as possible with the actual sites of displacement. This prompts one to gain a sense of immediacy about their spatial, social, economic and political histories and ongoing dynamics. Doing so allows one to trace what has been lost or changed through displacement, and how this has been experienced by differently positioned actors. I would emphasize, however, that there are seldom (perhaps never) single sites relevant to displacement processes, but rather many interconnected places, as well as in-between transitional spaces.

For my doctoral research in northwest rural Zimbabwe in the late 1990s, I spent time with an evicted community whose houses and granaries had been burnt down by the local district council in the process of their eviction. Close to 120 households had been chased away but had managed to return to their homesteads and fields after living for five months 'out in the open', some twenty kilometres away. Their return, however, was for an uncertain length of time, and they lived constantly under the threat of another eviction. Yet at the same time they continued to find ways to farm again, and to organize themselves to try and strengthen their political and legal position in the area. The following short excerpt from my thesis describes a moment when a particular evictee family at its reclaimed homestead insisted on showing me the evidence of destruction and suffering they had experienced at the hands of the council the previous year:

> Together, we would walk around the dusty yard, scrawny chickens and lean dogs underfoot, and someone would point to the site where a particular sleeping hut or grain store had once stood, the foundations peering out of the dry earth like an accusation. The charcoaled edges of burnt construction poles, shattered clay storage pots and broken farm implements still littered corners of the yard… Once, several plastic sacks were dragged into the open from a nearby hut and their contents emptied onto mats, where the charred relics of a past life were displayed with archival precision: fragments of clothing, kitchen utensils, even full maize cobs, all blackened by fire and underscored by the pungent smell of smoke.

These 'walking narratives' and the embodied memories shared with me were not only an invitation to witness – and record – what had taken place there, but were equally a form of critique by those displaced of the post-colonial state's violence towards its own citizens. At the same time, I was shown fields that were being harvested, and granaries that had been rebuilt and were slowly being refilled just a few years after the eviction and return. This, too, was part of an assertion of defiance, as well as pride regained after the indignities of the eviction. Later there would also be tales of the evictee leadership accessing resources that they distributed only to those loyal to them, and excluding others deemed disloyal or undeserving.

Importantly, then – and it was necessary to keep this constantly in mind – this was only one part of a more complex local politics that was linked simultaneously to a much larger national story concerning struggles over resources, territory, sovereignty and citizenship. At the same time, it was a story that resonated both with older histories of colonial land dispossession and with post-independence practices of eviction. It was also interwoven with the effects of structural adjustment policies introduced in the 1990s. Finally, it also played into ongoing and intensifying partisan politics both at the political-geographical centre and on the margins. Eventually it would connect with the dynamics of the so-called land revolution and a new form of narrow nationalism that would unfold in the 2000s. This would generate mass urban and rural displacements, but would especially see the radical reshaping of the agrarian landscape. Yet while being interconnected in complex ways, all of these dynamics had – and would continue to have – their own specific, place-based stories to reveal.

Positionality

Both former and changing social positions have an impact on the ways in which people experience and manage their displacement. Similarly, in a more specifically spatial sense, people who are physically displaced are affected by questions of proximity and returnability in relation to places of dislocation. Critical, too, are the conditions of welcome and security (or not) in sites of relocation, as well as the time scale and changing conditions of possibility that allow one to build, or dream. In other words, *both who one is and where one is situated socially, spatially and temporally* are highly significant for understanding the causes, experiences, opportunities and outcomes of particular displacements. That is to say, displacement is shaped – and differentially experienced – by class, gender, race, ethnicity and age, and by the geographies of difference these imply. Displacement can and does also profoundly alter familiar patterns of power and possibility associated with these positionalities.

I provide a few examples here from post-2000 Zimbabwe of shifts in positionality resulting from displacement and at the same time further deepening its effects. First, the focus is on an urban setting, where the meanings of age, gender and class have been, and are still being, redefined in new ways. In a context in which labour and the economy itself has been dramatically displaced over the past decade – with formal unemployment in Zimbabwe officially having reached over 80 per cent by the late 2000s, and even much of the previously extensive informal-sector structure having been violently dismantled by the state in 2005 – old forms of status and social mobility associated with 'professional' life have radically altered. Jeremy Jones' (2010) innovative research describes how a new economic logic emerged during the 2000s, especially in the high-density townships of Zimbabwe. This is the logic of *kukiyakiya*, of 'getting by' in ChiShona, through 'cleverness, dodging, and the exploitation of whatever resources are at hand with an eye to self-sustenance'. Jones terms this (somewhat ironically) '*kiya*nomics'.

In this context, doing things 'straight' or 'properly' – in 'the old way', as many of the older generation have been well schooled to do – no longer worked. It no longer provided even the basics of survival. Even those with education and professional qualifications, usually the older members of families, could no longer hold families together. This particularly affected male breadwinners who had formal jobs and either lost them as the economic crisis worsened and companies closed, or were still employed but whose salaries barely covered transport to and from work. In fact, many even *with* jobs – teachers and civil servants, as much as factory workers – abandoned them to take up more lucrative, but less stable, forms of livelihood, often illicit. In the worst period of political violence and hyperinflation in the late 2000s, many even ended up as farmworkers across the border in South Africa (Bolt 2010). In Zimbabwe's townships, much younger men (particularly adept at navigating the plethora of uncertainties and cutting 'zigzag deals'), or women selling sex or engaged in cross-border trading largely became the primary providers. This profoundly changed family dynamics.

Second, in rural contexts over the same period, other kinds of radical repositioning have occurred following the widespread land invasions and evictions that displaced not only thousands of white commercial farmers, but also hundreds of thousands of black farmworkers and ordinary opposition party supporters. In some cases, where white farmers lost their lands but managed to remain in the general vicinity, unexpected relationships of cooperation emerged between them and some of the new black settlers. Conrade Zawe (2006) describes how, in several cases where irrigation cooperatives were established on occupied farms by the new 'settlers', the latter paid former white farmers to advise them on how to operate the mechanical infrastructure and to supply inputs and services that ranged from tillage and planting to transporting produce to market. This is especially significant if one considers that the state's promises to support new settlers, many of whom were on the front line of the land invasions supported (or even precipitated) by the state, largely remained unfulfilled. As Zawe comments: 'It is striking and ironic to note that the very "enemies of the state", i.e. the white commercial farmers, proved to be the most reliable partners available to the invader settlers in their endeavours to make the fast track resettlement programme a farming success' (Zawe 2006: 291).

In an entirely different context researched from the mid to late 2000s, evicted white commercial farmers from Zimbabwe who sought ways to survive and generate a living by migrating to Mozambique were confronted with new kinds of vulnerabilities (Hammar 2010). On the one hand, they faced the disorientation and the social, linguistic and bureaucratic barriers common to cross-border displacees everywhere. On the other hand, they were also confronted by another round of displacements when their deals with a multinational tobacco company (which had naively hoped to replicate Zimbabwe's high-end tobacco production through them) turned sour.

In other cases involving former commercial farms in Zimbabwe, paradoxical conditions emerged for those farmworkers who lost their jobs following the land invasions, but managed to remain 'displaced-in-place' on the farms (Magaramombe 2010). On the one hand, the so-called 'fast-track land reforms' created immense hardships for former farmworkers, removing regular incomes and producing widespread destitution. But as Magaramombe argues, the new insecurities and loosening of formal obligations to employers created new, if uneven, opportunities to engage in other livelihood strategies, ranging from piecework for the new farmers, to various forms of independent entrepreneurship, including beer brewing, firewood vending and gold panning. Some workers, especially women, claimed to feel 'empowered' by a new independence not only from white farmers, but also from their husbands. This new 'residential autonomy', as Magaramombe calls it, was precipitated by the de-linking of accommodation from work. This has meant that old forms of 'domestic governance' – a term coined by Blair Rutherford (2001) to describe the sovereign authority wielded by white farmers over black workers – no longer exist on commercial farms. On the other hand, recent research (as well as anecdotal evidence) points to other forms of exploitation of some farmworkers by new black farm owners.

Yet in Zimbabwe – as in other contexts of chronic crisis, displacement and uncertainty – repositioning is not a linear or even process, and new positions are unlikely to be fixed for long. This could not really be otherwise under conditions where, as now, security of access to, or control over, property is always in doubt, and where the value of such assets is unstable. Similarly, these are conditions in which certain avenues for wealth creation and accumulation have been permanently destroyed, and where displacement has generated permanent relocation, yet uncertain grounding in the new spaces of re/settlement and replacement.

Productivity

The last set of examples link to a third paradoxical dimension of displacement, namely the issue of productivity. Here I take this word to refer both to the more material notion of production itself, and to the idea of something having generative capacity.

The point I wish to reiterate here is that there is a need not only to consider what conditions and dynamics *generate* displacement, but also to investigate what displacement itself *generates*. Somehow, we more readily recognize the negative aspects of this: in particular, the various degrees and forms of violence, dislocation, confinement and loss, and their multiply destructive effects. In relation to Zimbabwe, much of the scholarly and the activist literature over the past decade has been understandably devoted to recording and analysing this. Many analysts, academic and otherwise, have discussed the dramatic fall in production levels and foreign currency earnings, for example, in the agricultural, mining, tourist and manufacturing sectors. There has also been a dramatic rise in food insecurity, and a severe decline in many public sector services and infrastructure, such as health, education, water and electricity. While it is clearly important to record all this, far less attention has been paid to the emergence of new and complex social relations and identities, new economic logics and practices, new forms of nationalism and citizenship, or new institutional mechanisms both inside and outside the state. This is critical in order to broaden the scope of evidence that will deepen our understanding of the crisis and its consequences. Positively, though, an increasingly diverse and robust scholarship is filling the gaps to some extent.

Part of the difficulty has been the challenge for scholars of trying to do research under an authoritarian regime, even after the establishment of a Government of National Unity in early 2009. In particular, there are ongoing sensitivities around questions of property ownership. Yet even less focus has been given to the concrete changes and continuities in production, trade and accumulation that the past decade of crisis and cumulative mass displacement has generated. Among the early exceptions to this were the results of a long-term study into the livestock sector or 'beef value chain' in Masvingo Province, southwest Zimbabwe, undertaken by Ian Scoones, together with a number of

Zimbabwean colleagues (Mavedzenge et al. 2008; Scoones et al. 2010). Despite – or partly because of – the collapse of the long-standing *export* beef sector, precipitated by the wide-scale evictions under the fast-track land reform programme, and the disappearance of large-scale commercial ranching accompanied by a decline in the quality of beef, there has been what Mavedzenge et al. (2008: 620) describe as:

> a major transition from a highly concentrated and regulated commodity chain dominated by a few players to a huge diversity of actors at all levels of the commodity chain. This has been accompanied by a decline in state control and management of the market system to a growth in independent, increasingly informal economic activity and entrepreneurialism.

For some traditional players in the sector, this more complex and diversified production and marketing system was considered 'haphazard', 'disorganized' and 'chaotic', a real retreat from 'order' and from a neat and narrow route to 'progress'. For others, even if the market has become less predictable and less efficient – and, with reduced government capacity to monitor veterinary regulations, somewhat less sanitary in some contexts – it has allowed space for a much wider range of actors at various levels, including intermediaries active in buying and transporting beef. Ever since the liberalization of meat markets back in the 1990s, associated with a structural adjustment programme, there has been a further mushrooming of private abattoirs, but this has further extended to the slaughter of animals directly at local butcheries.

Yet while this local 'boom' in one sector, and one part of the country, hardly represents a global upturn in productivity in Zimbabwe's agricultural sphere, it is not an isolated exception either. At a more general level, Scoones (2008) has argued that, even if the statistical production indicators in agriculture were down for the majority of agricultural commodities, what this reflected was 'the collapse of the old, formal, commercial agricultural economy but not the whole agricultural economy'. The picture on the ground, he claims, is far more mixed than global figures or generalizations would suggest, especially in relation to the smallholder sector – and even more specifically in relation to the livestock sector in the southwest. Scoones and his Zimbabwean colleagues, however, problematically used their findings from Masvingo to make more generalized claims for Zimbabwe as a whole in a somewhat controversial book (Scoones et al. 2010). This has been highly criticized in some quarters – not so much for what it includes, as for what it excludes. Among other things, it fails to engage in any meaningful discussion of the partisan political dimensions and intentions of the land reform programme or of its wide-scale violence and devastating displacement effects. In addition, it generalizes its claims for Zimbabwe as a whole, and ingeniously represents the reform process as largely a success. No matter what overall conclusions are drawn about the Zimbabwe crisis, the realities attest to the complex layers of actors and interests and paradoxical effects associated with what has unquestionably been an intense and uneven process of displacement, replacement and resettlement lasting more than a decade. Clearly, this could not possibly be analysed sufficiently using merely technocratic-humanitarian analytical tools.[21]

Conclusion

I would like to return now to the question we might ask more generally: why does studying displacement – and displacement in this way – matter?

In a very pragmatic, even demographic sense, one could say that displacement affects millions of people on the African continent and beyond in multiple ways, so that merely in terms of scale it is in itself a valid arena of study. Yet, as argued in this chapter, too much of the understanding and representation of those forcibly removed or immobilized is defined by the abstract, technocratic terms of humanitarian agencies that, ironically, often diminish those they aim to assist. Such restrictive terminologies, and the institutional and financial frameworks associated with them, simultaneously reinforce stereotypes of Africans as passive, suffering victims and reproduce older global dynamics of 'othering' and inequality. This needs to be countered with empirically grounded knowledge and to include alternative (especially African) voices and perspectives that reflect the complex conditions and diverse experiences of displacement, and the independent ways in which people confront and navigate its worst effects and unexpected opportunities.

Moving beyond the over-bureaucratization – and at times implicit criminalization – of the displaced is essential if one is to counter critical invisibilities and reverse the conceptual (and sometimes legal) reduction of dislocated people to non-beings, and instead to recognize their resourcefulness and rights. With implications for the ways in which national and international policies

21 An intellectual project that is exploring productive ways of analysing similar complexities in settings across the African continent is a volume edited by this author entitled *Displacement Economies in Africa: Paradoxes of crisis and creativity* (*Hammar, 2014*). Collectively, the authors aim to refine the conceptual and methodological tools for analysing the paradoxical landscapes of displacement, with a particular emphasis on the reshaping of economic logics, spaces, relations and practices.

towards the displaced are formulated and applied, this is not an entirely automatic prospect. Yet it is the job of scholars to keep making visible what is repeatedly ignored or erased. Invisibility produces its own violence, and studies of African realities, over the centuries and including the present, are replete with what Jemima Pierre (2006) calls 'the violence of languages of silencing and exclusion'.

There is much work to be done to counter such silence and invisibility. In the words of US-based Malawian scholar and fiction writer Paul Zeleza (2006: 29), a past chair of the African Studies Association in the US:

> The challenge for committed African and Africanist scholars is to ensure that we continue to struggle for the production, organization, dissemination, and consumption of knowledges that enhance, rather than undermine, Africa's possibilities.

Thinking about displacement in relation to this challenge, I would suggest that it implies looking at the concept from different spatial and social locations, as well as from different disciplinary vantage points. What is further needed is to try to understand the diverse yet interconnected perspectives of those who have been displaced, those that displace and replace them, and those, too, that host, manage, or further displace them in various ways. It also means taking a longer historical view of particular displacements, tracing earlier and later continuities, as well as ruptures, and making links with other occasions or patterns of violence, movement and enclosure. Finally, as noted earlier but reiterated here as perhaps the most critical conceptual provocation – and one taken up more fully elsewhere (Hammar 2014) – it means not only considering what range of complex conditions and relations *produce* displacement, but also investigating what displacement itself *produces*.

References

Barnett, Laura (2002). 'Global governance and the evolution of the international refugee regime', *International Journal of Refugee Law*, 14:2/3, pp. 238–62.

Bøås, Morten and Ingunn Bjørkhaug (2014). 'The IDP economy in northern Uganda: A prisoners' economy?' in Amanda Hammar (ed.), *Displacement Economies in Africa: Paradoxes of crisis and creativity*. Zed Books, London.

Bolt, Max (2010). 'Camaraderie and its discontents: Class consciousness, ethnicity and divergent masculinities among Zimbabwean migrant farmworkers in South Africa', *Journal of Southern African Studies*, 36:2, pp. 377–93.

Bourdieu, Pierre (1999). 'Rethinking the state: Genesis and structure of the bureaucratic field' in George Steinmetz (ed.), *State/Culture: State-Formation after the Cultural Turn*. Cornell University Press, Ithaca and London.

Brockington, Daniel and James Igoe (2006). 'Eviction for conservation: A global overview', *Conservation and Society*, 4:3, pp. 424–70.

Christensen, Asger and Niels Harild (2009). *Forced Displacement: The development challenge*. World Bank (Social Development Department), Washington, DC.

De Bruijn, Mirjam Rijk Van Dijk, Dick Foeken (eds) (2001). *Mobile Africa: Changing patterns of movement in Africa and beyond.* Brill, Leiden, Boston and Köln.

Downing, Theodore E. (2002). *Avoiding New Poverty: Mining-induced displacement and resettlement*, Mining Minerals for Sustainable Development Project Report No. 58, International Institute for Environment and Development, London, at: http://www.indiaenvironmentportal.org.in/files/7_17.pdf.

Finnström, Sverker (2008). *Living with Bad Surroundings: War, history and everyday moments in northern Uganda.* Duke University Press, Durham, NC.

Hammar, Amanda (2001). '"The day of burning": Eviction and reinvention in the margins of northwest Zimbabwe', *Journal of Agrarian Change*, 1:4, pp. 550–74.

Hammar, Amanda (2006). 'Criminality, security and development: Postcolonial reversals in Zimbabwe's margins' in Lars Buur, Steffen Jensen and Finn Stepputat (eds), *The Security-Development Nexus: Expressions of sovereignty and securitization in Southern Africa.* Nordic Africa Institute, Uppsala.

Hammar, Amanda (2008). 'In the name of sovereignty: Displacement and state making in post independence Zimbabwe', *Journal of Contemporary African Studies*, 26:4, pp. 417–34.

Hammar, Amanda (2010). 'Ambivalent mobilities: Zimbabwean commercial farmers in Mozambique', *Journal of Southern African Studies*, 36:2, pp. 395–416.

Hammar, Amanda (ed.) (2014). *Displacement Economies in Africa: Paradoxes of crisis and creativity*. Zed Books, London.

Hammar, Amanda, JoAnn McGregor and Loren Landau (2010). 'Introduction: Displacing Zimbabwe: Crisis and construction in Southern Africa', *Journal of Southern African Studies*, 36:2, pp. 263–83.

Hanlon, Joseph and Teresa Smart (2008). *Do Bicycles Equal Development in Mozambique?* James Currey, Rochester, NY.

IDMC and Norwegian Refugee Council (2010). *Internal Displacement in Africa*, at: http://www.internal-displacement.org/publications/global-overview-2010-africa.pdf.

Jackson, Michael (2004). *In Sierra Leone*. Duke University Press, Durham and London.

Jones, Jeremy (2010). '"Nothing is straight in Zimbabwe": The rise of the Kukiya-kiya economy 2000–2008', *Journal of Southern African Studies*, 36:2, pp. 285–99.

Lubkemann, Stephen (2008). 'Involuntary immobility: On a theoretical invisibility in forced migration studies', *Journal of Refugee Studies*, 21:4, pp. 454–75.

Lubkemann, Stephen (2010). *Culture in Chaos: An anthropology of the social condition in war*. Chicago University Press, Chicago and London.

Magaramombe, Godfrey (2010). 'Agrarian displacements, replacements and resettlement: "Displaced in place" farm workers in Mazowe district', *Journal of Southern African Studies*, 36:2, pp. 361–75.

Mavedzenge, B.Z., J. Mahenehene, F. Murimbarimba, I. Scoones and W. Wolmer (2008). 'The dynamics of real markets: Cattle in southern Zimbabwe following land reform', *Development and Change*, 39:4, pp. 613–39.

Massey, Doreen (2005). *For Space*. Sage Publications, London and New Delhi.

Pierre, Jemima (2006). 'Anthropology and the race of/for Africa' in Paul Tiyambe Zeleza (ed.), *The Study of Africa*, Vol. I, *Disciplinary and Interdisciplinary Encounters*. Codesria, Dakar.

Roy, Arundhati (1999). *The Cost of Living*. Flamingo, London.

Rutherford, Blair (2001). *Working on the Margins: Black workers, white farmers in postcolonial Zimbabwe*. Zed Books, London and Weaver Press, Harare.

Rutherford, Blair (2008). 'An unsettled belonging: Zimbabwean farm workers in Limpopo province, South Africa', *Journal of Contemporary African Studies*, 26:4, pp. 401–15.

Scoones, Ian (2008). 'A new start for Zimbabwe?', Livelihoods After Land Reform (LALR) website, 15 September 2008, at: http://www.lalr.org.za/news/a-new-start-for-zimbabwe-by-ian-scoones.

Scoones Ian, Nelson Marongwe, Blasio Mavedzenge, Felix Murimbarimba, Jacob Mahenehene and Chrispen Sukume (2010). *Zimbabwe's Land Reform: Myths and realities*. Weaver Press, Harare; Jacana, Johannesburg; and James Currey, Rochester, NY.

Scudder, Thayer (1973). 'The human ecology of big projects: River basin development and resettlement', *Annual Review of Anthropology*, 2, pp. 45–55.

Solidarity Peace Trust (2009). *'Gone to Egoli'. Economic survival strategies in Matabeleland: A preliminary study*. Solidarity Peace Trust, Port Shepstone, South Africa.

Stahn, Carsten (2007). 'Responsibility to protect: Political rhetoric of emerging legal norm?', *American Journal of International Law*, 101:1, pp. 99–120.

Turton, David (2003). 'Refugees and "other forced migrants"', Refugee Studies Centre Working Paper 13, International Development Centre, University of Oxford.

Vigh, Henrik (2008). 'Crisis and chronicity: Anthropological perspectives on continuous conflict and decline', *Ethnos*, 73:1, pp. 5–24.

Watts, Michael (2004). 'Resource curse? Governmentality, oil and power in the Niger delta, Nigeria', *Geopolitics*, 9:1, pp. 50–80.

Worby, Eric (2010). 'Address unknown: The temporality of displacement and the ethics of disconnection among Zimbabwean migrants in Johannesburg', *Journal of Southern African Studies*, 36:2, pp. 417–31.

Zawe, Conrade (2006). 'Reforms in turbulent times: A study in the theory and practice of three irrigation management policy reform models in Mashonaland, Zimbabwe', unpublished PhD thesis, Wageningen University.

Zeleza, Paul Tiyambe (2006). 'Introduction: The disciplining of Africa' in Paul Tiyambe Zeleza (ed.), *The Study of Africa*, Vol. 1, *Disciplinary and Interdisciplinary Encounters*. Codesria, Dakar.

Zetter, Roger (2007). 'More labels, fewer refugees: Remaking the refugee label in an era of globalization', *Journal of Refugee Studies*, 20:2, pp. 172–92.

CHAPTER 7

Primitive Accumulation: Concept, Similarities and Varieties

Rune Skarstein[1]

Introduction

> ...instead of the economic system being embedded in social relationships, these relationships were now embedded in the economic system.
>
> POLANYI 1947

Since the fall of communism in the Soviet Union and Eastern Europe, economic development is generally – and most often implicitly – understood as *capitalist* development. Mainstream development economics emphasizes primarily structural change, the growth of national and export markets, the way in which market-driven competition stimulates technological progress and a rise in labour productivity. It also discusses the importance of entrepreneurship and the role of the state in establishing infrastructure to foster structural change and economic growth. Pre-capitalist peasant agriculture is "modernized", and peasants are drawn into market relationships and wage labour in a harmonious process virtually without any resistance or conflicts. According to mainstream development economics, the triumph of capitalism implies only winners and no losers.

Marx's Concept of Primitive Accumulation

This view is rejected by classical social scientists as diverse as Karl Marx and Karl Polanyi. They both emphasize that a basic characteristic of capitalism is that land (as a collective term for all natural resources) and labour are *commodified* in processes involving grave conflicts, resulting in several winners but also many losers.[2] Referring to the rise of capitalism in England, Marx – in chapters 26–28 of

1 I am indebted to Amit Bhaduri, Kjell J. Havnevik and Roberto Iacono, as well as two anonymous referees, for comments and suggestions on earlier drafts of this article.

2 Of course, I could add several other theorists sharing the view of Marx and Polanyi on this particular issue, e.g. Max Weber (1923/1991).

 | DOI 10.1163/9789004305465_008

the first volume of *Capital* – analyses the process of the commodification of land and labour, which he (in an ironic allusion to Adam Smith) terms "so-called primitive accumulation" (Marx 1867/1976: 873–904).[3] He notes that, historically, the accumulation of capital "seems to turn around in a never-ending circle, which we can only get out of by assuming a primitive accumulation ... which precedes capitalist accumulation; an accumulation which is not the result of the capitalist mode of production but its point of departure" (ibid.: 873). The "point of departure" of capitalism is robbery of the immediate pre-capitalist producers of their means of production and livelihoods, of land, forests, water and other resources, forcing them to become vagabonds and beggars or, at best, people dependent on selling their labour power: "In actual history, it is a notorious fact that conquest, enslavement, robbery, murder, in short, force, play the greatest part... As a matter of fact, the methods of primitive accumulation are anything but idyllic" (ibid.: 874). Marx goes on to specify the essential aspects of primitive accumulation:

> The process, therefore, which creates the capital-relation can be nothing other than the process which divorces the worker from the ownership of the conditions of his own labour; it is a process which operates two transformations, whereby the social means of subsistence and production are turned into capital, and the immediate producers are turned into wage-labourers. So-called primitive accumulation, therefore, is nothing else than the historical process of divorcing the producer from the means of production. It appears as "primitive" because it forms the pre-history of capital, and of the mode of production corresponding to capital. ... The expropriation of the agricultural producer, of the peasant, from the soil is the basis of the whole process.
>
> MARX 1867/1976: 875–876

In short, the basic features of primitive accumulation are twofold. One aspect is the expropriation of the pre-capitalist immediate producers from their means of production and livelihoods, transforming land and other natural resources, as well as labour, into commodities. The other aspect is that the expropriated populations will have "nothing to sell but their labour power", and they are thus ready to be exploited by capital, as wage labourers. In other words, Marx's message is that the accumulation of capital depends on land and other natural

3 In a footnote Marx quotes Smith's *Wealth of Nations*, Introduction to Book II: "The accumulation of stock must, in the nature of things, be previous to the division of labour." In the original German edition Marx uses the expression "ursprüngliche Akkumulation" – "original accumulation" – which I think is a more appropriate term.

resources as its material basis, as well as on labour power to add value to material "inputs". For the capitalist mode of production to expand, the immediate producers therefore have to be expropriated from their land and other natural resources, being turned into a "reserve army of unemployed", i.e. both land and labour power are made ready to be integrated into the circuit of capital.[4]

Primitive accumulation will be repeated whenever capitalism increases its territory, i.e. conquers and destroys pre-capitalist modes of production, in a process always called "development" in the mainstream literature. Precisely because this process takes place outside the circuit of capital and is a process of conquering land and labour for the accumulation of capital, "conquest, enslavement, robbery, murder, in short, force, play the greatest part". Therefore, primitive accumulation is a deeply political process. As long as the "never-ending circle of capital" does not encompass all natural resources and all labour power, there is scope for further expansion of the capitalist mode of production. In other words, primitive accumulation is not history, but an ongoing process where the capitalist mode of production is expanding by destroying pre-capitalist modes of production, under the name of "development".

Karl Polanyi: Society becoming an "Adjunct to the Market"

In this respect, Marx's view is shared by Karl Polanyi, although Polanyi uses different terms. He notes that:

> The outstanding discovery of recent historical and anthropological research is that man's economy, as a rule, is submerged in his social relationships. He does not act so as to safeguard his individual interest in the possession of material goods; he acts so as to safeguard his social standing, his social claims, his social assets.
>
> POLANYI 1957: 46

Polanyi argues that, before the advent of capitalism, economic life was governed by three principles: *householding* (i.e. production for own use), *reciprocity* and *redistribution* (ibid.: 47–55). Of course, some kinds of market transactions existed also under these principles, long before the era of capitalism:

---

4 "The circuit of capital is a unified process of circulation and production, it includes both… [T]his whole process presupposes the capitalist character of the production process and hence this production process itself as a basis, as well as the specific social relations determined by it" (Marx 1884/1978: 139, 142).

> No society could, naturally, live for any length of time unless it possessed an economy of some sort; but previously to our time no economy has ever existed that, even in principle, was controlled by markets. In spite of the chorus of academic incantations so persistent in the nineteenth century, gain and profit made on exchange never before played an important part in human economy. Though the institution of the market was fairly common since the later Stone Age, its role was no more than incidental to economic life… [U]p to the end of the Middle Ages, markets played no important part in the economic system; other institutional patterns prevailed.
>
> IBID.: 43, 55

Like Marx, Polanyi holds that the commodification of land (including all types of natural resources) and labour represents the decisive step in the establishment of what he calls "the market system" or "the market economy" – what Marx calls "the capitalist mode of production". He agrees with Marx that this transformation has always taken place by means of force, repression and fraud. But, unlike Marx, he claims that land and labour are not, and cannot be, real commodities:

> The crucial point is this: land, labour and money are essential elements in industry; they also must be organized in markets; in fact these markets form an absolutely vital part of the economic system. But labour, land and money are obviously not commodities; the postulate that anything that is bought and sold must have been produced for sale is emphatically untrue in regard to them… The commodity description of land, labour and money is entirely fictitious. Nevertheless, it is with the help of this fiction that the actual markets for land, labour and money are organized; their demand and supply are real magnitudes; and any measures or policies that would inhibit the formation of such markets would *ipso facto* endanger the self-regulation of the system… Undoubtedly, labour, land and money markets *are* essential to the market economy. But no society could stand the effects of such a system of crude fictions even for the shortest stretch of time unless its human and natural substance as well as its business organization was protected against the ravages of this satanic mill.
>
> IBID.: 72–73

Polanyi emphasizes that the commodification of land, labour and money implies a profound change in society:

> [T]he control of the economic system by the market is of overwhelming consequence to the whole organization of society: it means no less than the running of society as an adjunct to the market. Instead of economy

> being embedded in social relations, social relations are embedded in the economic system… A self-regulating market demands nothing less than the institutional separation of society into an economic and political sphere.[5]
>
> IBID.: 57, 71

David Harvey: "Accumulation by Dispossession"

David Harvey raises two points of criticism against Marx's notion of primitive accumulation. First, he claims that Marx "does not consider this possibility except in the case of the creation of an industrial reserve army through technologically induced unemployment" (Harvey 2005: 143). However, as we have seen, Marx actually argues that the most fundamental aspect of primitive accumulation is capital's expropriation of the immediate producers from their livelihoods and means of production. In Marx's words: "The expropriation of the agricultural producer, of the peasant, from the soil is the basis of the whole process." Second, David Harvey holds that Marx considers "so-called primitive accumulation" as a finished historical process that is "no longer relevant", in other words, that it does not take place any more (ibid.: 144). Implying that Marx had another view, he (rightly) argues that "All the features of primitive accumulation that Marx mentions have remained powerfully present within capitalism's historical geography up until now" (ibid.: 145). To emphasize that his view diverges from that of Marx, he writes: "Since it seems peculiar to call an ongoing process 'primitive' or 'original' I shall…substitute these terms by the concept of 'accumulation by dispossession'" (ibid.: 144).

This is a misrepresentation of Marx. Certainly, in *Capital* he analyses the history of primitive accumulation in England, noting that "only in England, which we therefore take as our example, has it [primitive accumulation] the classical form". But he also stresses that primitive accumulation is an ongoing process:

> In Western Europe, the homeland of political economy, the process of primitive accumulation has more or less been accomplished… It is otherwise in the colonies. There the capitalist regime constantly comes up against the obstacle presented by the producer, who, as owner of his own conditions of labour, employs that labour to enrich himself instead of the capitalist… Where the capitalist has behind him the power of the mother country, he tries to use force to clear out of the way the modes of production and appropriation which rest on the personal labour of the independent producer.
>
> MARX 1867/1976: 931

5 See also Polanyi (1947: 112, 114).

While Marx's concept of primitive accumulation deals with capital's conquest and destruction of pre-capitalist modes of production, Harvey's "accumulation by dispossession" seems to be a rather broad concept, encompassing a long range of phenomena that are more or less internal to the circuit of capital. In his narrative, fundamentally different institutions or social groups are "dispossessed". For example, he includes the loss of pension funds due to the collapse of Enron; the "speculative raiding carried out by hedge funds and other major institutions of finance capital"; privatization of different types of public utilities or assets; selling off of publicly owned companies, etc. (Harvey 2005: 145–161). Certainly, Marx did not consider privatization of public property or public utilities as primitive accumulation, for two reasons. First, he rightly considered the state at his time as "the executive of the ruling class". Second, to the extent that public property existed, he considered that property as already conquered by capital and controlled by the ruling class.

Harvey's view implies that numerous internal aspects of the capitalist process itself can be labelled "accumulation by dispossession". Also, in my assessment, Harvey diverges from Marx by arguing, with reference to Rosa Luxemburg, that an important purpose and function of accumulation by dispossession is to help to "stave off the overaccumulation problem, at least for a while" (ibid.: 158). This means that Harvey's very broad concept of accumulation by dispossession differs considerably from Marx's precise concept of primitive accumulation.[6] My criticism does not imply that "accumulation by dispossession" cannot be useful in analysing some aspects of capitalism. However, I am left with an uneasy impression that David Harvey is trying to demonstrate originality at the cost of Karl Marx.

England: The Classic Case of Primitive Accumulation

The classic and much-analysed example of primitive accumulation is England, where this process was characterized by two waves of enclosures – the first in c.1400 to c.1520, and the second in the period from c.1660 to c.1800. The Black Death around 1350 was an important turning point which triggered a process that finally led to primitive accumulation. The plague led to a dramatic decline in population and, as a consequence, to a shortage of serfs in English feudal agriculture. The class power of serfs vis-à-vis the landed nobility was thus strengthened, and the peasantry started a long-lasting struggle for freedom, which culminated in the great peasant uprising of 1381. The peasants won their freedom, but the landlords succeeded in keeping the land (see Brenner 1976; Hilton 1977). By 1500,

6 For a more comprehensive criticism of Harvey, see e.g. Levien (2011: 454–458).

serfdom had disappeared in England, but the resumption of population growth from the early 1400s onwards strengthened the power of the landed nobility against the peasant tenants, who became increasingly more exploited.

The first wave of enclosures had a defensive character, as a direct aftermath of the Black Death and the subsequent outbreaks of the plague. At times in conflict with the Crown, big landlords, including the Church and monasteries, enclosed vast areas of abandoned as well as still cultivated holdings, and also some common land. The enclosed land was turned into less work-demanding sheep pastures, and wage labourers were hired as fence-builders, herdsmen, slaughterers and shearers. In this way the landlords mitigated the lack of peasant serfs, and they succeeded in maintaining control over their land and reinforcing their property rights. Through the wool exports to the Flemish market, the landlords, as capitalists-to-be, established close networks with the urban bourgeoisie, which represented an important step towards a capitalist agriculture (Tawney 1967/1912: 187–188). Gradually, the process which started with the enclosure of abandoned holdings, led to displacements of numerous small peasants from their plots of cultivated land, and even from their pastures and from firewood resources in the commons. This process was so comprehensive that, between c. 1450 and 1525, about 10 per cent of the villages in the southern part of the Midlands were destroyed (Allen 1992: 66, 163–167).

The second wave of enclosures (from c. 1660 to the late 1700s) had an offensive character. It is often called "parliamentary enclosure", because it was backed by law enacted by a parliament where only the landed nobility was represented. The main aspect of that wave was enclosure of the remaining open fields and amalgamation of the small peasant holdings into large farms, to be rented out to tenants for cultivation using wage labour. Under pressure from competition and the landlords' rent hunger, the tenant farmers sought to reduce costs through the typical capitalist form of technical change, viz. labour-saving innovations.[7] In the process, large numbers of peasants were evicted from their holdings, and the number of employed per acre fell to about half of what it was in 1600. As a result, average labour productivity in English agriculture more than doubled between 1600 and 1800, while land productivity increased far more modestly (Wrigley 2004: 43). Through this process, a large industrial reserve army was created:

7 An important aspect of labour saving was the increased use of horses in agriculture, as well as outside agriculture. E.A. Wrigley shows that in agriculture horses replaced human labour, e.g. in freight work (pulling of carts) and soil tillage. Increased use of horses combined with improved implements for horse-draught (carts, ploughs, harrows) appears to have been the most important labour-saving innovations. In the year 1800, English agriculture (including Wales) had three times more horse power than in 1300 on virtually the same area of cultivated land of c.4.5 million hectares (Wrigley 2006: 456).

> By enclosure it was argued in 1663, people were added to the manufacturing population who previously did not increase the store of the nation but wasted it… A wage-earner who had lost his common rights would be much more dependent on his employer than one who had not. Enclosure, Adam Moore argued in its favour, "will give the poor an interest in toiling, whom terror never yet could enure to travail".
>
> HILL 1991: 51–52

Robert Allen provides several examples of how the amalgamation of holdings into large farms implied a "social revolution", which actually represented the rise of agrarian capitalism. He concludes that:

> Not only were most rural people becoming exclusively dependent on wage income, but the demand for that labour was falling. Enclosures and large farms were the cause of the rise in productivity, but they also caused low wages and unemployment for the majority of the population, and high rents for the rich minority. *Inequality and productivity growth were inextricably linked…* The conclusion is unavoidable – most English men and women would have been better off had the landlords' revolution never occurred.
>
> ALLEN 1992: 8, *21; my italics*

Allen points out that industry, including proto-industries, absorbed very little of the labour force evicted from agriculture (ibid.: 239–262). Actually, the migration of people from England to the "New World", including North America, contributed much more to alleviating the problem of unemployment and poverty caused by the emergence of agrarian capitalism in England. According to the first US Census of 1790, 1.87 million persons were of English ancestry. This figure corresponds to 32 per cent of the estimated population of England in 1751, and 47.5 per cent of the total population of the USA in 1790.[8]

Karl Polanyi notes that the intellectual support for enclosures "appears to take for granted the essence of purely economic progress which is to achieve improvement at the price of social dislocation", and that it hints at how the poor man is "doomed by the rich man's desire for a public improvement which profits him privately". He adds that enclosures turned the majority of the displaced peasants "from decent husbandmen into a mob of beggars and thieves" (Polanyi 1957: 34–35).[9]

The first wave of enclosures in England fuelled the rise of an enormously land-demanding capitalism based on *organic energy*. The central aspect of the second wave was amalgamation of peasant holdings into large capitalist farms,

8 Cf. http://en.wikipedia.org/wiki/1790_United_States_Census.

9 See also Hill (1991: 39–56).

which forced large numbers of peasants out of agriculture to constitute the industrial labour class. This represented the prelude to industrial capitalism based on *fossil fuels* (cf. Wrigley 1988). At the time of the second wave of enclosures, English settlers and trading companies had already started *external colonization*, acquiring land in India, North America and Oceania, and making land in these regions a tradable commodity.

Primitive Accumulation and Colonization

To a large extent, primitive accumulation and colonization appear to be different terms for the same phenomenon. Of course, the trajectories of primitive accumulation have been quite different in different cases and under different historical conditions. At a general level, we may distinguish between the *internal primitive accumulation* (e.g. in England, the first capitalist nation) and the *intruding primitive accumulation* that has taken place through colonization, for example in Africa and India. The former may well be called *internal colonization*, characterized by the landlords' expropriation of the peasants and the attainment of "absolute property rights", leading to capitalism in England. The latter may be called *external colonization*, characterized by European colonizers' and settlers' land grabbing, their expropriation from the indigenous peasantries and the forced conversion of the latter into wage labour. However, in Africa and India today there is a combination of the two forms of colonization, represented by the corporate-led and state-supported acquisition of land and the displacement of people (cf. Bhaduri 2010). Bearing in mind that the basic features of primitive accumulation are overall the same, I will consider these differences in a bit more detail, using North America, India and Africa as examples.

USA: Primitive Accumulation through Conquest of Indigenous Lands

The European colonization of the Americas represents basic patterns of primitive accumulation of a very special kind: violent land grabbing combined with virtual extinction of the indigenous populations.[10] Here we will

10 However, with respect to objectives and organization, the Spanish conquest of South America also exhibits essentially feudal aspects (cf. de las Casas 1552; Stannard 1992: esp. 57–103).

take a closer look at the territories which today constitute the USA, where the process of primitive accumulation can be roughly divided into three stages.

The first stage was classical external colonization, where the state supported and organized the land grabbing of intruding settlers of European origin, while displacing violently the Indian population from their lands. Many of the original settlers became tillers of small and medium-sized family farms, which characterized US agriculture until the early 1900s. In the second stage, there was a dramatic amalgamation and increase of the average size of farms, and a corresponding decline in their number. The number of individual farms dropped by 73 per cent, from 6.7 million in 1930, to 1.8 million in the mid-1990s. Today, only 6 per cent of all US farms account for 75 per cent of total US farm output (cf. Lewontin 1998: 72; Sumner 2014: 147). The average size of commercial farms more than doubled in the period 1987–2007. In that period, acres of maize per corn farm rose from 200 to 600 acres (Sumner 2014: 148).

In the third stage, which after 1950 is closely related to the second one, a rapidly increasing number of US farmers have become "contract farmers", being directed and controlled by agro-corporations on the supply side (credit, investments, seeds, fertilizers, insecticides, veterinary services/control), as well as on the demand side (quality/quantity of output, price, terms of delivery and payment,). As R.C. Lewontin notes, "The farmer does own some of the means of production, land and buildings, but has no control over the labor process or over the alienated product. The farmer has become the typical 'putting out' worker…" There has been a "change in the farmer's position from an independent producer, selling in a market with many buyers, into a proletarian without options…" (Lewontin 1998: 82–83). Large agro-corporations reap the huge profits, while agriculture accounts for only 10 per cent of the value added in the agrifood system (ibid.: 74). Today agro-corporations direct and control US agriculture both "upstream" and "downstream". Agriculture has become a subordinate link in the valorization and accumulation of capital. Primitive accumulation has been completed. In the following we will consider only the first stage of this painful process.

At the time of the European conquest, a large number of Indian people were spread over the vast North American continent. There are great discrepancies in estimates of the size of the Indian population when the first European settlers arrived in what is today the United States. The most recent studies estimate that between 8 million and 12 million people were living north of Mexico, "while some of the more outstanding scholars in the field have begun to suspect that the true figure was even higher than the highest end of this range" (Stannard 1992: 268; cf. also Anderson 2014: 27). The large majority of this population lived in the territories of today's USA (Thornton 1987: 26). By 1800, it had declined to about 600,000, and in the 1890s it was down to 250,000 individuals, most of them living west of the Mississippi (Thornton 1987: 42–43, 47; Thornton 1998: 18–19). This dramatic decline in population – by 95 per cent from 1500 to 1890 – was the result of loss of land and livelihood, war, genocide, malnutrition and the spread of European diseases (such as smallpox, measles, typhoid, syphilis, tuberculosis and influenza epidemics). Thornton notes that we do not know how many Indians were killed in wars with Europeans and Americans up to 1890.[11] But he adds: "the mortality figures are substantial: 150,000?, 250,000?, 500,000? Suffice it to say, American Indians suffered substantial population loss due to warfare stemming from the European arrival and colonization" (Thornton 1987: 49).

The Declaration of Independence, penned by Thomas Jefferson, stated that "all men are created equal", but did not include the Indians who had lived in America for at least 6,000 years, or the black people who were forced to work as slaves on the plantations in the South.[12] Around 1815, the total Indian population east of the Mississippi River was still nearly 100,000, with 200,000 more west of the river. In the period 1801–25, "So much land [in western territories] had been acquired that government surveyors could not keep up with the work required to measure it" (Anderson 2014: 149). In 1817, General Andrew Jackson (later president) stated that, "white settlers in [eastern] territories were 'citizens' and Indians were 'subjects'. As such, Indians had 'no right' to the soil but merely a 'possessory right yielded by the liberality of the United States through humanity'" (Anderson 2014: 144, 148). In other words, the Indian tribes were treated as foreign nations in their own country. Jackson's view became official policy after he was elected president in 1828.

Acquisition of Indian lands was – to begin with – negotiated and had to be ratified by the Senate, as any other international agreement. After negotiations, the settlers received the conquered land virtually free of charge. However, as Ronald Gerste points out, the reality was far uglier: "In most cases, these people were already exhausted by war and were forced to sign the treaties" (Gerste 1990: 34). Whenever settlers or speculators wanted "permanent Indian land", there was a new spiral of violence and displacement of Indian people, supported by the federal state.

11 In 1894, the US Bureau of Census reported that, since 1775, there had been more than 40 Indian wars under the US government (Thornton 1987: 48).

12 However: "Very recent and compelling archeological evidence puts the date for earliest… North American habitation at around 40,000 years B.C. …" (Stannard 1992: 10).

In 1830, Congress accommodated the whites' westward expansion by passing the Indian Removal Act, which authorized the government to displace Indians from their homelands within established states to lands west of the Mississippi River. The Act authorized the president to exchange "unorganized land" in the West for Indian lands in the East. By 1842, only a few thousand Indians were left in the eastern states:

> Of the roughly 100,000 Indians…identified in 1830, over 80,000 had been forcefully removed. The land taken from these Indians was worth billions of dollars, and its sale financed the federal government for years to come.
> ANDERSON 2014: 171

In 1834, Congress adopted more legislation – the Act to Regulate Trade and Intercourse with Indian Tribes and to Preserve Peace on the Frontiers. All that part of the United States west of the Mississippi River and not within the states of Missouri or Louisiana or the territory of Arkansas, should be Indian country, where no white persons would be permitted to settle or to pass through without the consent of the Indians. The borders to Indian land should be protected by the military force of the United States. However, before the law could come into force, a new wave of white settlers swept westwards. The first Indians to face forced expulsion from their lands west of the Mississippi River were in Texas, which entered the American Union in 1845 (Anderson 2014: 175). As a consequence of the westward wave, the Congress shifted the "permanent Indian frontier" from the Mississippi River to the ninety-fifth meridian (Brown 1972: 5–6; Anderson 2014: 173–191).

However, in 1848, gold was discovered in California. Within a few months, thousands of fortune-seeking white easterners were crossing Indian territory. In 1849 alone, some 50,000 "Americans" mounted the trail (Anderson 2014: 192–193). As a consequence of the social and economic aspects of the gold rush, the Indian population in California was reduced from an estimated 150,000 in 1845 to about 35,000 by 1860, and less than 18,000 in 1890 (ibid.; Stannard 1992: 145). In 1850, California became the thirty-first state of the Union. But none of the hundred or more Indian tribes along the Pacific coast had been consulted on the matter beforehand. In 1858, Minnesota became a state, its boundaries being extended a hundred miles beyond the "permanent Indian frontier" (Brown 1972: 7–8).

To justify the brutal westward expansion and the systematic breaches of the "permanent Indian frontier", the newspaper editor John L. O'Sullivan in 1845 coined the phrase "Manifest Destiny", as the "design of Providence" – a perfect parallel to Kipling's "white man's burden". "Manifest Destiny" was eagerly taken up by the policy makers in Washington, who now insisted that the Europeans and their descendants were ordained by destiny (i.e. the Christian God) to rule all of America. They were the dominant race and therefore responsible for the Indians – along with their lands, their forests and their mineral wealth. Only the New Englanders (who had already destroyed or driven out all the Indian population) spoke against "Manifest Destiny" (Brown 1972: 7–8).

Ironically, the most cooperative Indian tribes were among the first victims of colonization. Benjamin Hawkins, assigned as US agent to the south-eastern tribes, advised them in establishing private property, in European-style farming, and even in taking up slaveholding for work on plantations. These tribes also established their own school system. However, in 1838 President Jackson used military force to gather and transport the Cherokees to infertile lands west of the Mississippi River. About 17,000 Indians, along with approximately 2,000 black slaves held by the Cherokees, were brutally expelled from Georgia. This forced displacement led to the death of an estimated 3,000 to 4,000 Cherokees on the "Trail of Tears" (Carter 1976: 232–238, 253–266; Gerste 1990: 34; Anderson 2014: 117–127, 157, 170). Russell Thornton summarizes the US government's destruction of the livelihoods of the Indian population as follows:

> Among the concerted efforts to destroy Indian ways of life were the Spanish missions in California, Florida and Texas; the US government's attempts to make Plain Indians into cattle rangers and Southern Indians into American farmers; and efforts by churches and governments to undermine Indian religious, governmental, and kinship systems. Most dramatic and perhaps most important, however, were the often deliberate destructions of flora and fauna that American Indians used for food and other purposes. Such destructions were "the strategy universally adopted by European troop commanders, who warred against Indians...destroying their crops, knowing that they thus destroyed the tribes' basic food supply" (Jennings 1975). The most glaring example of animal reduction – probably the most destructive to American Indians – was the near extinction of the buffalo, which culminated during the last half of the nineteenth century.
>
> THORNTON 1987: 51

In many Indian tribes, women carried out sophisticated cultivation of several varieties of crops, such as maize, beans and squash. However, in virtually all tribes, hunting and fishing represented essential components of their nutrition. Hunting demanded large areas of land per person. For example, the Sioux (or Dakota) – the last of the great Indian nations to be defeated by the whites – were basically nomads who followed the annual movements of the buffalo. For them, the buffalo represented the most important means of subsistence, and it also had religious significance. From the buffalo they got meat for food, skins for clothes, and cover for their *tipis*. But, as Thornton notes in the quotation above, within a few years the whites managed virtually to eradicate the buffalo, which was also a decisive step in destroying the Sioux population.

> Along with exterminating the bison, the whites also captured the land of the Sioux. During the ten years preceding the Civil War, more than 150,000 white settlers pushed into Santee country, thus rupturing the left flank of the once "permanent Indian frontier". As a result of two deceptive treaties, the woodland Sioux surrendered nine-tenths of their land and were crowded into a narrow strip of territory along the Minnesota River. From the beginning, agents and traders hovered around them like buzzards around the carcasses of slaughtered buffalo, systematically cheating them out of the greater part of the promised annuities for which they had been persuaded to give up their lands.
>
> BROWN 1972: 32

The Civil Rights Bill adopted in 1866 gave "equal rights to all persons born in the United States", *except Indians*. While the Civil War raged and Afro-Americans were proclaimed free, the US government continued its policies of submission, forced displacement and extermination of the Indian population. But apparently, the war gave the Sioux a little breathing space and improved their capacity to organize resistance against the whites' ruthless invasion. Under the leadership of the Oglala Chief Red Cloud, they forced the whites to sign a treaty (1868), renouncing patrolling by the military of the Bozeman Trail, which led straight through the land of the Sioux to the gold mines in Montana. The whites had to give up three established military forts. This was the first time that they had to back down in a confrontation with the Indians.

In the early 1870s, General George Armstrong Custer reported to the government in Washington that the Black Hills "were filled with gold 'from the grass roots down'... By 1874 there was such a bad clamour from gold-hungry Americans that the Army was ordered to make a reconnaissance into the Black Hills" (Brown 1972: 220). In plain words: a military invasion into the heartland of the Sioux people. However, the Indians remained calm and did not provoke the army in any way: "So the whites had to take the initiative without the slightest legitimacy for their aggression" (Gerste 1990: 34). The leader of the US Seventh Cavalry's attack at Little Bighorn River was General George A. Custer, "that egocentric man whose leitmotif was eternal fame and the road to the White House" (ibid.). The US soldiers met surprisingly strong resistance: "For the first time, the old impediments to Indian warfare – division and lack of discipline – had been overcome, but far too late" (ibid.). All the western Sioux, the Cheyenne and other tribes had united for that battle. In the attack on the morning of 25 June 1876, General Custer and all his 250 or so soldiers were killed (ibid.; Brown 1972: 230–236). The unbelievable and complete victory of the Sioux shattered the United States at the zenith of the celebration of the Union's 100 years.

But the victory of the Sioux at Little Bighorn was a pyrrhic one: they had already lost almost all their land, and were crowded together in reservation confinements, tortured by hunger and disease. The whites' cruel revenge for the defeat at Little Bighorn came in December 1890. Frightened by the murder of the legendary Chief Sitting Bull on 15 December, a group of Indians under the leadership of the seriously ill Chief Big Foot set off for Pine Ridge, where they hoped Chief Red Cloud and his people would accord them protection from the US soldiers: "Their only aim was security for themselves and their families" (Gerste 1990: 34). Near the cavalry camp at Wounded Knee Creek, they were halted and carefully counted: 120 men and 230 women and children (Brown 1972: 349). Surrounded by military watchmen, the hungry, frozen and exhausted refugees were assigned a campsite for the night near the military camp. In the morning of 29 December, the military commander Colonel George A. Forsyth informed the Indians that they should surrender all their weapons. They were disarmed without resistance, and a few (mostly antiquated) rifles were handed over to the soldiers (Gerste 1990: 34).[13]

Soon afterwards, about 500 soldiers, most of them from the reconstituted Seventh Cavalry under the leadership of General Forsyth, started massacring the virtually defenceless Indians.[14] One estimate placed the final death toll at nearly 300 of the 350 men, women and children. The US soldiers lost 25 dead and 39 wounded, most of them struck by their own bullets or shrapnel (Brown 1972: 351).

At Wounded Knee, the white American soldiers lived up to their slogan that "The only good Indian is a dead Indian." Many voices in the American public praised this "revenge for Custer". Colonel Forsyth was first removed from his position, but shortly thereafter reinstated by the war ministry in Washington. Even worse, the government awarded the gunnery officer Paul Weinert the highest US military decoration, the Medal of Honor, for his mass murder at Wounded Knee. The massacre was the last of the major violent confrontations between the whites and the Indians, and spelled an end to the Indians' hopes for a life with dignity.

To this day, the Indian population is compressed into reservation confinements, casinos represent the leading industry, and gambling revenue offers the main income. In the late nineteenth century, the United States established

13 Brown (1972: 350) writes that reportedly "The troopers found only two rifles, one of them a new Winchester."

14 This massacre is a central theme of the Hollywood film *Little Big Man* (1970).

boarding schools for the children of Indians. These were often run by Christian missionaries. The children were taken away from their homes, forbidden to speak their own language, indoctrinated with Christianity, and denied the right to practise their native religions. Investigations have documented the sexual, physical and mental abuse of the children that took place in these schools (Smith 2007). In these and other ways, the white Americans' humiliation of the Indian population continued long into the twentieth century: some of these boarding schools closed only in the 1960s.

In 2004, Republican Senator Sam Brownback (from Kansas) introduced a joint resolution to "offer an apology to all Native Peoples on behalf of the United States", for past "ill-conceived policies" by US governments. In 2009, President Barack Obama signed the historic apology into law. But even today, the majority of Native Americans wait in vain for a life of dignity in American society.

Contemporary India: Primitive Accumulation by Means of Internal Colonization

> ... If you have to suffer, you should do so in the interest of the country...
> J. Nehru, while laying the foundation stone for the Hirakud Dam in Orissa in 1948.

In an analysis focusing on India, Amit Bhaduri argues that the political independence of the former colonies only meant a change of direction in the hunt for natural resources in these areas, meaning also a change of direction in primitive accumulation:

> In post-colonial societies, decolonisation merely changed the direction but not the goal of this violent hunt for natural resources. As countries that were once formal or informal colonies gain political independence, the more successful among them join the march of civilisation in the name of "development" only to become colonisers themselves... If a lack of strength does not allow them to conquer other lands and people, regions inside the country are identified for the hunt of natural resources. Imperialism turns inwards, and the latecomers in the race wage war against their own citizens, but this time in the name of developing them. Nevertheless, with the hunt for resources turning inwards history begins to repeat itself, but this time perhaps as a farce. Development again becomes a class project despite the attempts at giving it the face of a nationalist project.
>
> BHADURI 2010: 12

The process of land acquisition and displacement of the local people for "development" purposes has accelerated since the mid-1990s, under the neo-liberal "reform" regime. Large areas of land and water resources have been expropriated from farmers and tribal people for the construction of hydro-power plants, for mines, manufacturing industries, and for highways. A massive land grabbing by large corporations is going on in various guises, systematically supported by the land-acquisition policies of both the federal and the state governments. While favouring the corporations, the central government has neglected agriculture and rural areas by reducing public investments, privatizing health services, etc.[15]

Special Economic Zones (SEZs) have become a main vehicle for the acquisition of land. By 2010, the central government had approved 513 SEZs in 19 states across India. The land area acquired for these zones, deemed "foreign territories", amounted to close to 200,000 hectares (ha), which is greater than the area of Delhi in the National Capital Region (Asher and Atmavilas 2011: 319–320). Similarly, mining rights and land for hydropower plants are being granted to national and foreign corporations, mostly on tribal lands (Bhaduri 2009: 51–52).

These zones are justified by the Indian authorities as necessary to achieve development, by attracting direct foreign investment, and to escape the imminent balance-of-payments crisis. Foreign direct investors are enticed by exemption from taxes and duties, and from labour and environment legislation, and are offered low-cost energy, water supply and other infrastructure (Asher and Atmavilas 2011: 333–334).[16] In other words, industrial sites with developed economic infrastructure offering generous tax holidays are important incentives in attracting national and foreign corporations to the SEZs.[17] Another important attraction is ample availability of low-cost, sufficiently educated and disciplined labour (e.g. Levien 2011: 461).

According to the SEZ Act of 2005, the Development Commissioner represents the authority and executive power of the central government over the SEZs. In practice, he can dismiss local resistance to the establishment and running of SEZs. The Scheduled Areas Act of 1996 requires the *panchayat*

15 Public investment in agriculture declined from 3.51 per cent of agricultural GDP in 1981–85, to 1.41 per cent in 2001–03 (Chand 2010: 49). The ratio of income per worker in non-agriculture to agriculture rose from 2.85 in 1978/79–1983/84 to 5.22 in 1998/99–2003/04, while the number of undernourished people in rural India rose from an estimated 190 million in 1993/94 to 357 million in 2004/05 (Reddy and Mishra 2010: 28–29).

16 The SEZ Act, listing the incentives to investors is available at: http://www.csez.com/documents/sezact.pdf.

17 "As a Mahinda manager told me, about 80% of the companies are interested in the SEZ solely for income tax benefit" (Levien 2011: 461).

(local government) to consult the *gram sabha* (local people's assembly) on land acquisitions. However, there are several examples, e.g. in Jharkhand and Odisha, of this stipulation being systematically ignored, and of the police surrounding ordinary members in the *gram sabha* meetings in a threatening manner (Bhaduri 2009: 52).

An amendment to the SEZ Act requires at least 50 per cent of the land acquired to be used for "processing", i.e. producing goods and services that target the domestic elite and foreign markets. On the rest of the land, the SEZ can develop luxury housing or "lifestyle activities" or whatever other projects it wants. This possibility represents an economic incentive not only for the establishment of SEZs, but also for rampant land speculation both inside and around the SEZ (Asher and Atmavilas 2011: 327–330; Levien 2011: 458).[18]

The SEZ developer is an economic and legal entity in its own right – most often a private real estate company.[19] The local state disposes of common-property land and can, in addition, acquire land through expropriation from the local population for sale to the SEZ for the development of infrastructure, such as water, sewerage and energy supply. These expropriations have, in most cases, taken place under the colonial Land Acquisition Act of 1894 (Asher and Atmavilas 2011: 324).

While the central government provides the overall policy framework for SEZs, states compete to offer further incentives to attract particular companies to set up SEZs in their state. Like other big projects, such as mines, steel plants and car factories, deals for large SEZs are regulated by a Memorandum of Understanding between the state and the SEZ, which is often kept secret (Levien 2011: 462). The SEZ will then lease out at least 50 per cent of the land to local or foreign enterprises to produce goods or services, mostly on long-term tenure contracts, and will keep the rest of the land for its own profit. In his study of the SEZ called Mahindra World City (MWC) in Rajasthan, Michael Levien gives a concise account of the expropriation process:

18 For example, at the Mihan SEZ in Nagpur, "about a million small and big investors have invested in plots or farmland beyond the city limits with the hope that prices will appreciate. Relators estimate at least 200,000 individuals to be engaged in land brokering in and around Nagpur" (Asher and Atmavilas 2011: 328). Asher and Atmavilas quote Kanchiram Rana, member of the Parliamentary Standing Committee reviewing SEZs, as saying that "There is heavy land speculation around all the proposed SEZs in India. Land prices in these areas are hitting sky-high levels" (ibid.: 328–329).

19 In September 2006, the Reserve Bank of India issued a notification asking commercial banks to treat SEZ s the same as any other real estate project when it comes to lending (Asher and Atmavilas 2011: 327).

> To enable this land development function [of the SEZ], the government forcibly acquired private farmland and public grazing land from farmers and sold it to Mahindra at a low price that only reflects its government-listed agricultural value plus administrative fees... Under its enacting legislation, the Jaipur Development Authority [JDA, the state's executive body] could...transfer the 1,000 acres of grazing land in the area to MWC without the approval of the local government (*panchayat*). For the privately owned farmland, the JDA started formal *eminent domain* proceedings, using the central Land Acquisition Act. There was no consultation with affected farmers, most of whom first learned of the project when notice of the land acquisition was posted in local newspapers... The SEZ developer is thus a capitalist rentier who, with state assistance, commodifies rural land for urban uses and captures the windfall between the artificially low price of dispossessed agricultural land and its industrial, commercial and residential value minus development costs.
>
> LEVIEN 2011: 459, 462

The establishment of corporate-led hydropower plants and mining, as well as industry projects within SEZs is based on forced displacement of very large numbers of people. The internally displaced persons (IDPs) and project-affected persons (PAPs), dispossessed of livelihood and habitat, are the true victims of land acquisition and of the neglect of agriculture. According to one estimate, the acquisition of 25 million ha of land for industrial sites, hydropower plants, mines and highways had resulted in around 60 million IDPs/PAPs up until 2004, i.e. *before* the SEZ Act came into effect. This total land area included 7 million ha of forests and 6 million ha of other common property resources (Fernandes 2011: 303).

The main victims of these acquisitions are the two groups of people at the bottom of the social ladder: the *adivasis* (about 8 per cent of the total Indian population) who have their homeland in some of the most resource-rich regions of India, and the *dalits* (16 per cent), who are treated as rejects of Hindu society – untouchables. Together, these two groups are among the poorest in rural India (Bhaduri 2010: 13). The "tribal" proportion among the IDPs/PAPs has been put at 40 per cent. Studies also show that more than 20 per cent of IDPs/PAPs are *dalits* (Fernandes 2011: 305). The so-called rehabilitation of the IDPs/PAPs has been negligible (Asher and Atmavilas 2011: 322, 331). The affected families are often not even paid the "compensation" they were promised for the loss of land (Dhagamwar 2011: 223). One report points out that almost 30 years after the massive Bhakra-Nangal hydropower project was completed, only 730 of the 2,108 displaced families had been resettled (Dharmadhikary 2005).

As well as destroying the livelihood of large tribal and lower-caste sections of the population, the acquisition of land causes distress to small farmers, who are very often displaced to less fertile land. The ratio of the number of landless agricultural workers to the total agricultural working population has risen considerably. In 1951, about 72 per cent were cultivators and 28 per cent landless agricultural workers. In 2011, 45 per cent were cultivators and 55 per cent landless workers (Bhaduri 2015: 18, note 8). As Fernandes points out: "An obvious result of landlessness is joblessness, because the land the IDPS/PAPS lose to the project is their sustenance, both in the form of food and work. So its loss deprives them of both" (Fernandes 2011: 309). Hence landlessness equates to impoverishment, and impoverishment forces many IDPS/PAPS into debt or labour bondage, or into child labour, prostitution and crime. Displacement also leads to increased pressure on the remaining non-privatized land (ibid.: 310–311).

As a result of increased misery and poverty, there is a rising rate of suicide among farmers. In India as a whole, the suicide rate among male farmers almost doubled from 10.5 per 1,000 in 1995 to 18.2 in 2006; in Andhra Pradesh it rose from 13.6 to 41.6; and in Maharashtra from 14.7 to 62.6 (Reddy and Mishra 2010: 31). Since the late 1990s, more than 15,000 impoverished peasants have committed suicide every year (cf. Sanhati Collective 2012: 2).

The corporate industries have not provided the expropriated and poor farmers with decent new employment opportunities. The growth of employment in the organized industrial sector has been minimal (or non-existent) since the market reforms started (Singh 2006; Bhaduri 2010: 59–60). Instead, the displaced people migrating to urban areas in search of a livelihood are brutally exploited:

> Subcontracting to the unorganized sector along with casualization of labour on a large scale become convenient devices to ensure longer working hours without higher pay. Self-employed workers, totalling 260 million, expanded fastest during the high-growth regime, providing an invisible source of labour productivity growth.
>
> BHADURI 2009: 69

What is going on in India is merciless acquisition of land and other natural resources and forced displacement of large numbers of poor people, implying destruction of the livelihood of the poor in the name of industrialization, mining and big dams for power generation and irrigation. At best, the displaced people are forced into casual labour, receiving almost starvation wages. This may aptly be characterized as "development turning perverse" and "development terrorism against the poor" (Bhaduri 2009: 51, 56). As long as this injustice persists, there will be resistance – both armed and unarmed – of the sort we have seen especially in the most resource-rich eastern and central states of West Bengal, Jharkhand, Odisha and Chhattisgarh.[20]

Contemporary Africa: Primitive Accumulation by Means of Land Grabbing

Africa has a bloody history of external colonization: land robbery by European settlers, for plantations and mines. Still today this continent of rich natural resources is being exploited by transnational corporations hunting for oil, copper, diamonds, uranium and gold. And even today local people are losing land or are being displaced, for example for the extraction of oil in the Niger Delta, or for gold mining in North Mara (Tanzania).[21] Mostly these activities take place in close collaboration with the national and local elites. Here I will discuss the more recent phenomenon, already noted, whereby transnational and local corporations, with the support of state and even local authorities, are grabbing the land of smallholders, to establish large farms for the production of food or biofuel feedstock.

According to the Land Matrix, across the world, formal contracts with private corporations for the acquisition of 39.6 million ha (396,000 km^2) had been completed by the end of 2014. That is an area considerably larger than Germany (349,000 km^2). In addition, contracts for about 16 million ha were under negotiation (cf. also Table 7.1).[22] Africa, and in particular Sub-Saharan Africa, appears to be in the forefront of the new wave of land acquisitions, accounting for 45.6 per cent of all land acquisitions in the world at the end of 2014 (Table 7.1). But the exact magnitude of land grabbing in Africa is difficult

20 The resistance, which the mainstream media and many researchers refer to as "India's Maoist menace", has lasted since the early 1990s. In recent years, Indian government politicians have proclaimed that the resistance had been practically extinguished. However, on 26 May 2013 rebels in Chhattisgarh killed 24 politicians of the Congress Party, people "who comprise the 'top brass' of the Party's Chhattisgarh leadership..., the rebels' most politically significant attack in over 20 years" ("India's Maoists far from a spent force", *Asia Times*, 3 June 2013, available at: http://atimes.com/South_Asia/SOU-01-030613.html).

21 On gold mining in North Mara, see Lugoe (2011). Sometimes the resistance to destructive projects succeeds. One example in this regard is the impeded Stigler's Gorge hydropower project in Tanzania, which would have destroyed the livelihood of numerous rice-cultivating smallholders and fishermen in the Lower Rufiji Basin. Cf. Havnevik (1993: 76–81, 263–283).

22 Cf. Land Matrix – February 2015: www.landmatrix.org. The Land Matrix represents a cooperative effort between several research institutions and non-governmental organizations.

TABLE 7.1 *Known formally concluded contracts on land acquisitions by end of 2014. Land area in'000 ha*

	Transnational contracts		Domestic contracts		Total	
Region	'000 ha	Per cent	'000 ha	Per cent	'000 ha	Per cent
Africa	16078	52.8	1982	21.6	18060	45.6
Europe	2903	9.6	1791	19.6	4694	11.9
America	2707	8.9	1012	11.0	3719	9.4
Oceania	2257	7.4	163	1.8	2420	6.1
Asia	6490	21.3	4214	46.0	10704	27.0
World	30435	100.0	9162	100.0	39597	100.0

SOURCE: HTTP://LANDMATRIX.ORG/EN/GET-THE-IDEA/AGRICULTURAL-DRIVERS/ RETRIEVED 25.02.2015

to estimate. The main reason for this is the lack of transparency surrounding these transfers and the reluctance of "host governments", as well as foreign investors, to publish the content of contracts on land deals (Cotula 2011: 1–3, 18; Mousseau et al. 2011: 16). The World Bank notes that "instead of relying on publicity of relevant documents, and independent third-party verification, agreements are surrounded by an air of secrecy that makes public reporting and monitoring near impossible" (World Bank 2011: 71). Therefore, among researchers there seems to be broad agreement that land grabbing is largely underreported. The Land Matrix points out that in particular domestic land acquisition contracts are strongly underreported.

According to information collected by the World Bank in the period from 1 October 2008 to 31 August 2009, 48 per cent of the registered projects and 70 per cent (39.7 million ha) of the area acquired worldwide was in Sub-Saharan Africa (World Bank 2011: 51). A report from 2010 reviewing the literature, estimated that land in Africa transferred to foreign investors amounted to between 51 million and 63 million ha (Friis and Reenberg 2010: 11–12). Especially for some countries, the World Bank reports substantially lower figures than Friis and Reenberg, while other studies report higher figures.[23]

23 The World Bank estimates that in the period 2004–09, total land acquisitions in Ethiopia amounted to 1,190 thousand ha, and in Mozambique 2,670 thousand ha (World Bank 2011: 62). On the other hand, Katundu et al. (2013: 21, 28) report that in Tanzania 117 companies had acquired more than 2 million hectares of land, corresponding to 5.9 per cent of the country's agricultural area. By contrast, Mousseau et al. (2011: 16) report that, with regard

TABLE 7.2 *Land resources and known formally concluded land acquisition contracts in East Africa by end of 2014*

Country	Estimated agricultural area, million ha	Number of contracts	Total contracted land area,'000 ha	Contracted land as % of total agricultural area
Ethiopia	36.5	58	990.9	2.7
Kenya	27.4	5	188.4	0.7
Madagascar	41.4	9	592.6	1.4
Malawi	5.7	3	57.5	10.1
Mozambique	49.9	68	2208.5	4.4
Rwanda	1.9	3	21.1	1.1
Tanzania	40.6	27	276.4	0.7
Uganda	14.2	11	47.0	0.3
Zambia	23.8	21	360.6	1.5
Zimbabwe	16.2	3	391.7	2.4
Total	257.6	208	5134.7	2.0

Agricultural area is defined as potentially cultivable land, not land which is actually cultivated. For seven contracts, corporations are not reported or the contract company is domestic. The remaining 201 contracts (97 per cent) were signed by foreign corporations. Nine contracts where the land area is not reported are not included in the table.
SOURCE: HTTP://WWW.LANDMATRIX.ORG/EN/GET-THE-DETAIL/BY-TARGET-REGION/EASTERN-AFRICA/DATA ON AGRICULTURAL AREA: FAOSTAT LAND RESOURCE DATABASE, HTTP://FAOSTAT3.FAO.ORG/DOWNLOAD/R/RL/E

Data from the Land Matrix Database indicate considerably lower figures than most other reports. That database provides information on formally concluded contracts for a total of 18 million ha of land in the whole of Africa, and formally concluded contracts of 5 million ha of land in East Africa (Tables 7.1 and 7.2). However, Africa is still in the global forefront of land grabbing, accounting for nearly 46 per cent of all concluded contracts and as much as 53 per cent of all transnational contracts, measured in land area (Table 7.1).

In East Africa, almost all land acquisitions are based on contracts between the "host country" and foreign corporations. As a share of potentially cultivable agricultural area, the contracted land varies from almost nil (Uganda) to more than 10 per cent (Malawi), with an average of 2 per cent (Table 7.2). However, the potentially cultivable area is generally many times larger than the actually cultivated area. For example, in Tanzania an estimated area of 14.7 million ha

to foreign investors, "data obtained from national government officials suggests that less than 70,000 ha had actually been formally leased as of December 2010".

of land is cultivated (URT 2013: 46–48). Thus the contracted land area reported in Table 7.2 represents 1.9 per cent of the cultivated area.

There are five important drivers of the new "scramble for land" in Africa. First, the global economic crisis since 2008 has made international capital investments outside the USA and Europe more attractive. Second, the price hike of food (maize, wheat, rice) in 2008–09, which was to a large extent caused by speculation, motivated investment in land for food production (World Bank 2011: 51).[24] Third, rising oil prices in the period 2000–13 and fear of a future scarcity of fossil fuels, combined with policies to avert climate change, have stimulated international investment in land for biofuel feedstock production, especially sugarcane, maize, jatropha and oil palms (Matondi et al. 2011).

Fourth, many governments in Africa consider smallholder agriculture to be an impediment to economic development, claiming implicitly that a transition to large-scale commercial agriculture is necessary in order to achieve higher agricultural productivity and exports, especially of food crops. This view prevails in the political class even in Tanzania, where the smallholders enjoy better legal protection than in probably any other African country. In its draft biofuel guidelines of 2008, the government states:

> Smallholder farmers responsible for 90% of all farm produce underutilize arable land, as production systems remain archaic in tillage, storage and processing.[25]

This is consistent with the government's Agricultural Sector Development Strategy of 2001, which emphasizes that: "*Government will work towards creating an enabling environment for medium and large-scale investors to make use of the abundant land resource in the country*" (URT 2001: not paginated; italics in original). This was followed up in the strategy launched in 2009, called "Agriculture First" ("Kilimo Kwanza"), to modernize agriculture. One "pillar" of that strategy is to make land more available to investors, in order to increase capital flows to the sector.

24 The World Bank reports a strong increase in foreign land acquisitions concomitant with the sudden rise in food prices. From 1 October 2008 to 31 August 2009, 464 projects involving a total of 56.6 million ha were registered. As much as 70 per cent of this area (39.7 million ha) was acquired in Sub-Saharan Africa (World Bank 2011: 51). These figures are much higher than those reported by the Land Matrix. The reason for that may be that the Land Matrix coverage is low, or that many of the projects the World Bank reported in 2011 have failed.

25 URT, *Guidelines for Sustainable Liquid Biofuels Investments and Development in Tanzania (draft)*, Ministry of Energy and Minerals, Dar es Salaam, 2008. Here quoted from Sulle and Nelson (2009: 36).

It should be noted that the governments of other Sub-Saharan countries, too, are sceptical about the possibilities of improving smallholder agriculture. On Mozambique, Timothy A. Wise (of Tufts University) reports the following from a conversation with the economic adviser to the minister of agriculture, Luis Sitoe, related to the huge and largely failed land acquisition project ProSavana, "the largest land grab in Africa":

> I asked Mr. Sitoe…if the lesson of ProSavana was that agricultural development needed to be based on Mozambique's three million small-scale food producers. He smirked again. No, he assured me, the government is committed to foreign investment, with its capital and technology, as the path to agricultural development.
>
> WISE 2015: 4

The fifth driver is the wrongly perceived abundance of land which has motivated international investors to target Sub-Saharan Africa.[26] For example, in Tanzania, which is considered to be one of the most land-abundant countries in Africa, the government has stated that,

> Unlike its neighbours, Tanzania has comparatively abundant land resources. Even though there are substantial areas under various forms of protection, and other areas infested with tsetse fly, there is still land available for expansion of cultivation.[27]
>
> URT 2000: 3

It is not just many African governments that apparently believe there is an abundance of land in Sub-Saharan Africa: the World Bank claims that the potentially cultivable land area is 201 million ha, corresponding to more than 45 per cent of total potentially cultivable land in the world (World Bank 2011: xxxiv).[28] This optimism ignores the fact that Africa's numerous smallholder families survive on very small holdings. For example, for Tanzania Mainland, the National Land Policy of 1995 estimated arable land at 48.7 million ha (NLP 1997: 4). However, the great majority of the more than 30 million people (almost 80 per cent of the population) involved in crop agriculture are members of 5.7 million smallholder families, cultivating about 14.7 million ha of land.

26 For an example of the belief in land abundance, see Purdon (2013). For criticisms of this belief, see Lugoe (2010); and Matondi et al. 2011: 7–10.

27 According to official estimates, about 12.9 million ha, i.e. 26 per cent of the pastoral areas, are affected by tsetse fly and cannot therefore be used for grazing (URT 2000: 28).

28 It appears from Table 7.2, that the Food and Agriculture Organization is even more optimistic, estimating that potentially cultivable land in East Africa alone amounts to 257.6 million ha.

The average land per household is 2.5 ha. Mainly owing to cultivation with fallowing, an average of only 1.6 ha is planted with annual crops (URT 2013: 46, 48). Most of these households also need additional land for collecting fuelwood.

Moreover, there is a considerable population of pastoralists who need large areas of grazing land for their animals. Official figures indicate that Tanzania is made up of about 61 million ha of pasture or grazing land, of which only 37 million ha are permanent pasture. However, the aggregate figure of pasture actually used is about 44 million ha (NLP 1997: 4). This means that a "sizable portion of grazing" is undertaken on about 7 million ha of non-permanent pasture, which "as experience has shown, is vulnerable to harsh weather and climatic conditions" (Lugoe 2010: 6).

In other words, under present conditions in Tanzania there is a large *deficit* of land for permanent pasture in livestock agriculture, while cultivating smallholders are in great need of more acreage. Land abundance turns out to be an illusion.[29] It should be added that more than 30 per cent of the land surface in Tanzania is made up of protected areas, where cultivation is prohibited and grazing severely restricted (USAID 2012: 25–28). A considerable increase in the area of large-scale commercial agriculture may lead to serious conflicts with cultivators and pastoralists, as well as hostilities between these groups, and could have grave ecological consequences (ibid.: 56).[30]

In most of Sub-Saharan Africa, land tenure has, for generations, been based on customary law, where the chief or the elders of the community allocate land to its members. However, most states have adopted national land laws superimposed on customary law. Even in countries where customary land rights enjoy legal protection, such as in Mali or Tanzania, national law considers most rural people to have qualified use rights on land "vested" by the (head of the) state (Shivji 1998). Lorenzo Cotula summarizes the situation as follows:

> The problem is that the customary rights of local people may have no or little recognition under national law. This circumstance is historically rooted in the colonial experience, when colonisers treated conquered lands without visible developments as being empty (*terres vacantes et sans maître*, in French) and brought them under the state ownership, and in decades of post-independence law-making shaped by single-party regimes or military dictatorships... Virtually all countries have legislation

29 Thus, Lugoe's comment appears to be highly relevant: "Statements floating around with regard to land abundance in Tanzania should be based on reality and not wishes as is currently the case" (Lugoe 2010: 7).

30 In the National Land Policy of 1995, this problem seems to be acknowledged: "There are growing social conflicts, environmental concerns and land use conflicts due to haphazard alienation of rangeland for large scale agriculture" (NLP 1997: 35).

> that enables government compulsorily to take [land] rights if it is in the public interest to do so.
>
> COTULA 2011: 17, 33

We have noted that the smallholders in Tanzania probably enjoy more secure land rights than smallholders in most other African countries. However, even in Tanzania customary law represents no guarantee of secure land rights. When a colonial act was abolished in 1963, the executive power of chiefs, headmen and elders in land administration based on customary law was replaced by elected village councils and assemblies. Customary law survived somehow in reality, if not formally. This fact was recognized by the Shivji Commission of 1992, which recommended two forms of land tenure with equal legal status, viz. "granted right of occupancy" and "customary right of occupancy" (Shivji et al. 1994: 160–162). These two forms of land tenure were upheld in the National Land Policy (NLP 1997) of 1995, as well as in the Village Land Act (VLA) of 1999. According to official estimates, 69.5 per cent of the land area in Tanzania Mainland is under customary law, whereas 15.8 per cent is land "owned by buying", and 5.5 per cent is land "under official land titles" (URT 2013: 46). However, customary tenure does not apply to village land only. It also applies to "general land" and some "reserved land", as well as to urban land and peri-urban areas (cf. Lugoe 2010).

According to the NLP and VLA, all land in Tanzania is public land and "vested in the President as trustee on behalf of all citizens". The legislation defines three categories of land: (i) *village land* within the demarcated boundaries of villages, which comprises customary, communal and vacant land; (ii) *reserved land* (about 30 per cent of Tanzania's total land area), which is set aside as protected areas for wildlife, forests, and marine and coastal protection; (iii) *general land*, which is neither village land nor reserved land and may also include unused or unoccupied village land.

Investors can acquire land in Tanzania only by obtaining a "granted right of occupancy". The transfer of customary land rights by citizens to non-citizens is prohibited (NLP 1997: 11). However, the president has the authority to "transfer any area of village land to general or reserved land for public interest", which includes "investments of national interest" (VLA, Part III: 26; NLP 1997: 15). If a company or a person wishes to invest in village land, the president must first convert that land to general land. Village land converted to general land comes under the administration of the Tanzania Investment Centre (TIC) which, functioning as a "land bank", will lease it out to domestic or foreign investors by granting them so-called "derivative rights of occupancy".[31] The NLP (1997: 9) states that "Consultation and

---

31 The leases are long term: 50 or even 99 years.

consent of a Village council will be required whenever alienation of Village lands is necessary." However, several reports argue that this requirement is not always followed up. One study states that "The whole process happens at government level, from introduction of business idea to the TIC, finding of appropriate general land, approving of land by the Ministry of Agriculture and finally application for derivative right of occupancy from the TIC" (Theting and Brekke 2010: 5).

An additional aspect is that the great majority of villages cannot defend their interests by referring to official documents demarcating the village borders. The World Bank notes that, "more than a decade after passage of Tanzania's Land Acts, only 753, or 7%, of the country's 10,397 registered villages have received a certificate of village land. Even where such certificates were issued, pastoralist rights continue to be neglected" (World Bank 2011: 102). The World Bank points out that in this regard Tanzania is not an exception. In Mozambique, only some 12 per cent of the 70 million ha estimated to be controlled by communities has been mapped (ibid.).

Another general aspect is that after leasing the land, the investor quite often does not implement the proposed project. The World Bank study found that "investors acquired land in quantities much larger than they could use, at least initially" (World Bank 2011: 63). The general picture is that "actual farming has so far started on only 20% of the announced deals, indicating that there is a large gap between plans and implementation" (ibid.: xxxii). For example, in Mozambique an enormous area of 2.7 million ha was transferred to investors in the period 2004–09.[32] However, a land audit in 2009 found that more than 50 per cent of the projects had either not started any activity or lagged significantly behind their development plans. In the Amhara region of Ethiopia, only 16 out of 46 large-scale agriculture projects were used as intended. In other projects, the land was either used for other purposes or simply rented out to smallholders, "in explicit contravention of contract" (World Bank 2011: 62, 118). A similar pattern is found in other countries, including Tanzania (Katundu et al. 2013: 21–27).

The reason for the acquisition of more land than "needed" may be to take advantage of (too) favourable lease terms, to eliminate future competition from other investors, to profit on expected future land price rise, or betting on higher prices of food and biofuels in the future.[33] In any event, the World Bank concludes that "many investments, not always by foreigners, failed to live up to expectations and, instead of generating sustainable benefits, contributed to [smallholders'] asset loss and left local people worse off than they would have been without the investment" (World Bank 2011: 71).

---

32 Note that this figure is considerably higher than the 2.2 million ha of concluded contracts reported by the Land Matrix (Table 7.2).

33 One study suggests that the cost of land acquisition in Africa is only about USD 50 per hectare (Mitchell 2011: 64–65).

Especially biofuel projects demand not only land, but enormous quantities of water. Water is therefore one potential issue of conflict between the biofuel investors and the smallholders in Sub-Saharan Africa. Even more than in other sectors of agribusiness, corporate profit in the production of biofuel feedstock is best assured when these plantations are on the most fertile lands, with ample water supplies, especially in sugarcane production, and close to major transportation routes. However, millions of smallholders in Africa occupy these lands, and they have become the main obstacle in the path of the biofuel rush. It is becoming clear that when biofuel crops are on the agenda, the pressure on the smallholders to leave their land intensifies (cf. Matondi et al. 2011).

Although Africa's wetlands cover only 4 per cent of its total landmass, they account for more than half of the world's liquid freshwater storage (Sielhorst et al. 2008: 3). The most popular biofuel crops require large amounts of water. The production of sugarcane yielding one litre of ethanol requires 4,000 litres of water, while maize needs 2,500 litres. On the other hand, the normal ethanol yield per hectare of land is 8,900 litres for sugarcane and 3,200 litres for maize, which makes sugarcane the preferred crop of international investors (ibid.: 31–32). Therefore, for local smallholders in wetlands, biofuel feedstock production may have a negative impact on the availability of both water and land. For this production to expand, smallholders will be forced to move to poorer lands, and the local food production can be affected by decreased availability of water, which is already a limiting factor for agriculture in large parts of Sub-Saharan Africa (ibid.: 35–36; Matondi et al. 2011).

We have seen that in India the forced displacement of tribal people and smallholders is taking place on a large scale. In Africa, too, such processes are becoming a reality. For example, an environmental and social impact assessment on a sugar plantation project in Mali concluded that land acquisitions will have a negative impact on local food security and pastoralists' access to grazing. The Resettlement Action Plan for the project estimated that 1,718 people would be directly affected, and that, of these, 1,644 people from 128 households would be physically displaced (Cotula 2011: 32). A study of five regions in Tanzania shows the same pattern. In Mvomero District, Morogoro Region, 247 smallholder farmers were displaced and dispossessed of their land to give way to land acquisition by foreign investors. The same happened to 14 smallholder farmers in Kisarawe, Coast Region, and eight smallholders in Kilolo, Iringa Region (Katundu et al. 2013: 21).[34] These forced displacements not only mean economic ruin for many smallholders, but also the destruction of their culture.

34 Tanzania Mainland has 21 regions. The five regions of the study are: Arusha, Iringa, Dar es Salaam, Morogoro and Pwani.

Some Final Comments

We have noted that the general character of primitive accumulation is expropriation of the pre-capitalist immediate producers from their means of production and livelihoods, turning them into wage labourers or members of the "reserve army of unemployed". But as the examples of England, the USA, India and Africa show, this process can take very different forms. It is virtually always characterized by atrocities and injustice, although to differing degrees. Primitive accumulation in England may be considered to have been quite lenient, compared to what happened in the colonies, including America. In South Africa, the black population was robbed of its land and confined in Bantustans, similar to the reservations in the United States. The colonization of Belgian Congo under King Leopold was possibly even more brutal than the extermination of the Indian population in the United States. The external (British) colonization of India was seemingly less brutal than that of Africa. On the other hand, the contemporary government-promoted land acquisitions in India appear to be more violent than what happens in most African countries.

These experiences suggest that primitive accumulation (internal or external colonization) is more brutal in ethnically heterogeneous societies than in ethnically quite homogeneous societies, and this tendency may be reinforced if the different ethnic groups are also different in terms of culture and religion. Ethnic and cultural differences may be used by the hegemonic group to rationalize their superiority and their atrocities against, and exploitation of the ethnic groups under their control. This is most striking in the USA, where the Indian population was almost eradicated, and in contemporary India, where the *adivasis* and the *dalits* are the main victims of primitive accumulation.

The historical and contemporary experiences of primitive accumulation make it essential to elaborate an alternative policy for a fundamentally different model of development – one that gives voice and power to the population at the lowest local level to control their land, their resources and their livelihoods; and one that implies a far more equal distribution of the fruits of our earth.

References

Allen R.C. (1992). *Enclosure and the Yeoman.* Clarendon, Oxford.

Anderson, Gary Clayton (2014), *Ethnic Cleansing and the Indian – The Crime That should Haunt America*, University of Oklahoma Ptress, Norman OK.

Asher, Manshi and Yamini Atmavilas (2011). 'Special economic zones: The new "land" mines' in Hari Mohan Mathur (ed.), *Resettling Displaced People: Policy and practice in India.* Routledge, New Delhi/London.

Bhaduri, Amit (2009). *The Face You were Afraid to See: Essays on the Indian economy.* Penguin, New Delhi/London.

Bhaduri, Amit (2010). *Essays in the Reconstruction of Political Economy,* Aakar Books , New Delhi.

Bhaduri, Amit (2010). 'Recognise this face?', *Economic and Political Weekly,* 45:47, pp. 10–14.

Bhaduri, Amit (2015), 'A Study in Development by Dispossession', unpublished draft manuscript obtained from the author, February 2015.

Brenner, Robert (1976). 'Agrarian class structure and economic development in pre-industrial Europe', *Past and Present,* 70 (February), pp. 30–74.

Brown, Dee (1972). *Bury My Heart at Wounded Knee: An Indian history of the American West.* Pan Books, London.

Carter, Samuel (1976). *Cherokee Sunset: A nation betrayed: A narrative of travail and triumph, persecution and exile.* Doubleday, New York.

Chand, Ramesh (2010). 'Capital formation in Indian agriculture – national and state level analysis' in D Narasimha Reddy and Srijit Mishra (eds), *Agrarian Crisis in India.* Oxford University Press, New Delhi/Oxford.

Cotula, L. (2011). *Land Deals in Africa: What is in the contracts?* IIED, London.

De Las Casas, Bartolomé (1552). *Brevísima relación de la destrucción de las Indias,* available as an e-book published by Biblioteka Digital Ciudad Seva at: http://www.ciudadseva.com/textos/otros/brevisi.htm Latest English edition: *A Short Account of the Destruction of the Indies.* Penguin Books, Harmondsworth, 2004.

Dhagamwar, Vasudha (2011). 'From Narmada to Nandigram: The never-ending clamour for land as the only route to resettlement' in Hari Mohan Mathur (ed.), *Resettling Displaced People: Policy and practice in India.* Routledge, New Delhi/ London.

Dharmadhikary S. (2005). *Unravelling Bhakra: Assessing the temple of resurgent India.* Manthan Adhyayan Kendra, Barwani, India.

Fernandes, Walter (2011). 'Development-induced displacement in the era of privatisation' in Hari Mohan Mathur (ed.), *Resettling Displaced People: Policy and practice in India.* Routledge, New Delhi/ London.

Friis, Cecilie and Anette Reenberg (2010). *Land Grab in Africa: Emerging land system drivers in a teleconnected world.* Global Land Project International Project Office, Copenhagen.

Gerste, Ronald D. (1990). 'So starb eines Volkes Traum', *Die Zeit,* 28 December 1990, pp. 33–34.

Harvey, David (2005). *The New Imperialism.* Oxford University Press, Oxford.

Havnevik, Kjell (1993). *Tanzania: The limits to development from above.* Nordic Africa Institute, Uppsala/Mkuki na Nyota, Dar es Salaam.

Hill, Christopher (1991). *The World Turned Upside Down.* Penguin, London.

Hilton, Rodney (1977). *Bond Men Made Free: Medieval peasant movements and the English rising of 1381.* Methuen & Co., London.

Jennings, Francis (1975). *The Invasion of America: Indians, colonialism, and the cant of conquest*. University of North Carolina Press, Chapel Hill.

Katundu, Mangasini A., Innocent M.A Makungo and Shakila H. Mteti (2013). 'Nature and magnitude of land acquisitions in Tanzania: Analyzing the role of different actors, key trends and drivers in land acquisitions'. Paper presented at the international conference on the Political Economy of Agricultural Policy in Africa, organized by Future Agricultures Consortium (FAC), Pretoria, 18–20 March.

Levien, Michael (2011). 'Special economic zones and accumulation by dispossession in India', *Journal of Agrarian Change*, 11:4, pp. 454–83.

Lewontin, R.C. (1998), 'The maturing of capitalist agriculture: Farmer as proletarian', *Monthly Review*, vol. 50, no.3, July/August. Special issue on Agriculture Food and Ecology, pp. 72–84.

Lugoe, Furaha N. (2010). *Land: Pillar No. 5 of Kilimo Kwanza*. Dar es Salaam Institute of Land Administration and Policy Studies (DILAPS), Dar es Salaam.

Lugoe, Furaha (2011). 'The land factor in mining gold reserves in Tanzania', ESRF Policy Brief No. 1/2011, Dar es Salaam.

Marx, K. (1867/1976). *Capital*, Vol. 1. Penguin, Harmondsworth.

Marx, K. (1884/1978). *Capital*, Vol. 2. Penguin, Harmondsworth.

Matondi P.B., K. Havnevik and A. Beyene (eds) (2011). *Biofuels, Land Grabbing and Food Security in Africa*. Zed Books, London/New York.

Mitchell, Donald (2011). *Biofuels in Africa: Opportunities, prospects and challenges*. World Bank, Washington, DC.

Mousseau, Frederic et al. (2011). *Understanding Land Investment Deals in Africa. Country Report: Tanzania*. Oakland Institute, Oakland, CA.

NLP (1997) [Ministry of Lands and Human Settlements Development], *National Land Policy*, 2nd edition, Dar es Salaam. (First edition: 1995).

Polanyi, Karl (1947). 'Our obsolete market mentality', *Commentary*, 3, February 1947, pp. 109–17.

Polanyi, Karl (1957). *The Great Transformation*. Beacon, Boston, MA.

Purdon, Mark (2013). 'Land acquisitions in Tanzania: Strong sustainability, weak sustainability and the importance of comparative methods', *Journal of Agricultural and Environment Ethics*, 26:6, pp. 1127–56.

Reddy, D. Narasimha and Srijit Mishra (2010). 'Agriculture in the reforms regime' in D. Narasimha Reddy and Srijit Mishra (eds), *Agrarian Crisis in India*. Oxford University Press, New Delhi/Oxford.

Sanhati Collective (2012). *Farmer Suicides in India: A policy-induced disaster of epic proportions*, available at: http://www.sanhati.com.

Shivji, Issa G. et al. (1994), *Report of the Presidential Commission of Inquiry into Land Matters. Vol. 1: Land Policy and Land Tenure Structure*. Report submitted to the president of the United Republic of Tanzania, 11th November, 1992. Published by The

Ministry of Lands, Housing and Urban Development, Dar es Salaam in cooperation with the Nordic Africa Institute, Uppsala.

Shivji, Issa G. (1998). *Not Yet Democracy: Reforming land tenure in Tanzania.* IIED/ HAKIARDHI/Faculty of Law, University of Dar es Salaam.

Sielhorst, Sven, Jan W. Molenaar and Don Offermans (2008). *Biofuels in Africa: An assessment of risks and benefits for African wetlands.* Wetlands International, Amsterdam.

Singh, S. (2006). 'Agriculture, agrarian crisis and employment: Some views', *Indian Journal of Labour Economics*, 49:4, pp. 757–78.

Smith, Andrea (2007). 'Soul wound: The legacy of Native American schools', *Amnesty International Magazine*, 26 March 2007, available at: http://www.amnestyusa.org/ node/87342.

Stannard, David E. (1992), *American Holocaust – The Conquest of the New World*, Oxford University Press, New York/Oxford.

Sumner, Daniel A. (2014), 'American farms keep growing: Size, productivity, and policy', *Journal of Economic Perspectives*, vol. 28, no. 1, pp. 147–166.

Sulle, Emmanuel and Fred Nelson (2009). *Biofuels, Land Access and Rural Livelihoods in Tanzania.* International Institute for Environment and Development, London.

Tawney, R.H. (1967/1912). *The Agrarian Problem in the Sixteenth Century,* Harper Torchbooks. Harper & Row Publishers, New York/London.

Theting, Hans and Brita Brekke (2010). *Land Investments or Land Grab? A critical view from Tanzania and Mozambique.* Spire, Oslo.

Thornton, Russell (1987). *American Indian Holocaust and Survival: A population history since 1492.* University of Oklahoma Press, Oklahoma City.

Thornton, Russell (1998). 'The demography of colonialism and "old" and "new" Native Americans', in Russell Thornton, *Studying Native America.* University of Wisconsin Press, Madison.

URT [Ministry of Agriculture and Food Security] (2000), *Tanzania Agriculture: Performance and Strategies for Sustainable Growth*, Dodoma.

URT [United Republic of Tanzania] (2001), *Agricultural Sector Development Strategy*, Dar es Salaam, October 2001.

URT [NBS/Ministry of Finance] (2013), *Tanzania in Figures 2012*, Dar es Salaam, June 2013.

USAID (2012). *Tanzania Environmental Threats and Opportunities Assessment.* USAID, Washington, DC.

VLA [The Village land Act, 1999], Passed in the National Assembly on the 11 February, 1999. Government Printer, Dar es Salaam.

Weber, Max (1923/1991). *Wirtschaftsgeschichte.* Duncker & Humblot, Berlin.

Wise, Timothy A. (2015), „The Great land Giveaway in Mozambique", *Triple Crisis Blog*, 11 March 2015: http://triplecrisis.com/the-great-land-giveaway-in-mozambique/.

World Bank (2011). *Rising Global Interest in Farmland: Can it yield sustainable and equitable benefits?* World Bank, Washington, DC.

Wrigley, E.A. (1988), 'Two Kinds of Capitalism, Two Kinds of Growth', *L.S.E. Quarterly*, no. 2, pp. 97–121.

Wrigley, E.A. (2004). *Poverty, Progress and Population.* Cambridge University Press, Cambridge.

Wrigley, E.A. (2006). 'The transition to an advanced organic economy: Half a millennium of English agriculture', *Economic History Review*, LIX:3, pp. 435–80.

CHAPTER 8

From Food Security to Food Sovereignty?

Kjell Havnevik

Introduction

This chapter will investigate how the concept of food security has evolved in line with changing global power relations and developmental contexts. In particular, it will inquire about the direction of the changes of the concept over time. One deficiency related to the concept of food security is its apparent inability to explain the causes of hunger. This may be an important reason why development interventions have not been able to reduce global hunger.

In 1990, the number of hungry people in the world was estimated to be 800 million. By 2013 the figure had increased to 870 million, according to the Food and Agriculture Organization (FAO, 13 March 2013). In 2009, it even topped 1 billion. The Millennium Development Goals (MDG) objective of reducing the number of people who suffer hunger to 400 million by 2015 (down 50 per cent from the 1990 level) will not be reached. There is accordingly a 'food security policy gap' of around half a billion people, most of them in Africa and South Asia.

This chapter will also discuss possible ways in which the concept of food security could develop, in order to incorporate within it an understanding of the causes of hunger and to address sustainability issues. Such an approach goes beyond techniques and measurements: it requires more profound changes in the mindsets of those states/regions and institutions with the power to set the global development and food security agenda.

Such a shift will require an analysis of the power relations that exist between dominant and marginalized countries/regions of the world, as well as of the relationships within countries. A first important step is to gain insights that will make it possible to acknowledge the way in which historical developments have created deep-seated problems and divisions between and within continents and countries and their populations (Said 1978). Such problems and divisions have been (and remain) visible in exploitation, colonization, racism and gender inequality. The reproduction of these mechanisms and processes takes place through the use of stereotypes and symbolism that support their legitimation. Hence it is not the identification of images as positive or negative that should be central, but an understanding of the processes of subjectification that are made possible through stereotypical discourse (Bhabha 1983).

 | DOI 10.1163/9789004305465_009

In order to be relevant in this broader perspective, analysis of the concept of food security over time should also address the cultural, socio-economic and political frameworks that determine and sustain the domination of some regions/countries and social classes over others and that reproduce hunger on a global scale. The conceptual analysis in this chapter rests on the author's understanding of the broader frames and of how their corresponding stereotypes generate and maintain global inequalities and power relations. The aim is to discuss whether an alternative concept – food sovereignty – might better capture the causes, power relations and patterns of food insecurity, both locally and globally.

Such an approach is required because international institutions are downplaying the failure of policy regarding hunger. This is partly done by emphasizing that global poverty reduction (another major MDG goal: i.e. to reduce world poverty by 50 per cent in relation to the 1990 level) *is* likely to be attained by 2015. The main reason for this success, however, lies not in the policies of the FAO, the UN or international financial institutions, but in the fact that by virtue of their own strategies, some of the transition economies (in particular China) have lifted millions of people out of poverty.

In addition, the FAO, the UN specialized agency for food and agriculture, and the dominant international financial institutions and agencies have changed the way they report on global hunger. Instead of speaking about an increase in absolute global hunger levels, they now report the prevalence of global hunger in percentage terms. In this way, they can show that between 1990 and 2013 the level of global hunger remained static, at 16 per cent of the world's population – though in actual numbers it has increased substantially. This is because, as the world's population grows, so there is a corresponding relative rise in the number of hungry people (HLPE 2012: 21).

Change in the Concept of Food Security over Time

The first Global Food Summit, which took place in Rome in 1974 in the context of rapidly increasing global food prices, proposed the establishment of strategic grain reserves to stabilize world food prices. The 1974 summit also established an intergovernmental Committee on World Food Security (CFS). After the summit, the then US secretary of state, Henry Kissinger, felt confident enough to proclaim that 'no child will go to bed hungry within ten years' (*The Economist*, 19 November 2009). The thinking was that natural disasters, adverse weather and climatic conditions and low agricultural production should not be allowed to affect global food provision negatively in the longer term, which would help stabilize global food prices. Increasing global food prices would most importantly hit large non-food-producing populations in developing countries, but it would also have a negative impact on welfare levels in industrialized countries. The build-up of grain reserves was subsequently promoted by international institutions and donors on a global scale.

These ideas were also advanced in the negotiations about the New International Economic Order (NIEO) that emerged on the UN agenda in 1974, triggered by rising oil prices. At that time, transnational companies controlled (directly or indirectly) 75–90 per cent of global mineral ore and metal resources, 30–40 per cent of agricultural raw materials and close to 40 per cent of food exports originating in developing countries. An international agreement on an Integrated Programme for Commodities was reached at the fourth session of UNCTAD (Resolution 93(IV)) in 1976. It also included a Common Fund to finance buffer stocks and to promote international commodity arrangements.

The NIEO negotiations aimed at a more economically and socially just global order and came about through a global shift in political power from the industrialized to the developing countries, including Arab oil-producing countries. The power shift (which proved temporary) was based on the industrialized countries' fear that production cartels for other strategic commodities (along the lines of OPEC) might be created, which would have further negative consequences for the economies of the North. Acknowledging their new-found power, developing countries pressed – though not always in unison – for permanent sovereignty over their natural resources. Their aim was also to reduce the influence and control that transnational companies had over their economies through the establishment of universally agreed codes of conduct. Developing countries likewise demanded better conditions for trade, including buffer stocks, and support for agriculture and food production. The South also demanded that technology transfers from the North to the South should lead to real development and that the share of global manufacturing production in the South should increase (cf. the Lima Declaration of 1979).

The Food Summit and the NIEO showed limited (or no) concern for environmental sustainability in food and agricultural production. Such concerns had been raised in the Declaration of the United Nations Conference on the Human Environment, held in 1972 in Stockholm. But it took until the end of the 1980s for environmental issues to be taken more seriously. When it came about, it was partly as a consequence of the publication of a major study by a UN-appointed committee – *Our Common Future* (UN 1987).

Against this background, I will argue that the discussion of food security in this early phase focused mainly on the production and provision of food. We could call this the *abundance aspect* of the concept of food security. It implies that the production and provision of food should be a necessary but not sufficient condition for global food security to be met. However, in the abundance aspect there was no consideration of any sustainability issues related to the nature of the production of the food.

In the early 1980s, new knowledge about the causes of large-scale hunger emerged in connection with a major famine in Ethiopia. It was shown that, notwithstanding the famine, sufficient food was being produced to feed the entire population of the country. The problem was that food produced within the country was spread geographically unevenly, and transport between deficit and surplus food-producing areas was difficult to organize. However, most importantly, in areas of sufficient food production and 'abundance', many people still remained hungry because they had no income or other means of buying or accessing the food available.

This triggered a shift in analysis of the food security concept, led by Amartya Sen, towards *food entitlement*. This implied a concept of food security that went beyond production and abundance and argued that food security mechanisms by which people *access* food should be included in the analysis (Sen 1981; Maxwell and Smith 1992). Such entitlement or access mechanisms could, for example, be waged labour that generated income to purchase food; ownership or user rights to land, so that people could produce food for their own consumption; and acquisition of food through family or community relationships. The new insight connected with entitlement to food showed that socio-economic and cultural aspects were also of critical importance for food security.

Studies within other academic areas, such as nutrition and anthropology, added further elements to the understanding of food security. Such disciplinary research that related to the dynamics within households led to the insight that food distribution was also uneven within households. This meant that the understanding of food security had to be taken down to the individual level (Ruel et al. 1998). Although African women are responsible for providing the bulk of food for the household through their own production or purchases, studies show that men and children are given priority in family food consumption in times of food shortage. Nutritionists were also able to show that care and external conditions prevailing during food consumption have an impact on the digestive system's ability to absorb the nutritious elements of the food: in situations where there was social instability or tension – either within the family or on account of conflict and war – the intake of food would thus 'overstate' the calorific value of the food consumed (Maxwell and Smith 1992; Ruel et al. 1998).

Another aspect of food security that was gradually acknowledged and given more prominence was food safety – i.e. issues connected with the quality of food, relating to proper food storage, processing and preparation. Food safety focused on the need for clean water, sanitation and hygiene in the production, storage and processing of food and in the consumption chain. Food safety also aimed at preventing pathogens from infecting food, so that illness among consumers could be avoided (Antle 1999; Bourn and Prescott 2002). This is of particular importance in the urban areas of many developing countries, where food cultivation and animal rearing go on side by side (Egal et al. 2001). Research shows that as much as 20 per cent of the food consumed in developing countries' urban areas is produced in those urban areas themselves.

Other aspects of food security have surfaced in connection with forced migration and are linked to the cultural acceptance of food. Some religions, for example, do not allow the consumption of pork (Rozin 1996). Another issue is that the acceptance of food by individuals, although voluntary, may be related to the consumer's perception of the source or impact of the food being produced. Some consumers will not eat food from living animals, while others decline to consume food whose production has a negative impact on the environment and/or on the health of animals and human beings.

In my first approximation of the definition of a food security concept, I will accordingly include: (i) *abundance*, i.e. sufficient production of food for all, (ii) *adequacy*, i.e. the food produced is of adequate *nutritional value* and the human body's digestive system can absorb that value, (iii) that the quality of the food is secured through safe storage, proper distribution and processing, i.e. *food safety*, (iv) that the food is *culturally accepted*, and (v) that people command entitlements that enable their *access* to food.

This definition of food security in concrete terms corresponds well to the more general and official definition taken by the FAO Food Summit 1996, which states that food security is attained 'when all people at all times have access to sufficient, safe, nutritious food to maintain a healthy and active life'.

Change in the Global Context and New Initiatives to Address Global Food Security

The above definitions of food security are, however, rather descriptive and do not capture well the causes of hunger and the power relations that generate and sustain food insecurity and environmental degradation over time. This has become particularly evident since the economic and financial crisis of 2008, which saw both food and energy security come to the fore as primary global political concerns. The driving forces behind this new global emphasis were also the attainment of 'peak oil', the growing fear of climate change and the rapid rise and instability of food prices (Matondi et al. 2011).

The current problems related to food insecurity (and their causes) are thus connected to profound global changes. The financial and economic crisis led to a rapid rise in the number of food-insecure people: this peaked at 1.023 billion in 2009. During this period as well, the mal-governance of international institutions promoting global food security was exposed. An urgent need arose for a deeper understanding of the causes of food insecurity.

The Invigoration of the Committee on World Food Security – Concern over the Governance Gap

A step in the right direction came with the restructuring of the intergovernmental Committee on World Food Security (CFS) under the auspices of the FAO. The committee had been dormant since 1974.

According to McKeon, there is a particular problem of global food security governance that operates on different levels (McKeon 2011; 2012). The system that exists for its monitoring and governance is fragmented and unaccountable. On the one side are actors such as the International Monetary Fund, the World Bank and the World Trade Organization – all market oriented and dominated by the North. On the other side are UN institutions: the FAO, the International Fund for Agricultural Development (IFAD) and some advocacy organizations and groups that seek to temper (at least to some degree) the relationship between economic liberalization and food security.

However, even this second set of actors/institutions is strongly influenced by expert policy networks and advice, and by private commercial sector lobbying for self-regulating mechanisms along the food chain. Private-sector actors have been able to carve out large and unregulated spaces for themselves, and have also managed to secure a key role in establishing the rules that aim to regulate their activities, e.g. the Codex Alimentarius. The private sector and the market-oriented institutions are unable to address the causes and complexity of food security, and they cannot promote constructive strategies and policy advice to reduce global hunger in line with the MDG objectives.

Concerned at the growing governance gap and the policy failure as regards food security, the UN Secretary General established a 'High Level Task Force' on the Global Food Security Crisis. The G8, for their part, signalled their concern by promoting rhetoric around a 'Global Partnership on Agriculture, Food Security and Nutrition'. Attached to such statements were promises of billions of dollars in new agricultural investment, mostly relating to green technology fixes. Support also came from philanthropic actors, such as the Bill and Melinda Gates Foundation. On the one hand, the rise of philanthropy on the development arena reflected the inability of public development assistance to bring about constructive change in Africa; on the other it reflected growing global economic inequalities. African governments for their part agreed to steer 10 per cent of government budgets towards agriculture. To this day, these promises have only been partially fulfilled.

In response to this high-tech and gap-oriented approach to hunger reduction, a number of actors, including some mentioned above, joined forces to promote a more comprehensive and inclusive way of addressing global food security. The new idea was to make the process more participatory, by working with social movements, civil society actors and a few dominant FAO member countries of the South. The idea was anchored in the FAO, and was thus still inside the legitimate international framework. The plan was to use and invigorate the CFS as a vehicle for genuine food security reform.

In October 2009, the proposal to reform the CFS was adopted. However, its new organization and activities emerged as a compromise between social movement/civil society organizations and some UN member governments that were reluctant to see the creation within the CFS of a new and genuine space for thinking, reflection and policy development connected to food security and nutrition.

Contestations over Guidelines

For its part, the G8 had stated in 2008 that large-scale foreign agro-investments in developing countries should be seen as a welcome move to increase food production and reduce global food insecurity. Only limited discussion took place as to whether large-scale agro-investments had the potential to create win–win situations for all stakeholders – international investors, states and rural smallholders alike. This was in spite of the fact that research, both historic and current, had shown that large-scale agro-investments lead to monocultures that undermine biological diversity; conflicts related to water access and problems with groundwater levels; and an increase in fertilizer and pesticide use, which reduces soil fertility by poisoning the soil and its products over time. Most large-scale agro-investments in Africa target well-watered lands that are already inhabited and used by rural smallholders. Such features of large-scale agro-investments have been documented by, among others, the UN Rapporteur on Food Security and Human Rights, advocacy groups worldwide, Washington's International Food Policy Research Institute (IFPRI) and London's International Institute for Environmental Development (IIED) (Havnevik 2011; Matondi et al. 2011; Fernandes et al. 2012).

With this knowledge in mind, a number of guidelines for responsible agricultural investment emerged in 2009. Although the various guidelines issued differently weighted and prioritized recommendations, there was consensus on the following, relating to large-scale land acquisitions and to the lease process connected with agro-investments: (i) there should be transparency in the negotiations, (ii) the rights of local communities, including customary land rights, should be protected, (iii) the benefits should be shared between local communities and investors, (iv) environmental sustainability should be ensured, and (v) food security should not be compromised. I will term these consensus areas the 'first generation' of guidelines for agro-investments. Scrutiny of the analysis and reflections on which the guidelines were based shows some consideration of power relations (Havnevik 2011).

The World Bank did not participate in the process that led to this 'first generation' of guidelines for responsible agro-investment. In fact, its 2007 report on agriculture devoted scant attention to the rapid increase in agro-investments worldwide. However, although it acknowledged the important role of smallholders, it was sympathetic to a shift from smallholders to large-scale agricultural cultivation:

> An emerging vision of agriculture for development redefines the role of producers, the private sector and the state. Production is mainly by smallholders, who often remain the most efficient producers, in particular when supported by their organizations. *But when these organizations cannot capture economies of scale in production and marketing, labor-intensive commercial farming can be a better form of production, and efficient and fair labor markets are the key instrument to reducing rural poverty.*
>
> WORLD BANK 2007, *my italics*

The World Bank's 2007 report on agriculture overlooked many of the problems relating to large-scale agro-investment (Havnevik et al. 2007). The italicized statement above also implies that the World Bank acknowledged that economies of scale exist in agriculture that could lead to economic growth and social improvement. Historical analyses, on the contrary, show that economies of scale occur predominantly in manufacturing and not in agriculture. Hence countries that historically prioritized large-scale agriculture over manufacturing were outmanoeuvred by industrial economies. This was foreseen by the Argentinian economist Raúl Prebisch, based at the UN Economic Commission for Latin America, who recommended industrialization of the continent as the only way of bringing about its broad-based development.

The World Bank, international institutions and donors are, however, strongly influenced by the standard theory of international trade, which maintains that – under certain assumptions – all partners will benefit from free trade based on comparative advantages. Investments and trade in agricultural products are, therefore, considered a pathway to global economic growth and poverty reduction. In this spirit, in 2009 the World Bank initiated a global study on large-scale agro-investments. The final version was published in 2011 (Deininger et al. 2011).

Here the World Bank attempts, in cooperation with some partners, to identify the framework for the global discussion and analysis of large-scale agro-investments and recommends a new set of guidelines for such investments. These first of all came to be known as Responsible Agricultural Investments (RAI).

The World Bank's RAI were later renamed Principles for Responsible Agricultural Investments (PRAI). They incorporated many of the elements of the first generation of guidelines, but the PRAI had nevertheless been formulated in 'closed door discussions by the World Bank and other multilateral institutions' (McKeon 2012). The CFS was subsequently asked by the World Bank to give its seal of approval to the PRAI. The CFS, however, disapproved.

The CFS had by now developed into a forum for knowledge generation about a broad range of food security issues, in consultation with researchers and civil society worldwide. The CFS also organized a High Level Panel of Experts on Food Security and Nutrition (HLPE) from which studies could be requested on various aspects of food security (e.g. HLPE 2012; 2013a; 2013b).

New Committee on World Food Security Initiatives

CFS-led intergovernmental negotiations assisted in the finalization of an FAO initiative that began in 2009 to develop Voluntary Guidelines on Responsible Governance for Tenure of Land, Forests and Fisheries (the so-called 'voluntary guidelines' or VGGT). The final text was negotiated in early 2012, and in May of that year the CFS endorsed the VGGT, which aimed at 'helping governments safeguard the right of people to own or access land, forests and fisheries' (FAO Media Centre, 11 May 2012).

The process leading up to the VGGT had been strongly supported by the civil society forum that grew up alongside the official FAO Food Summits of 1996 and 2002. This forum provided an alternative base for global networking on food security, where rural social movements could also participate. People's organizations in particular had a decisive role within this forum, alongside non-governmental organizations (NGOs). The forum had entrusted a creation of its own, the International Planning Committee on Food Sovereignty (IPC), with taking its action agenda forward. The IPC is currently an autonomous, self-managed committee, supported by a global network of 45 people's movements and NGOs and comprising more than 800 organizations worldwide.

The IPC network and associated organizations denounced the World Bank's PRAI guidelines as an attempt to legitimize the corporate takeover of the territories of rural people. The argument was that the right to decide about land resources is not a technical, but essentially a political matter that involves conflicting interests and power relationships (Global Campaign for Agrarian Reform/Land Research Action Network 2010). According to McKeon, civil society interventions in the intense final negotiations within CFS regarding the VGGT were decisive in bringing about the finalization of the guidelines (McKeon 2012: 15).

The VGGT, however, primarily operate at the national level, as a tool for developing countries' governments to protect people's assets and their access to land, forest and fisheries. Aware of the national limitation of the VGGT, in late 2011 the CFS decided to develop a new set of 'Principles for responsible agricultural investments (rai) in the context of food security and nutrition' (CFS 2013). These were to be termed 'rai' (with small letters, to distinguish them from the World Bank's PRAI). According to the CFS, the rai are to be developed in a broad consultative process, where member governments, civil society, private business and relevant international organizations shall participate (Swedish Ministry of Rural Affairs, Memorandum, 26 February 2013). The terms of reference (ToR) for the rai were adopted by the CFS in October 2012, and the new rai was endorsed on October 15 2014 (CFS 2014).

According to the ToR, the rai principles shall (i) seek to promote investments that enhance food security and nutrition, (ii) contribute to realizing the right to food, (iii) be voluntary and not binding, and (iv) be interpreted in correspondence with national and international law and with reference to the voluntary initiatives by states under international instruments (Swedish Ministry of Rural Affairs, Memorandum, 26 February 2013, my translation). The rai principles are to address investments along the entire food chain and to embrace all categories of investor worldwide. According to the ToR, the rai are also to build on and complement the VGGT (in particular chapter 12) and the PRAI principles developed with the World Bank as the lead.

In August 2013, the CFS released a Zero Draft of rai to provide information about the outcomes so far and to request inputs to the process (CFS, August 2013). Discussion of the rai in the Zero Draft is organized into four parts: (i) food security, nutrition and sustainable development (economic, social, environmental and cultural issues), (ii) policy coherence and sector development, (iii) governance and grievance mechanisms, and (iv) review and accountability. In each part, the draft principles are spelled out and a summary of their rationale, objectives and application is presented. After each part, the roles and responsibilities of stakeholders and actors are outlined, but without being targeted at the different categories of investors. In total, eight draft principles are presented: four for Part I, one for Part II, two for Part III and one for Part IV.

The Zero Draft of rai takes a broad approach to responsible investments for food security and nutrition. It includes agricultural research, education, infrastructure and other relevant services. There are many actors included: 'private and public, domestic and foreign at small, medium or large scale. The incentives and capacities to invest of all these actors are significantly affected by the presence of an enabling environment, including a conducive policy framework' (CFS, August 2013: 1).

The Zero Draft of rai specifically recognizes the important role of small-scale food producers and processors – women and men – in investing on-farm, and it also takes account of the fact that this group is disproportionately represented among the food insecure and poor. In addition, all other actors are acknowledged, including large-scale investors in agriculture and food systems (ibid.: 2).

The VGGT guidelines emphasize the protection of smallholders' rights (to land and food) and the promotion of production conditions to encourage sustainable agricultural outputs. The rai principles, by contrast, emphasize more strongly the need to enhance people's food security and nutrition within the context of progressive realization of the right to food. The four rai principles of Part I of the Zero Draft include: to enhance people's food security and nutrition and to contribute to the realization of the right to food in the national context (Principle 1); to generate positive socio-economic impacts for all (women and men alike), to respect core labour standards, and to apply the VGGT (Principle 2); to use, develop and regenerate natural resources sustainably and to contribute to climate change mitigation and adaptation (Principle 3); and to respect the cultural heritage, landscapes and traditional knowledge in a way that is consistent with international agreements and is considered legitimate by local and other relevant stakeholders (Principle 4) (ibid.: 3–5).

As to the roles and responsibilities in relation to Principles 1–4, the Zero Draft states that all of them have implications for all categories of investors involved in investments in agriculture and food systems, 'but some of these implications are more relevant to medium and large-scale investors' (ibid.: 6). There is, however, no discussion of what applies to large-, medium- or small-scale investors. The rai, in other words, do not link various types of responsibilities to different categories of investors. The principles do not reflect the fact that the current expansion of large-scale agro-investments means that often they are in competition with smallholder agriculture for land and water and that this leads to conflict with, and to the alienation and displacement of, rural populations. Large-scale agro-investments are highly mechanized and require little labour. In addition, they promote monocultures and undermine biological diversity. A fundamental problem with large-scale agro-investments, as evidenced by research from Latin America, is that their technical, agro-ecological, economic and social features make them incapable of promoting sustainable development (Fernandes et al. 2012; Coulson 2013).

In essence, the rai principles, as presented in the Zero Draft, take the moral high ground in arguing both for the concern for smallholders, the environment and the climate and for the enhancement of food security, nutrition and sustainable development; but they make no attempt to operationalize the principles by placing responsibilities on different types of investors. Hence some agro-investors, e.g. those that are large in scale, may not fully understand how the principles relate to their activities; others who do understand may not feel sufficiently challenged to act in the spirit of the principles; while a third group of investors – those who understand the implications and their responsibilities – is given free rein to act as it chooses. Anyway, the principles are of a voluntary nature. Some parts of the UN system and the business world that focus on human rights and business enterprises (under the UN 'Protect, Respect and Remedy' framework) seem to understand the weaknesses of the rai type of principles. In this human rights framework, the process aims at identifying and placing the human rights issues and responsibilities with specific corporations or businesses (United Nations Human Rights Council 2011).

In the area of agricultural investment, one need go no further than the CFS itself to be reminded that dominant FAO member states favour large-scale agricultural investment by transnational companies. For instance, at its meeting in October 2012, the US acted to block endorsement by the CFS of the first draft of a global framework for food security (the Global Strategic Framework or GSF). This happened in spite of the fact that negotiations on the text in principle had been finalized in July 2012. Later, however, 'the US had informed that it would tear up the last part of the framework, relating to questions around which there is no consensus and that may be in need of further work, e.g. questions relating to patents and [genetically modified organisms]' (report by an NGO representative of the Swedish Church, Axelsson Nycander, 26 October 2012). And further, in the VGGT, which the Zero Draft of rai encourages investors to follow, the protection of people's ownership and access to land, forest and fisheries is at the discretion of nation states. Historical and more recent research shows, however, that African states, instead of protecting and supporting their own smallholders, have been more inclined to align themselves with large-scale investors and agri-business, both foreign and domestic (Gibbon et al. 1992; Depelchin 2004; Matondi et al. 2011; URT 2009; Coulson 2013).

The longest documented history of alliances between the state, large landowners and agri-business is to be found in Latin America and Brazil; it shows clearly that those who suffer are indigenous peoples, rural smallholders and the environment (Wolf and Hansen 1972; Branford and Glock 1985; Fernandes et al. 2012). Currently in Brazil, large-scale agriculture and agri-business control 75 per cent of the productive land, but produce only 60 per cent of the gross agricultural value. Smallholders, on the other hand, farm only 25 per cent of the land, but produce 40 per cent of the gross value of agriculture. In addition, they employ 15 people per 100 hectares of cultivation, whereas for the same area large-scale agriculture employs only two people. Hence, smallholders perform better in terms of securing employment, enhancing food security and addressing environmental concerns (Fernandes et al. 2012). The creation in 1983 of the Movement of Workers Without Land (MST) and the establishment of the Workers' Party (PT), which gained political power in 2003, have not been able to stop the expansion of large-scale agricultural investment, both domestic and foreign, in the mono-cropping of sugarcane and soy beans. Land conflicts have thus been spreading across Brazil, and both the environment generally and the forests have been degraded (ibid.; Hermele 2012; Mendonça et al. 2013 and Carter 2015).

Research from the African continent has recently emerged to reveal similar conflicts between large-scale agro-investments and smallholder agriculture that have had a negative impact on food security and nutrition (Matondi et al. 2011; Neville and Dauvergne 2012; FAO 2013). The lessons of history in Brazil, at least in part, may indicate what is taking place and what will happen in Africa. Brazilian companies, too, are engaging in large-scale agro-investment in Africa (Cheru and Modi 2013: chapters 7–9).

In my assessment, the draft rai principles, which are voluntary, are inadequate to address the real problems and challenges unfolding in relation to different types of agricultural investment. This is mainly due to lack of operationalization in terms of targeting or assigning responsibility for the various implications of agro-investments to different categories of investors. Therefore rai will have difficulty in relating to real issues on the ground, and in particular to conflicts between different scales of agricultural investment. This, in my view, will happen in spite of the fact that Part III of the Zero Draft addresses governance and grievance mechanisms, and Part IV review and accountability. These features of rai are likely to render the principles ineffective in promoting responsible agro-investment. The draft rai are conceptualized within the framework of the dominant states and regions, and it will be unable to challenge their drive and support for large-scale agro-investment. Hence attention is diverted from the important potential that smallholder agriculture regimes have to enhance food security, nutrition and sustainable development. In my assessment, the rai principles have to be made more concrete through a more active and conscious use of experiences and knowledge relating to agricultural production, food security, nutrition and sustainability. The rai principles also need to be complemented with associated guidelines that can provide concrete advice and recommendations for investors, smallholders, host governments, NGOs, social movements and international institutions (see Havnevik 2014). This was not done in the final version of rai of October 15 2014 (CFS 2014).

To move outside the societal frame of the dominant states and global interests implies a need for rai to address in an integrated way the impacts of, and the conflicts between, different scales of agro-investment in relation to environmental sustainability, food security and global social justice. This would require of rai that it links responsibilities to different categories of agricultural investment/investor. In my assessment, only in this manner can a pathway open up that goes beyond the dominant framework and towards a concept – food sovereignty – that takes power relations and conflicts into account in the understanding and promotion of enhanced food security and nutrition, sustainable production and social justice (Havnevik 2014).

A Paradigm Shift in Understanding Food Security

Environmental Sustainability

Environmental sustainability is connected to the way in which food is produced. It is associated with the scale and the character of production in terms of the use of land, soil, water, forests, energy and other natural resources, and also in terms of its effects on biological diversity, environmental services and ecological systems. The production regimes of food affect the climate as well, through direct and indirect land-use changes, including deforestation. The indirect land-use changes, which often have a negative impact on climate, are difficult to ascertain; the overall effect of land-use changes on climate may be far larger than one would guess just by looking at direct land-use changes.

Environmental sustainability in the wider sense is also connected to the distribution of resources and benefits between generations and between human beings and other species inhabiting the world (Dobson 1998). Environmental sustainability is thus closely linked to the reproduction of ecological systems for generating life-supporting services. The greatest challenge to humanity is to address the limits of the ever-expanding dominant global production and consumption system. This capitalist system can only reproduce itself through expansion, i.e. through increased levels of consumption and resource exploitation. The rise of emerging economies and other developing countries is bound to intensify consumerism, which will undermine ecological systems and environmental services on a global scale (Bauman 2007).

Economic system expansion and reproduction are thus dependent upon the 'creation' of 'needs' that generate demand and economic growth. The 'cost' of economic growth (e.g. in terms of environmental system damage and climate change) is taken into account in superficial ways, through compensatory payment schemes that help to legitimate the high levels of consumption (Buscher 2011).

Those developing countries that have contributed least to environmental degradation and climate change will be hardest hit by their effects. Hence the developed North is imposing on the transition economies and poor developing countries a regime that it did not accept for itself. Large-scale agro-investment in Africa in order to enhance food and energy security at home is but one manifestation of this unwillingness to address environmental sustainability, high and increasing inequalities and consumerism (Bauman 2007; Matondi et al. 2011; FAO 2013).

Global Social Justice

Rising global income inequalities are a major challenge to food security – one that leads in the direction of the broader issue of *social justice*. Current global food production can provide every human being with sufficient food for a healthy life. Yet about 16 per cent of the world's population find themselves malnourished or hungry.

The emphasis on food security on the global political agenda of the last few years is associated not only with increased food insecurity, but also with the character of food as a commodity. Food is necessary to sustain life, and for this reason the scarcity of food can easily be transformed into political tension and conflict. This was evidenced when food riots broke out in a number of poor countries after the economic and financial crisis of 2008. Experience shows that the global challenge is not only to produce enough food to feed everyone in the future, but also to distribute equitably the food currently being produced.

Global economic *inequalities and social injustices* are important contributory factors in food insecurity. This relates to the distribution of power and assets, as that is what regulates access to food. In terms of global incomes and poverty, two continents or regions are lagging behind: South Asia and Africa. In rural Africa, food insecurity and poverty are closely related to lack of assets, insecure land tenure systems, low agricultural productivity and low incomes. Recent trends towards large-scale external agro-investment in Africa for the production of food and energy for export have led to a further alienation of rural smallholders from their land and water resources (Oestigaard 2012; Olanya 2012). The rise of large-scale agro-investment indicates that alliances are also being forged between African states and domestic elites and international commercial interests, both state and private, so that smallholders and rural dwellers are excluded and displaced.

In response to economic hardship, African smallholders have diversified their economic activities (Havnevik 1993; Havnevik and Hårsmar 1999; Djurfeldt et al. 2005). This takes place in a context where their mechanisms for accessing land and natural resources are weak and fragile. There are various indications (associated with smallholders' assets, market access and the institutional context) to suggest that smallholders face different problems and opportunities and that support initiatives and mechanisms need to be contextualized (HLPE 2013b; Havnevik 2014). Poor rural dwellers also respond to continuing hardship by migrating to urban areas and overseas. A mechanism for accessing food that could be seen as a last resort is through familial and social relationships and community networks. Such access relates to reciprocity and redistribution mechanisms that still operate in the African countryside, although they are weakening.

Human Right to Food

The deterioration in global food security has taken place in spite of the fact that human rights (including the right to food) have become increasingly prominent on international agendas. The fundamental right to be free of hunger was recognized separately in the United Nations International Covenant on Economic, Social and Cultural Rights (ESCR) of 1966. This covenant came into force in 1976, and by 2012 160 states had ratified it; in 106 countries, the right to food is applicable via constitutional arrangements and under various international treaties. The definition of adequate food used is: 'The right to adequate food is realized when every man, woman and child, alone or in community with others, has physical and economic access at all times to adequate food or means for its procurement' (United Nations Committee on Economic, Social and Cultural Rights 1999). The principal obligation of a state under the ESCR is to take steps to achieve progressively the full realization of the right to adequate food for everyone under its jurisdiction. There are three levels of obligations: (i) respect, i.e. the state is not to take any measures that prevent access to adequate food, (ii) protect, i.e. the state is to ensure that enterprises or industries do not deprive individuals of their access to food, and (iii) fulfil, i.e. the state is (a) to facilitate and proactively engage in strengthening people's access to food, and (b) to provide the right to adequate food directly when individuals or groups, for reasons beyond their control, are unable to access food.

The UN special representative on the issue of human rights and transnational business enterprises is working in close cooperation with all stakeholders to promote the framework relating to ESCR. This process has, in more concrete ways than the draft rai, been able to link responsibilities to different types of actors (UN Human Rights Council 2011).

For its part, the FAO has concretized recommendations on how governments can work to achieve the right to food by adopting the following seven initiatives: (i) identify the hungry and poor, (ii) conduct an assessment of existing policies, institutions, laws and programmes, (iii) develop right-based food security strategies, (iv) assign roles and responsibilities to institutions and ensure their coordination, (v) strengthen the legal framework, (vi) monitor the progressive realization of the right to food, and (vii) ensure effective recourse in the event of any violation of the right to food.

The UN special rapporteur on the right to food claims that states violate this right by selling or leasing land to investors, and as a consequence local people are alienated from productive resources that are required for their livelihoods. It would also be a violation of the right to food if deals were concluded without some mechanism to ensure that they do not undermine food security. On the basis of existing international legal frameworks, the UN special rapporteur on the right to food has put forward 11 minimum principles that address activities and responsibilities relating to all stakeholders, not just states (de Schutter 2009; 2010). Some of these aspects are contained in what I call the 'first generation' of guidelines for agro-investments.

An International Code of Conduct on the human right to adequate food was launched in 1997 and has widespread support among non-governmental organizations that advocate on behalf of the hungry.

Food Supply and International Trade

Although abundance is a necessary condition for food security, it is by no means a sufficient one. As well as production, the concept of *food supply* encompasses trade, to enable the distribution of (and access to) food, as well as technical and knowledge-related innovations that increase food and agricultural productivity. In the wake of environmental disaster, conflict and war, the last decades have seen emergency food aid play an increasing role. Food supply is also dependent upon the existence of a reasonable infrastructure for distributing available food, and on proper conditions for promoting food safety.

Food supply can also be enhanced through international trade. However, standard international trade theory employs certain assumptions, many of which do not hold true in real life. For instance, the assumptions of no externalities, stable prices, equal dynamic comparative advantages and no cross-border mobility of factors of production are not true reflections of the world today. It could be argued that absolute advantages are gradually becoming more important than comparative advantages in trade. This would recast the whole trade arena, where gains would flow to countries that hold, or that can create, such absolute advantages (Skarstein 2007). The history of trade between the rich and developed and the developing countries shows – at both the theoretical and the practical level – that trade should rather be understood in conjunction with concepts such as power and hegemony. One may ask what real choice Africa has had to acquire positive externalities (e.g. in the areas of technology and industrialization), given that its productive systems were basically imposed from outside.

As regards trade in food, recent developments show that important stakeholders and states no longer have confidence in the 'free trade doctrine' to safeguard their own food supplies. This has led to a rising global interest in farmland, for example in Africa, to produce food for export to the investing countries themselves (Deininger et al. 2011). In addition, bilateral investment and trade agreements are being signed to protect the external investments and to ensure a stable flow of food for export. With food and energy security at the top of global political priorities, the search for land on which to produce food and energy for export has expanded worldwide, but it has Africa in focus.

It is claimed that around 50 per cent (around 200 million hectares) of the 'available' global land reserves are in Africa (Deininger et al. 2011). What will happen when such external investments for food or energy, mainly with sugarcane as a feedstock, seek the well-watered areas that these crops require? If all 40 million hectares of the land acquired by external interests in Africa in 2009 come under cultivation, a staggering volume of water will be required for irrigation. The Oakland Institute has estimated that if the annual rate of land acquisitions in Africa continues at 2009 levels, the demand for fresh water from new land investments alone will overtake the existing supply of renewable fresh water on the continent by 2019 (Oestigaard 2012; Olanya 2012). There are indications, however, based on research, that large-scale investments in Africa, particularly those focusing on sugarcane/ethanol, are facing problems in accessing land in Africa (Matondi et al. 2011; Neville and Dauvergne 2012; FAO 2013; Abdallah et al. 2014). Many such investments are delayed; others have gone bankrupt. This development is also linked to the prospect of a weakening global market for ethanol, as the EU and other stakeholders become more sceptical about the use of land-based energy to fuel their transport fleets (Patnaude and Werber 2013).

Biotechnology and Alienation of Smallholders

As to the potential for increasing food production and supply, the spread of new biotechnology innovations has been advanced as an option. Biotechnology is, however, not likely to bring about greater sustainability in world agriculture. It may well increase agricultural productivity, but this is likely to be at the expense of sustainability and food security. True, certain biotechnologies could increase agricultural sustainability and some could increase food security. They *might* even generate economic development. But it is unlikely that they will do so, because they were created – and will exist – in a world in which these issues are (at best) of secondary importance to those who control the development of the technology. New technologies often lead to new ways of appropriating, substituting and standardizing living nature, so as to make it more amenable to the goals of agri-business. As such they 'change the rules of the game', where intellectual property rights have been extended to living organisms and global biodiversity has become a resource for incorporation into new processes and products (Busch 1997). Hence smallholders are losing their power and influence over seed production, which is being monopolized globally (Lipton 1989). In 2015 Monsanto presented a US$ 45 billion takeover bid of rival Syngenta AG which, if approved, would lead to near monopoly of the new company in the global supply of seeds and pesticides" (The Wall Street Journal, July 15 2015).

From Food Security to Food Sovereignty?

I have discussed how the concept of food security has changed over time, and gradually issues relating to *power*, *rights* and *sovereignty* have been introduced in this chapter so that we can get a better grasp of the principles, guidelines, agreements and processes that converge on global food security. The existing dominant technical and descriptive definitions and analyses of the concept have thus far been unable to generate successful interventions to reduce world hunger. The current strategy of international institutions and donor agencies is to promote large-scale agro-investment in order to address global hunger. Research has shown that the large-scale production of food and energy for export is leading to the further alienation of rural smallholders from land and water, thus undermining the core food producers in Latin America and increasingly in Africa.

The growing support for large-scale agro-investment has diverted the international focus away from the potential role of smallholders in addressing food security and national development, in terms of both employment and income generation. Research shows that smallholder agriculture has higher yields, employs more labour, is less damaging to biological diversity and the climate, and has more favourable agro-ecological features. All this makes it better able than large-scale agriculture to address food security over the coming years (Lipton 1989; 2010; Pingali et al. 1987; Binswanger-Mkhize and Gautam 2010; Fernandes et al. 2012; Coulson 2013). Economic, social, environmental, agro-ecological and cultural aspects of smallholder agriculture show that this production regime has a greater potential to address global hunger than other agricultural production systems.

The marginalization and displacement of smallholder agriculture in developing countries over the past decades have been stronger in Brazil and Latin America than in Africa and Asia. But the rise in large-scale agro-investment – in particular in food production for export – is currently affecting smallholders and pastoralists in Africa. Why does this neglect of smallholder agriculture in developing countries prevail among international financial institutions, international donors, global commercial companies and nation states?

I believe that the answer to the question of why these institutions and agencies are prioritizing large-scale, high-technology agriculture by international agri-business and domestic actors can be found in the broad framework within which the dominant states and global actors and interests operate. The attainment of food and energy security in the rich and transition economies now requires more agricultural land. In order to achieve this objective, the North, its institutions and companies align themselves with many developing states, global agri-business, domestic capitalists and large landowners. The Chinese state, for its part, promotes alliances between itself and its state companies and recipient states on other continents. China is going much further than the North in involving itself concretely in building infrastructure and industrial capacity often connected with the transfer of Chinese workers, but investments and interventions by the North still remain strong (Dietz et al. 2011).

Large-scale agriculture is closely connected with improved seeds, fertilizers and pesticides, and with advanced agricultural technologies that are monopolized by major global companies, e.g. Monsanto and Syngenta (Busch 1997; Fernandes et al. 2012). Smallholder knowledge and organization do not fit the large-scale investment models for agricultural modernization, which seek to maximize production and income over the shortest possible time.

The current smallholder development trajectory will therefore have to be changed primarily by the smallholders themselves. In part, this needs to come about by their organization at all levels to push for infrastructure, technical and market developments that address their hopes of influencing their own conditions of production. This would include pressing for enhanced security over the land they cultivate (Amanor 2012; Fernandes et al. 2012; FAO 2013; Havnevik 2014), for models of trade with the external world that are mutually beneficial, and for the state to fulfil its duties of protection, as stipulated by the Covenant on Economic, Social and Cultural Rights and the 'Protect, Respect and Remedy' framework of the UN.

The current concept of food security does not address the needs and aspirations of rural smallholders in their quest for increased productivity and improved livelihoods. The concept should therefore be rethought in line with the paradigm shift discussed above. The concept must have a strong focus on power relations and conflicts that affect all aspects of food security and on critical issues of how smallholder livelihoods and production can be supported and promoted. Due to the lack of concretization of the rai principles for responsible investments in agriculture, they are likely to be inadequate to break the dominant/dominated stereotypes and power relations that reproduce global inequality and hunger.

The reconceptualization of food security thus has to be located outside the 'dominant framework'. This process was initiated by the global smallholder organization La Via Campesina in 1996, when it introduced the concept of *food sovereignty*. The attainment of food sovereignty requires global and local structural and mindset changes that will weaken or break the stereotypes that reproduce inequality, hunger and resource degradation, and ensure that food is sustainably produced and equitably distributed. Since 2002, the International Planning Committee on Food Sovereignty has taken it upon itself to promote the food sovereignty concept.

The concept of food sovereignty reveals that large-scale agriculture and investments, advanced technology, improved inputs and various principles and guidelines are unable to challenge the historic and current stereotyping and symbolism of dominant global interests. The knowledge, technology and organization of such interests will prevail over those of 'the other'. This leads to the undermining of indigenous knowledge, cultural heritage, locally adapted technologies and local seed development – all of which are crucial for rural smallholders in terms of influencing their production conditions and livelihoods.

There is a critical need for those institutions, societies and groups that dominate and set the global development agenda to gain a deeper understanding of their historical and cultural foundations and frames (Said 1978). But this cannot come about while there is a binary perspective of the self and 'the other' – of 'us' and 'them'. In this relationship, ambivalence is an important dimension. The content and form of the interrelationship between 'I' and 'you', 'we' and 'they' have to converge in creating a 'third space' that can promote joint creativity and innovation. Only then will the reproduction of the stereotypes and symbols that legitimate exploitation and alienation between the dominant and the dominated, the North and the South, men and women be considered (Bhabha 1983: 372–373). The major obstacle to moving from food security to food sovereignty is related to the lack of such deeper understanding.

Such a transition can only happen slowly, since it does require a more profound understanding and an acknowledgement of the self that can help generate new mindsets, reflections and perspectives. Such a transition can be helped by better knowledge of agro-ecology, by better organizational, social, human and technical choices, and by better relationships that can improve global social justice and environmental sustainability.

References

Abdallah, J., L. Engström, K. Havnevik and L. Salomonsson (2014). 'Large-scale land acquisitions in Tanzania: A critical analysis of practices and dynamics' in M. Kaag and A. Zoomers (eds), *The Global Land Grab: Beyond the Hype*. Zed Books, London.

Amanor, K.J. (2012). *Land Governance in Africa: How historical context has shaped key contemporary issues relating to policy on land.* International Land Coalition Framing the Debate Series No. 1, Rome.

Antle, J.M. (1999). 'Benefits and costs of food safety regulation', *Food Policy*, 24:6, pp. 605–23.

Bauman, Z. (2007). *Consuming Life.* Polity Press, Cambridge.

Bhabha, H.K. (1983). 'The other question: the stereotype and colonial discourse', *Screen*, 24: 4, pp. 18–36.

Binswanger-Mkhize, H. and M. Gautam (2010). 'Towards an internationally competitive Tanzanian agriculture', Draft report, World Bank, Dar es Salaam.

Bourn, D. and J. Prescott (2002). 'A comparison of the nutritional value, sensory qualities and food safety of organically and conventionally produced foods', *Critical Reviews in Food Science and Nutrition*, 42:1, pp. 1–34.

Branford, S. and O. Glock (1985). *The Last Frontier: Fighting over land in the Amazon.* Zed Books, London.

Busch, L. (1997). 'Biotechnology and agricultural productivity: changing the rules of the game' A. Bhaduri and R. Skarstein, *Economic Development and Agricultural Productivity*. Edward Elgar, Cheltenham.

Buscher, B. (2011). 'The neoliberalisation of nature in Africa' in T. Dietz, K. Havnevik, M. Kaag and T. Oestigaard (eds), *African Engagements: Africa negotiating an emerging multi-polar world.* Brill, Leiden and Boston, pp. 84–110.

Carter, M. (ed) (2015). *Challenging Social Inequality. The Landless Rural Workers Movement and Agrarian Reform in Brazil.* Duke University Press.

Cheru, F. and R. Modi (2013). *Agricultural Development and Food Security in Africa: The impact of Chinese, Indian and Brazilian Investments*. Zed Books, London and New York.

Committee for World Food Security (CFS) (2013). 'Principles for responsible agricultural investment (rai) in the context of food security and nutrition', Zero Draft, mimeo, August.

CFS (2014), *Principles for Responsible Investment in Agriculture and Food Systems.* October 15, Rome.

Coulson, A. (2013). 'The end of the peasantry? Reflections based on Henry Bernstein's *Class Dynamics of Agrarian Change*', mimeo.

De Schutter, O. (2009). 'Large-scale land acquisitions and leases: A set of core principles and measures to address the human rights challenges', at: http://www.oecd.org/site/swacmali2010/44031283.pdf.

De Schutter, O. (2010). 'Responsibly destroying the world's peasantry: Land grabbing's grim reality' in Right to Food and Nutrition Watch Consortium, *Land Grabbing and Nutrition: Challenges for global governance*, at: http://www.rtfn-watch.org/fileadmin/media/rtfn-watch.org/ENGLISH/pdf/Watch_2010/watch_engl_innen_final_a4.pdf.

Deininger, K., D. Byerlee, J. Lindsay, A. Norton, H. Selod and M. Stickler (2011). 'Rising global interest in farmland – can it yield sustainable and equitable benefits?', World Bank, Washington, DC.

Depelchin, J. (2004). *Silences in African History. Between the syndromes of discovery and abolition.* Mkuki na Nyota Publishers, Dar es Salaam, Tanzania.

Dietz, T., K. Havnevik, M. Kaag and T. Oestigaard (eds) (2011). *African Engagements: Africa negotiating an emerging multi-polar world.* Brill, Leiden and Boston.

Djurfeldt, G., H. Holmén, M. Jirström and R. Larsson (2005). *The African Food Crises: Lessons from the Asian green revolution.* CABI Publishing, Wallingford.

Dobson, A. (1998). *Justice and the Environment: Conceptions of environmental sustainability and dimensions of social justice.* Oxford University Press.

Egal, F., A. Valstar and S. Meershoek (2001). 'Urban agriculture, household food security and nutrition in Southern Africa'. Paper presented at an FAO conference, Stellenbosch, South Africa, 15–18 January.

Fernandes, B.M.C., C.A Welch and E.C Gonçalves (2012). *Land Governance in Brazil: A geo-historical review of land governance in Brazil.* International Land Coalition Framing the Debate Series No. 2, Rome.

Food and Agriculture Organization (FAO) (2013). *State of World Food Insecurity.* FAO, Rome.

Gibbon, P., K.J. Havnevik and K. Hermele (1992). *A Blighted Harvest: The World Bank and African agriculture in the 1980s.* James Currey, London, and Africa World Press, Trenton, NJ.

Global Campaign for Agrarian Reform and Land Research Action Network (2010). 'Why we oppose the principles for Responsible Agricultural Investment (RAI)', at: http://www.viacampesina.org//en/images/stories/pdf/whyweopposerai.pdf.

Havnevik, K. (1993). *Tanzania: The limits to development from above*. Nordic Africa Institute, Uppsala.

Havnevik, K. (2011). 'Grabbing of African lands for energy and food: Implications for land rights, food security and smallholders' in P. Matondi, K. Havnevik and A. Beyene (eds), *Biofuels, Land Grabbing and Food Security in Africa*. ZED Books, London and New York.

Havnevik, K. (2014). 'Responsible agricultural investment in developing countries – how to make principles and guidelines effective.' Study prepared for the Swedish FAO Committee/Swedish Ministry for Rural Affairs, Stockholm.

Havnevik, K. and M. Hårsmar (1999). *The Diversified Future: An institutional approach to rural development in Tanzania*. Expert Group on Development Studies, Swedish Foreign Ministry, Stockholm.

Havnevik, K., D. Bryceson, L.-E. Birgegård, P. Matondi and A. Beyene (eds) (2007). *African Agriculture and the World Bank: Development or impoverishment?* Policy Dialogue No. 1, Nordic Africa Institute, Uppsala.

Hermele, K. (2012). 'Land matters: Agrofuels, unequal exchange, and appropriation of ecological space', PhD dissertation, Lund University, Sweden.

High Level Panel of Experts on Food Security and Nutrition (HLPE) (2012). *Social Protection and Food Security*. Committee on World Food Security, HLPE report No. 4, Rome.

HLPE (2013a). *Biofuels and Food Security*. Committee on World Food Security, HLPE report No. 5, Rome.

HLPE (2013b). *Investing in Smallholder Agriculture for Food Security*. Committee on World Food Security, HLPE report No. 6, Rome.

Lipton, M. (2010). 'From policy aims and small-farm characteristics to farm science needs', *World Development*, 38:10, pp. 1399–412.

Lipton, M. with R. Longhurst (1989). *New Seeds and Poor People*. Unwin, London.

Matondi, P., K. Havnevik and A. Beyene (eds) (2011). *Biofuels, Land Grabbing and Food Security in Africa*. Zed Books, London and New York.

Maxwell, S. and M. Smith (1992). 'Household food security: a conceptual review' in S. Maxwell and T. Frankenberger (eds), *Household Food Security: Concepts, indicators and measurements*. IFAD and UNICEF, Rome and New York.

McKeon, N. (2011). *Global Governance for World Food Security: A scorecard four years after the eruption of the 'food crisis'*. Heinrich Böll Foundation, Berlin.

McKeon, N. (2012). 'From food crisis to food governance?', *New Routes*, 3, pp. 12–16.

Mendonça, G.L., F.T. Pitta and C.V. Xavier (2013). 'The sugarcane industry and the global economic crisis'. TNI Agrarian Justice Programme, June.

Neville, K.J. and P. Dauvergne (2012). 'Biofuels and the politics of mapmaking', *Political Geography*, 31:5, pp. 279–89.

Oestigaard, T. (2012). 'Water scarcity and food security along the Nile: Politics, population increase and climate change', *Current African Issues*, 49. Nordic Africa Institute, Uppsala.

Olanya, D. (2012). 'From global land grabbing for biofuels to acquisitions of African water for commercial agriculture', *Current African Issues*, 50. Nordic Africa Institute, Uppsala.

Patnaude, A. and C. Werber (2013). 'Biofuels face uncertainty in Europe', *The Wall Street Journal*, 11 September, at: http://online.wsj.com/news/articles/SB10001424127887323595004579068742133643768.

Pingali, O., Y. Bigot and H. Binswanger (1987). *Agricultural Mechanization and the Evolution of Farming Systems in Sub-Tropical Africa*. John Hopkins University Press, Baltimore.

Rozin, P. (1996). 'The socio-cultural context of eating and food choice'. H.L. Meiselman and H.J.H. MacFie, *Food Choice Acceptance and Consumption*. Blackie, London.

Ruel, M., J.L. Garrett, S.S. Morris, D. Maxwell, A. Oshaug, P. Engle and L. Haddad (1998). 'Urban challenges to food nutrition security: A review of food security, health and caregiving in cities', FCND Discussion Paper No. 51. International Food Policy Research Institute, Washington, DC.

Said, E.W. (1978). *Orientalism: Western Conceptions of the Orient*. Routledge and Kegan Paul, London.

Sen, A.K. (1981). *Poverty and Famines: An essay on entitlements and deprivation*. Clarendon, Oxford.

Skarstein, R. (2007). *Ökonomi på en annen måte* [*Economics in another way*]. Abstrakt, Oslo.

The Wall Street Journal (July 15 2015). "How a Monsanto-Syngenta Merger Could Happen." (by Jacob Bunge), New York.

United Nations (1987). *Our Common Future*. Report of the World Commission on Environment and Development. New York.

United Nations Committee on Economic, Social and Cultural Rights (1999). General Comment No. 12, at: http://www1.umn.edu/humanrts/gencomm/escgencom12.htm.

United Nations Human Rights Council (2011). 'Report of the Special Representative of the Secretary-General on the issue of human rights and transnational corporations and other business enterprises. Guiding Principles on Business and Human Rights: Implementing the United Nations "Protect, Respect and Remedy" Framework. Advance Edited Version, March 21. A/HRC/17/31. New York.

United Republic of Tanzania (URT) (2009). *Kilimo Kwanza*. Dar es Salaam.

Wolf, E.R. and E.C. Hansen (1972). *The Human Condition in Latin America*. Oxford University Press, New York.

World Bank (2007). *Agriculture for Development*. World Bank, Washington, DC.

Index

Page references in italics refer to figures and tables. For example *98f5.2* refers to figure number 5.2 on page 93; *157t7.2* refers to table 7.2 on page 157.

www.ingramcontent.com/pod-product-compliance
Lightning Source LLC
LaVergne TN
LVHW011130300926
849160LV00008B/592
* 9 7 8 9 0 0 4 3 0 5 4 1 0 *